An Unexamined Life

A Memoir

Susan Broidy

For Sophie

ISBN 978-1098379742

Cover design by Sophie Greenfield

High Country Weather

Alone we are born
And die alone
Yet see the red-gold cirrus
over snow-mountain shine.

Upon the upland road
Ride easy, stranger
Surrender to the sky
Your heart of anger.

James Baxter, NZ poet 1926-1972

"An unexamined life is not worth living" is from Plato's Apology, a recollection of the speech Socrates gave at his trial.

Contents

My father, Norman Lamont, in 1916 with his

parents, and older brother and sister.

1. New Zealand 1940 -1945

New Zealand was at war when I was born. By the end of 1940, New Zealanders were being called up or were volunteering to fight in North Arica against Rommel. Over the next few years, the country was depleted of its young men, including boys lying about their age, as they left to join the thousands already overseas. Between 1940 and 1943, about 140,00 volunteers sailed away, a huge proportion when the total population was only about 1,600,000.

Entire shearing gangs signed up, abandoning New Zealand's sheep farms to the farmers' wives to manage as best they could. One of my aunts managed the tobacco farms for her husband and his brothers while they went off to fight in Italy, and another aunt successfully ran their butcher shop while raising her young family. It was a matter of pride that women could drive trucks and tractors, raise their children, and pay the bills while their men were on the other side of the world engaged in a patriotic endeavor to save the mother country from Fascism.

But my parents were different. My father was a Quaker and a conscientious objector. As a result, my mother was somewhat ostracized by the neighbors in the small town of Masterton where I spent my first five years. Only the

Methodist minister and his wife who lived on our street were understanding and I was christened in their church in gratitude. My father could have been sent to a detention camp along with many other conscientious objectors but was instead directed by the New Zealand Department of Agriculture to the essential service of growing food for the troops in the Pacific war. More than a third of all food received by American troops in the South Pacific came from New Zealand, with farmers growing great quantities of potatoes and cabbages. It was said that the acreage of cabbages multiplied to such an extent that the Americans revolted and dumped large quantities of the despised vegetable at sea.

My father was stationed in nearby Featherston and managed a large market garden operation with labor from the nearby Japanese prisoner of war camp. I have a hazy memory of going to the fields with him, in a coke-burning, gas-producing truck, modified in response to the gasoline shortage. It had a place to heat the kettle for inevitable cups of tea. Mile after mile of grey-green cabbages stretched off into the mist and on every row, it seemed, was a bent-over figure in prison blue, hoeing weeds. I was completely happy to be with my father, watching his competent hands make tea, keeping me safe and warm in the cab of his truck.

About 900 prisoners were housed at the camp, mostly Koreans and conscripts who had been captured at Guadalcanal. Many were young farmers who were happy enough to be working again in the fields instead of building airstrips on tropical islands.

A smaller group of prisoners arrived later. These men were about 240 officers and other ranks of the Imperial Japanese Army, Navy and Air Force. About half of them were crew from the Japanese cruiser *Furutaka*, which had been sunk during the Battle of Cape Esperance.

Ashamed to be prisoners, they refused to work, refusing to concede that compulsory work was allowed under the 1929 Geneva Convention on Prisoners of War. However, Japan had not agreed to the convention and the men subscribed to the Japanese concept of bushido, a warrior's code of honor that demanded suicide rather than surrender. Fear of disgrace haunted the prisoners and they dreaded the dishonor of eventually being returned alive in shame to Japan.

On 25 February 1943, a group of about 240 staged a sit-down strike in their compound, refusing to work. Armed guards were brought in. One lieutenant, Adachi, refused to come out of the compound, and sat with his men. They demanded a meeting with the commandant, who instructed his adjutant to get them back to work.

Accounts vary on what happened next. It is believed that the camp adjutant shot and wounded Adachi. The

Japanese then rose, either starting to rush or seeming about to rush at the guards. Although there had been no order to shoot, the guards opened fire with rifles and sub-machine guns as the Japanese threw stones and moved towards them.

The shooting lasted about 30 seconds. Thirty-one Japanese were killed instantly, 17 died later, and about 74 were wounded. One New Zealander was killed and six were wounded. (Te Ara, Encyclopedia of New Zealand)

Today, a plaque commemorates the site with a 17th-century haiku:

Behold the summer grass   All that remains   Of the dreams of warriors.

My father's role in the Featherston mutiny remains unknown. I wish I had questioned him more while he was still alive. As a Quaker pacifist he would have been appalled at the bloodshed and if he had been at work that day, he would have probably been in the fields, pipe in mouth, cup of tea in hand as he watched the other prisoners tending the vegetables. He was well-liked by the laborers – one of them gave him an intricately carved wooden plaque depicting a Japanese scene of cherry blossom, a wooden bridge, and a tea house – but cut in half so that each piece could be hidden under the prisoner's shirt and given separately to my father. It hung on a wall at home for many years, the glued split down the middle a reminder of those tragic days.

My mother subscribed for a while to Christian Scientist beliefs and during the war years she believed in natural remedies for childhood maladies. I remember gagging down the carrot juice which she made herself in the wash house by the kitchen – grating, pressing and straining carrots by the sack load. The smell of wet cement washtubs and her firm hand on my arm stick in my memory just as the lump of unstrained carrot stuck in my throat. She also collected rose hips from the wild roses that straggled along the country roads, turning them into rose hip syrup as a source of vitamin C for us in winter. She must have been very idealistic to have refused to have us vaccinated against whooping cough and would not let us have our tonsils removed as we grew older. That was a matter of some regret for me later when my schoolfriends boasted of living on ice cream for days after their tonsillectomies.

Our town had an American army base for troops for rest and recreation away from the war in the Pacific. The base was built on the showgrounds of Solway Park for some 2400 Marines. It must have been a considerable culture shock for men brought up in American suburban homes with central heating. The New Zealand winters were unpleasant, and the local diet of roast lamb was an unwelcome substitute for hamburgers. Many Americans were surprised by the spartan existence of wartime New Zealanders with no imported goods and a lack of luxuries due to rationing.

My parents had befriended an American –we called him GI Joe - an Italian American from San Francisco and homesick for his family. He came to our house for meals bringing gifts and I remember tasting a Hershey bar for the first time and falling in love instantly with America. Our main treat at the time was battleship-grey penny ice creams made from home-grown beet sugar.

The American presence in Masterton certainly changed its social structure. Quoted first in *The Miami Daily News,* April 1944 as 'over-paid, over-sexed and over here', the Americans brought a taste of glamour to the wartime austerity of New Zealand and while they were welcomed by lonely women, they were also a cause of unrest among New Zealand soldiers overseas. I suspect my favorite aunt was a casualty of American charm; I found out years later from another aunt that she could not have children because of an abortion during the war.

> *Suddenly, in strolled the Americans: all smiles, perfect teeth and looking like Clark Gable. Their uniforms were smart and well-tailored (at least by comparison with the New Zealanders' 'baggies'). They had money (about £5 – $400 – a week in pay, about twice what New Zealand soldiers were paid), and they were looking for fun. Their lucky date could expect taxi rides,*

meals out, exciting new tastes such as ice-cream sodas
or cocktails with Manhattan names, evenings spent
dancing wildly to bands or snuggling up at the movies,
and a gift of nylons to clinch the deal. (NZ History, US
Forces in NZ).

This caused some unrest among the soldiers overseas, imagining the worst about their women at home. There was a story about a young Maori soldier whose unit captured an Italian outpost in Libya and proceeded to drink the red wine they had "liberated." The young soldier was tired of desert warfare and was concerned that his girlfriend back home was forgetting him, so, full of alcohol-fueled courage, he stole a motorcycle and headed off "to New Zealand." As the cool desert air sobered him, he realized the tanks he was passing had German insignia on the sides and they were heading for his friends. He did a u -turn and sped back through the night, unchallenged by the Germans, and managed to warn his friends in time, for which he received a medal for gallantry in action. It made me think of the random nature of war – from deserter to hero by one lucky decision.

The last Marines left Masterton in 1943, to capture Tarawa in the Gilbert Islands. This landing turned into an American Gallipoli, with men mowed down by the Japanese as they waded ashore at low tide. More than 900 were killed and over 2000 wounded, leaving many New Zealand women young widows.

When the base in Solway Park closed, it was decided to destroy or bury all surplus US equipment rather than allow it to be sold and skew local markets. Buildings were knocked down, tents, beds, canteen equipment as well as Bren gun carriers, trailers and jeeps all went into two huge trenches. It was said to have taken nearly a week of convoys of army trucks to transport the equipment to the burial site. Local townspeople were aghast at such profligate waste at a time when everything was scarce or impossible to buy.

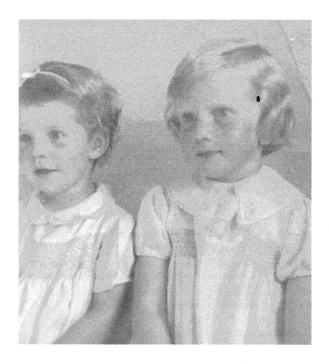

With my older sister Jane in 1942

About this time, my sister, little brother, and I were all ill with whooping cough at the same time. I remember waking in terror in the eerie landscape of my temporary bedroom in the living room by the firelight, sheets and blankets draped over table and chairs to dry as my mother struggled to keep up with the laundry. She talked in later years about taking us up to the fence surrounding the base, watching with bitterness as the Americans buried and burned blankets, sheets, pillows that she could have used for us.

She would talk about how I was such a good little girl during those early years, and how I would sit in a corner for hours playing quietly with my dolls. I remember it more as seeking refuge from my sister's torment and teasing, having learned that to seek attention from my mother was to result in retaliation from my jealous big sister. I was often blamed for Jane's misdeeds and it was pointless to cry out, "It's not fair!" Another of my usual cries was "Wait for me!" I loved taking refuge in the garage when my father was working at his carpenter's bench. I would pick up the curled wood shavings from his plane and tuck them under my doll's bonnet for curls.

One memorable day, Jane cut off my little brother's blond curls and encouraged me to use those for my doll instead. I was punished by my irate mother who refused to listen to my tearful protestations, and once again I would retreat, sucking my thumb for comfort from the unjust world.

As the war was ending my father was sent by the New Zealand government to America to study irrigation methods with the Tennessee Valley Authority, so that he could bring back state of the art technology to improve productivity on the Canterbury Plains. He left on a troop ship taking American servicemen home and his absence was marked for us by a flow of colorful postcards which we cherished and fought over. His return several months later was even more eventful with a trunk full of toys and treats that made us the envy of the neighborhood children.

I remember vividly a little pilot figure with a parachute attached – you simply folded the parachute around him and threw it high in the air to watch him floating down. My sister snatched it from my little brother and threw it onto the roof, causing tears and consternation until my father came home from work and rescued it with his ladder.

A fleeting memory of that time was when I was alone in the garden and suddenly the white wooden rose trellis started swaying alarmingly; if it was the big earthquake of 1942, I was not quite two at the time. Another flashback was when I was sent on my own to the dairy on the corner to fetch the milk. The dairy was what we called the corner grocer's shop where milk was not yet sold in bottles. I was on my way home trying not to spill the full white enamel billy can and must have been walking in the gutter or close to the edge of the road. An enormous US Army truck swept by me, its noise, exhaust, and rush of air startling me so much that I dropped the can of milk. I remember the men's concerned faces looking back at me from the truck as I burst into tears and ran home.

Another memory was of my kindergarten teacher coming to the house to show my mother a penguin I had modeled from plasticine. The door had hardy closed when my sister snatched the little model and reduced it to a crumble. I was too astonished at her gratuitous spite to be upset. My teacher's pride was consolation and for the first time I realized that I did not have to rely on my family for approval, and it was the beginning of my lasting pleasure in schoolwork.

As the war ended and the prisoners were sent back to Japan from the camp in Featherston, my father was transferred to Ashburton in the South Island. For some reason, my father and I travelled separately from the rest of the family and all I can remember from that overnight ferry trip to Nelson was my father's clumsy fingers as he tried unsuccessfully to tie a ribbon on my hair the next morning, the first time I discovered my father, my hero, was fallible.

We stayed a while with my aunt on the tobacco farm in Motueka, my uncle still away at the war. I have a memory of another truck sweeping by. I had been befriended by some of the land girls working the fields and they asked if I could go with them to a movie in town. If I was allowed I should let them know. If they did not hear from me they would know I was not able to go. I got the message wrong. I was waiting at the gate for them to pick me up and was desolate when the truck sped by, the girls waving back as I tried to get them to stop. I suppose it taught me something about precise communication, but it was a hard lesson at age four.

Another vivid memory was of miscommunication or maybe I was just trying to show my independence. I had been delivered by my father to stay with a family friend in a strange town under circumstances that I never understood. The family had a son, three or four years older than me and we walked to and from the local elementary school together, my first experience of being at school. On a hot dry, windy day a spark from a passing train on the nearby railway track lit the nearby grassy field on fire. Billowing smoke filled the classrooms and all the children were marshalled in the playground and told to go home. I looked for the boy but could not find him. I set off, away from the smoke, believing I knew the way home. I walked and walked, hot and thirsty, it seemed for miles. I decided I would go as far as the distant mirage-like shine on the tarred road and was disappointed when a car stopped and my parent's friend took me back to where I was meant to be, scolding me for not waiting to be met. I was wistful that I had never discovered the reason for the mysterious shiny glare on the road.

These are the memories of early childhood that linger – of confusion, loss, fear of abandonment and so very much to learn. There must have been many happy times and it is sad they do not come to mind as readily as those that convince you that your childhood was unhappy. As Tolstoy said in his novel Anna Karenina, "Happy families are all alike; every unhappy family is unhappy in its own way."

2. Ashburton 1945-1949

For so many young families, the housing shortage after the war was a hardship, and my parents rented first in Littleton, near Christchurch, where I encountered another penguin. Our family went to the beach on a sunny windy day to watch history being made. It was the final departure from New Zealand waters of the three-masted tea clipper, the Pamir. She was one of the famous sailing ships owned then by a German shipping company and had been seized as a prize of war by the New Zealand government in 1941.

She was sailing close to the coast as she headed for the Cape of Good Hope and we set out along the long beach for the best vantage point. I trailed behind, kicking at the long strips of kelp, and pulling them up to make the sand hoppers jump. My parents got tired of hearing me call "wait for me" and went on ahead into the blustery haze of the afternoon to join other onlookers on the beach. Suddenly I found a perfect little dead penguin, half covered in sand. I brushed it off and wrapped it in my cardigan, an unexpected treasure from the sea. As I hurried to catch up, I saw the grownups pointing out to sea and there was the sailing ship, white sails gleaming in the sunlight, a fairy tale ship from an unknown world. I was transfixed and promised myself that I would sail away on such a ship, some day.

My parents impressed on us that we had seen something memorable that day, something we would never see again – but I was only intent to get my little dead penguin home unnoticed. I wanted to put it into a safe warm hiding place, where I thought it would revive. When no one was looking I tucked it behind the clean sheets and towels in the warming closet. The smell of fishy decay soon alerted my mother, and that was the end of my pet penguin.

I was bitterly upset as I watched her bury it in the back garden. She probably tried to explain the meaning of death to me, but she had enough to cope with as it was. We all had mumps that year, and while I cannot recall the pain of swollen glands, I can remember scalding my foot as I swung out of my lower bunk bed and stepped into the bowl of porridge my mother had momentarily set down. I think it was probably around now that my mother finally decided to have us vaccinated against childhood diseases.

The house we were renting was a summer cottage and inconvenient for my father's job. So we moved further south to Ashburton and lived for a time with a resident landlady. I remember my mother's efforts to close our door with a little ball of screwed up paper behind it – so that we would know if the landlady had snooped in our absence. My father had bought an apple orchard within walking distance of the local Primary School, and he was able to hire a building contractor to frame and roof our future new home. My parents intended to finish it themselves because of the shortage of contractors and in the meantime we lived a gypsy existence that summer in a caravan and a couple of tents. I hated the outhouse and the bathtub which was under a hinged countertop, but it was an adventure while the weather was still warm.

Unfortunately, my father developed pleurisy from spraying the underside of the flooring with the pesticide Boracure – to prevent woodworm – and mother had to struggle with a sick husband in bed for weeks, and three restless children as the weather grew colder. My refuge from family tensions was the giant macrocapa hedge at the back of the orchard where I hollowed out a hiding place and could lie back and watch huge clouds billowing by. I could also spy on Bruce, an older boy who convinced us there was treasure buried in the potato field if only we knew where to dig. Bruce also had illicit cigarettes and persuaded my little brother to smoke, thankfully putting him off for life.

I loved school. I would walk there against the Southerly Busters that roared up from Antarctica I thought, or certainly were chilled by the snow-covered Alps that formed the backbone of the South Island. I suffered a lot from earache and wore knitted pixie hats to keep my ears warm, which my sister Jane took pleasure in snatching and throwing over hedges on the way to school. It did not prevent a trip to hospital for a mastoid operation, where I was gratified to receive a visit from my first year teacher, Miss Brown, who brought me a big empty writing book and some sharpened pencils, so that I could "write stories."

I was proud to be the milk monitor in my classroom, handing out the bottles each day with their cardboard tops with a hole for the straw. I would drink below the thick almost yellow topping of separated cream, leaving it to tease the magpies who would flutter round the emptied crates after break. I was also designated as reading help to some of the younger slower pupils in the class, which made me proud.

That was the year I broke my front tooth and learned how grownups could get things wrong. I was chasing Johnny, a handsome little boy in my class, around the school building and I doubled back to meet him headlong on the corner. I was laughing when I ran into him and my front tooth broke off in his forehead. He was bleeding and got all the attention – I was shocked and in pain and picked up my piece of tooth and ran home in tears. My mother later overheard two women discussing the incident – did you hear about that vicious little girl who bit a boy so hard that her tooth broke off in his forehead?

1948 was the year of the polio epidemic in New Zealand when schools, public pools and libraries were closed, and we all did lessons by correspondence. I raced through my week's assignment and was usually done by Wednesday, leaving me bored and lonely. I decided to write a play for the neighborhood children to act and I ended up being director and star in a short version of Cinderella. My parents encouraged my initiative and we charged admission for the performance, raising one pound sixteen shillings to buy books for the children's ward, donated mostly I think by my uncle and aunt who drove down from Christchurch for the occasion.

I remember being humiliated by my actors' poor performances, requiring much prompting from me as we stumbled through the story and I vowed never to rely on others in future. I believe I got my name mentioned in the local paper however, which was very satisfying.

The new house was finally finished, and I remember my mother's pride in her tangerine and cream kitchen. My favorite apple tree had been cut down and a lawn and gardens established. I cannot remember how long we lived there, but it wasn't long and must have been a terrible blow to my mother when the New Zealand Department of Agriculture decided my father would go to Fiji to manage a research and training station. The house was sold, belongings packed, and we set sail from Auckland in 1949 on the SS Matua.

Six years old

3. Fiji 1949-1953

We arrived in Suva Harbor on a steamy hot day, with grey rainclouds settled over Joske's Thumb, the high point of the surrounding hills. My first impression was the humidity and the overpowering smell from the nearby Delano margarine factory, which used processed coconut oil, and to this day I can remember how the gagging smell caught in my throat. We stayed for a few days at the Metropole Hotel, greeted at the entrance by a raucous white cockatoo chained to a perch, eating an exotic orange fruit with black seeds. My introduction to pawpaw or papaya was the first of many discoveries – bananas and pineapples were on the table every day and we got to choose from a menu. Curries and fish in coconut were probably too exotic then but I relished the smell of garlic and spices. The hotel staff intrigued me – the native Fijians with big hair and smiles, barefoot and wearing sarongs or sulus. The Indian staff were the cooks and waiters, and the front desk was run by part-Europeans – "we do not call then half-castes," my mother said, firmly.

After Jane and I had been enrolled at the Suva Girls Grammar School at the top of a hill, and Robert at the Boys Grammar School down by the sea, we were taken to be measured for school uniforms and the weekend wear of khaki shorts and casual shirts called bula shirts in Fiji, aloha shirts in Hawaii. Clothes and sandals were made to order by Indian tailors and shoemakers and my father was outfitted in the Civil Service "uniform" of white shirts and Bermuda shorts and knee length white socks. Downtown Suva was exciting – one store I loved because of its heady, dusty perfume of sandalwood and Chinese spices, with intricately carved camphorwood boxes and ivory figurines for sale. I was also intrigued by the new currency – pennies with holes in the middle and an octagonal threepenny piece with a native hut or bure on it.

Our temporary house in Suva was up on Government Hill, a sprawl of bungalows set in green lawns with a blaze of color from flowering trees– jacarandas, poincianas, frangipanis and brilliant hibiscus and alamanda bushes. I explored the neighborhood as soon as I was allowed, meeting a little girl and her mother who invited me to their house. I met the girl's grandfather, a retired Indian Army Colonel, who became an important part of my life over the coming years. Colonel taught me to appreciate art and music, and good Indian food. I do not know what he saw in me, but he must have recognized my loneliness and my hunger for beautiful things. I treasured the times I could visit him and would clean and polish his intricate Indian carvings while his batman or manservant from the Army days in India cooked delicious puris and samosas. On one memorable day he turned up at school, sending his chauffeur in to the Headmistress's office to demand I be released from class, so that he could take me shopping. We went to Widdowson's the jewelers and I got to choose my first wristwatch for a birthday gift. As my birthday was on Christmas Day, he said I could choose whichever one I wanted. He was pleased when I chose the most expensive one without knowing the price – "You have excellent taste," he said, "I have taught you well."

I was sorry to leave the city when it was time to move again. The Koronivia Agricultural Research Station where my father would be working was some distance from Suva and our new home was still being completed. To my mother's dismay, we were assigned to live temporarily near a village called Naduraloulou, in a former District Officer's enormous wooden bungalow overlooking the Rewa River. There was no electricity, so every evening my father would light the benzene and kerosene lamps, while my mother struggled through the day with a wood stove. I remember her stirring a pot on the stove, sweating and tearful when I recited Rupert Brooke's poem, beginning,

If I should die, think only this of me

That there's some corner of a foreign field

That is for ever England.

She swatted me with her wooden spoon, irritated and nostalgic not only for her kitchen in New Zealand but also for her childhood home in England.

We would wake each morning to the sound of the young Indian boy, Johnny, pumping water to fill the big, corrugated iron tank for our daily needs. On the rare occasions when guests came to dinner, Johnny was paid extra by my father to be punkah wallah, sitting cross legged on the floor just beyond the dining room door, rhythmically pulling the rope attached to the punkah or big wooden board over the table, stirring and cooling the air.

My mother disapproved of British colonial traditions like this and was unprepared to be a memsahib with servants, though was happy enough to have a Fijian woman to help with daily laundry and cleaning. Sala walked up from a nearby village, where my mother visited one day and was horrified to see the village children covered in sores, which turned out to be yaws. At her insistence, a Medical Officer was dispatched from Suva to treat them and we were forbidden to go there and play with the village children. We had our skin problems too – every scratch or mosquito bite became infected as we adjusted to the climate and for months we were covered in sticking plaster and iodine.

I hated the house – none of the screen doors seemed to fit and during the night, ugly cane toads would get in and head for the bathroom. I had to remove them with a dustpan and brush before I could shower. There was record rainfall that year, and the brown river surged by at flood level with the sugar cane barges sweeping down to the Colonial Sugar Refining mill in the nearby little town of Nausori. Sugar was the primary crop in Fiji, and my father's main job was to introduce other cash crops such as bananas, pineapples, and vanilla as well as to develop a dairy industry and better pastures for cattle raising.

Life was so much better when we were able to move to Koronivia to the new house on the hill, a short walk from the Research Station. We did not have so far to go in the school bus over the rutted main road to Suva -dusty or muddy according to the season - and we could roam the farm on the weekends, getting in the way of the students at milking time in the model dairy and riding the retired polo ponies who had been put out to pasture. I loved Kabutri, a bony old horse who hated being saddled up and urged to jump ditches, but she put up with me and my barefoot kicking, welcoming the turn for home by breaking into a trot and trying to scrape me off on the barbed wire fence.

Fiji was changing fast as the islands emerged from the war years. The population was about half native Fijians, 118,000, and half descendants of the East Indian indentured laborers, 120,00, with Europeans and Part Europeans numbering around 10,000. There was friction between the two main races because the Indians had been unwilling to fight for the British Empire in other parts of the world, whereas there had been an enthusiastic response from the indigenous Fijians.

The islands were largely untouched by the war in that the Japanese advance had stopped before they could invade, but the Americans had rushed ground, air and naval assets to the main island of Viti Levu, with a garrison of 10,000 Marines who later fought at Guadalcanal and the Solomons. Fiji remained a remote area for staging and logistics during the rest of the Pacific war, leaving a legacy of soured relations between the Indians and Fijians.

We picked up a little of each language, useful mainly in the weekend market. Dalo or taro and tapioca were the staple root crops which needed help to make them palatable - parboiling followed by roasting or mashing and frying made them an acceptable substitute for potatoes. Green vegetables were limited to long bitter snake beans, tough lettuce, and a variety of spinach, slimy when cooked, that we naturally rebelled against.

My mother used to buy frozen beef from New Zealand for our Sunday roast which we learned to describe as "as tough as Baker's boots", Thomas Baker being an unfortunate missionary who was killed and eaten in 1867. The leftover soles of his shoes, the leather tops of which were cooked and reputedly chewed by the cannibal tribe, are on display today in the Fiji Museum.

I must have been ten when my class was taken to the local cinema to see the movie *Great Expectations*. I was terrified when the escaped convict appeared in the misty graveyard, frightening Pip but shocking me to my core. I had recurring nightmares for years afterward and my sister delighted in opening my bedroom door and hissing "Great

Expectations" when I was trying to sleep. Sure enough, I would wake screaming in the night, usually wetting the bed, and finding solace only by sucking my thumb and rocking myself back to sleep. I could never have sleepovers with friends from school because of this and every time I passed my sister and her group of cronies at school, I was sure that they knew and were laughing about me.

I always tried to keep my distance from my sister. We would sit apart on the school bus, the Blue Bus, that raced the Yellow Bus on the dusty, corrugated road between Nausori and Suva. There were canvas curtains that rolled down over the open windows during heavy rain, so we were either choked by dust or stifled in the airless atmosphere. Sometimes on the way home, the bus driver would agree to stop by a patch of wild guavas that we knew, and we would run and fill our school satchels with the ripe yellow fruit. To this day, I can recall the taste and perfume of that first bite of the pink flesh and the gritty seeds, as the anxious driver urged us back onto the bus.

We ate other strange things – big rough skinned lemons or molis, that we would peel and eat with salt, my taste buds reacting even now at the memory – and newspaper twists of gooey brown tamarind pulp that we would buy for a penny at the local Indian store. Peanuts and hot peas were sold at the bus station in newspaper cones and if we had the pennies to buy them, yellow sticky sweets with a cloying after taste. I do not remember candy or chocolates except as special Christmas treats, but we made coconut fudge whenever we could.

1953 was a momentous year for the family. My father was due for home leave after three years in Fiji and we were to go to England for six months, plus extra time for study leave for my father and two months travel time by sea, so it was nearly a year altogether. It was Coronation year and my sister and I were to represent Fiji Girl Guides at Coronation events; my parents would rent a house and we would go to school in England, so the future was both exciting and alarming.

We left Fiji by flying boat, in one of the converted Air Force Sunderlands left over from the war which took us to New Zealand and then on to Rose Bay in Sydney. We had new dresses for the occasion and Mother wore hat and gloves; I had just had my twelfth birthday.

We boarded the SS Himalaya in January —a gleaming white P&O liner which had been launched in 1949. She towered over the wharf, a band played and passengers at the rails threw paper streamers down to friends. As the ship moved slowly and majestically away from the dock, I felt emotional too as the band played *Now is the Hour* and the streamers slowly parted. It became a favorite thing to do in later years after school to go down to the wharf and watch the tourist liners leave after a day in Suva. The Fiji Military Forces band, brilliant in scarlet and white, would play *Isa Lei*, the traditional Fijian farewell and it never failed to bring a lump in my throat.

The Himalaya soon became home to a tribe of children who explored its decks and "Staff Only" areas. We had some interesting fellow passengers. Ratu Sir George Cakobau, Fiji's paramount chief, was on his way to England for the Coronation, as well as brothel owner Tilly Devine, Sydney's "queen of the night" who was quoted as saying she was going to London "to see the other queen." I was disappointed to see how ordinary she looked, when I was hoping at least for scarlet shoes and a feather boa. Ratu Cakobau, described by the press as a cannibal chief, made the news also, when it was said he refused the menu offered by the waiter, saying "bring me the passenger list."

Shipboard life was endlessly fascinating. I used to follow an elegant young woman who was going to London to audition for the Sadlers Wells Ballet Company and would watch her as she rehearsed each day using the ship's rail as a barre. Early in the morning, there was usually an audience of awed children as a man practiced shooting empty beer cans which he tossed off the ship's stern. He was going to Rhodesia to avenge his brother's death at the hands of the Mau Mau. We also followed friendly crewmembers – the quartermaster who taught us how to make a Turks Head knot and the young lift operator who sometimes carried his white cockatoo on his shoulder. He took us down to the kitchen storeroom once and showed us where we could help ourselves to a huge container of broken cookies. It was exciting to be closer to the ship's noisy engines and their powerful vibration. I would often hang over the aft ship's rail, mesmerized by the enormous power of the ship's propellers churning up the ocean and leaving a wake as far as I could see. I loved the sense of being carried off to new worlds, without any agency of my own. This was something I learned later in life to resent instead.

Our first port of call after the Australian ports of Melbourne, Adelaide and Perth was Colombo in Ceylon, now Sri Lanka. It felt familiar with its Indian population and the British Colonial architecture, but the women's sarees seemed more brilliant than in Fiji and the buildings more imposing. It felt as if it had much more history than Fiji and its proximity to India meant it had experienced a similar path to independence in 1947. I was delighted when my parents took us all to have high tea on the terrace at the Mount Lavinia Hotel, a favored watering place among British expatriates, with its cool verandahs and colonnades and dramatic flowering trees in the spacious grounds. I sensed that it was a symbol of a Colonial past that was soon to disappear.

The long voyage across the Indian Ocean to the Suez Canal was wonderful – days filled with sunshine, swimming, roaming the decks, exploring the library, and enjoying the children's mealtime in the dining room before the grownups took over. As the sun set, the decks were ours again to prowl and overhear adult conversations, giggling at the silliness of some people after the cocktail hour, engaged in shipboard romances.

There was tragedy too. Across from my mother's cabin was a woman with two little girls. Mother could hear her crying in the night, and she found out that one of the daughters had been playing with a friend cutting out paper dolls. They had fought over the scissors and the visiting child had fallen onto the open points and had died as a result. The mother was going to England to try to get over the depression she was suffering, unable to come to terms with the fact that her daughter had caused the death of another child. I was distressed to learn this and wondered for a long time if the mother ever found peace.

We entered the Suez Canal at a time of political and social unrest. King Farouk had been deposed six months previously after increasing violence from Egyptian nationalists and the deaths of 54 British soldiers. Armed soldiers patrolled the canal banks as we slowly made our way through the locks. We were amused to see Arabs take off their sandals and wave them at us as we passed – we learned it was an insult in Arab custom to show the sole of your shoe to someone, but we children thought it hilarious. Where the canal widened, small boats came out and vendors shouted out to us to buy souvenirs, stuffed camels, and leather pouffes, but we were told not to buy them because the stuffing was said to have come from hospital waste. I was wistful as the camels were beautifully made.

I remember winning a prize at the children's fancy dress contest going as the exiled King Farouk – a pillow under a steward's borrowed white jacket, with a fez, a penciled-on mustache, and sunglasses.

The weather began to get colder as we entered the Mediterranean and the stewards came around with hot beef tea for passengers wrapped in rugs in their deck chairs as we approached Gibraltar. The rock was impressive, and I heard the legend surrounding the Barbary apes on the island. Once protected by the British army in Gibraltar, it is said that if they disappear, then British dominion over the Rock will cease. I learned later that the monkey population had little to do with the continuing struggle between Britain and Spain for sovereignty. In two referendums, the Gibraltarians rejected proposals for Spanish sovereignty. In 2002 the idea of shared sovereignty was also rejected. So the Rock remains British, and as the Himalaya rounded Gibraltar and we entered the English Channel, the next stage of our adventure, England, lay ahead.

4. England 1953

The white cliffs of Dover signaled that the voyage was over, and I was sad because the wild freedom of shipboard life was ending. Hating the unaccustomed cold weather, I was thankful to be welcomed by a chauffeur with warm rugs for us in a rented Daimler. The Home Office had done us proud with such an imposing car, the driver telling us he had taken a duchess to the dentist the day before. He drove us to our rented house in the countryside outside Romsey in Hampshire near where my mother had spent part of her childhood. It snowed as we were unpacking and my brother Rob and I shocked our landlady as we ran barefoot in the new snow, reveling in the novelty - short-lived as our feet became chilled. Only gypsies go barefoot, we were told.

We were back to family life under one roof and its restrictions and it was hard to escape from my older sister and her incessant teasing. I would be dependent on her over the next few months as we negotiated a new school environment and became used to English ways - lunch was dinner, dinner was tea and then there was supper. The Girl Guides Association in London welcomed us and approved some needed additions to our light cotton tropical uniform – a brown cardigan and beret and shoes and socks instead of sandals. We were given a detailed program of events for the Coronation including a week in Scotland. It was hard to get too excited when my greatest fears were of being cold and getting lost – both of which were realized on more than one occasion.

London was grim and grimy in 1953. Bomb sites were still evident, and buildings were black with soot as the Clean Air Act had not yet come into effect. My collar and cuffs would be grey after a day in the city and you could taste the grit in the air. I loved it though, the museums, the crowds in the streets, our visit to the BBC headquarters and most of all, a matinee at Sadlers Wells of the ballet, *Giselle*, starring Alicia Markova. I was so overcome by the experience that I could not stop crying. My sister kept hissing at me to stop and digging me in the ribs, so I was grateful for the kindness of the woman in the next seat. She patted my knee and lent me her handkerchief, saying," I know, it is really beautiful, isn't it."

Coronation Day in June was cold and wet. We had spent three days camping in some muddy fields with Girl Guides from all over the world, including some young Muslim women from Sudan who were horrified when bacon was served for breakfast. They are only 14 and are already married, we heard, and I was fascinated to think they were only a year older than me and yet already inhabited a different world and generation. We went to London the day before the Coronation and slept on groundsheets on the floor of Caxton Hall, the registry office where celebrities got married, including Elizabeth Taylor the previous year. I was unimpressed as I tossed and turned, cold and unable to sleep on the hard floor.

The next day for me was a mix of patriotic fervor and absolute misery, as we Girl Guides took our position on Parliament Square, waving our little Union Jacks as we watched the pageantry of the processions to and from the Abbey. It rained steadily and when I got home the next day my face broke out in blisters from the cold wind. That night we had gone down the Mall to Buckingham Palace to watch the young Queen wave to the crowds from the balcony, along with hundreds of thousands of excited Londoners. The crush was so great that my strong leather belt was wrenched off and I found myself alone in the crowd. Trying not to panic, I worked my way to the edge and somehow found my way back alone to Caxton Hall. It was one of many occasions when I wished my big sister would look back to see if I were following. My parents said later, "We watched it all on the telly and reassured ourselves that you were safe at Girl Guide headquarters and not in the crowd in front of the Palace."

I got used to going by bus to school in Dorking at the County Grammar School, where the children left me alone once they got used to the fact that just because we came from Fiji we were not cannibals. The boys would follow me around singing "She wears red feathers in her hula hula skirt," but ignored me when I started beating them at distance running and high jumping.

With Jane and the Fiji Brownie leader, Buckingham Palace.

The class I was assigned to was already ahead of me with Math and Latin, so I floundered along in those subjects, but I was ahead in English and Biology so was not entirely a misfit. Summer came and we were free to roam the countryside, exploring the nearby villages of Gomshall and Abinger Hammer, where I would watch for the mechanical blacksmith to strike the bell on the village clock. My father spent some time at Wye College in Kent, a well-known study and research center for the environment and agriculture. I remember him coming home one evening quite reverent about the fact that he had walked that day on pasture that had been undisturbed by a plough for over a thousand years.

We got to know some of the local children and explored a nearby beauty spot known as the Silent Pool. A young woman had drowned herself there, so legend had it, as she tried to escape the evil intentions of wicked King John around 1200. The only good thing that King John did, it seemed, was to sign the Magna Carta, but that was under duress from his barons. My sister and I were once invited to tea by two sisters, also named Jane and Susan, the daughters of a local doctor. Their house was impressively large and comfortable, and I remember vividly my first taste of marzipan cake. So secure in their middle-class upbringing, they were astonished that I had never tasted it before, and I felt like asking if they had ever tasted raw fish in coconut cream, a typical Fijian dish. I was also invited to tea by a girl whose father worked for the railways and they lived in a small cottage near the station. We played Beetle, the parlor game all the rage that year and we ate baked beans on toast, and nobody made me feel uncomfortable there.

My grandfather and his second wife visited us while we were in Surrey. His Scottish accent was almost impenetrable despite his years in New Zealand. He had left Glasgow as a young man, not wanting to be a coal miner like his father and grandfather, and instead found work in a diamond mine in South Africa where he made a small fortune. It was enough for him to return to Scotland and marry the local laird's daughter and take her to a new life in New Zealand. They were unhappy – he was a bigoted Calvinist and she was a liberal thinker – and they divorced when my father was still at school. He remembered bitterly how he had to ride his bike to his father's office every Friday to collect the alimony, and how his father made him wait for hours in the foyer.

We called his second wife Aunt Lillian – a retired English nurse she kept the old man alive until his nineties, after retiring in poor health when he was 40. She was not used to children, having none of her own and like my other grandmother Lillian, she was more likely to dispense discipline than affection.

Our time in England was running out. Looking back, it was our stay in Romsey that I enjoyed most. One cold, snowy morning I had gone with some Girl Guides to follow a hunt, the horses and hounds gathering at the former home of Florence Nightingale. The elegance of the horses and their riders in their red hunting jackets, the eager hounds, and the sound of the horn when they set off was thrilling. We stumbled along the muddy lane and watched them cross fields and ditches before we lost sight of them in the mist and returned home. Another place I loved was Romsey Abbey, a refuge of stillness and symmetry, the grey stones of its soaring roof seeming to me to contain the hopes and dreams of thousands of worshippers for a thousand years. In later years I would remember TS Eliot's phrase, a place "where prayer has been valid", when visiting old churches and cathedrals in the English countryside.

Our return home in October was on the New Zealand Shipping Line SS Rangitata, and this time we would be going through the Panama Canal, thus completing our round the world voyage. Not so imposing as the Himalaya, the ship was nevertheless a familiar temporary home, as we explored the decks and companionways, sliding deckchairs on the decks after they had been hosed down by the Lascar seamen, playing deck quoits and shuffleboard.

I tagged along with a group of about fifteen boys who were on their way to New Zealand as assisted immigrants under a migration policy that later was described as one of the most disgraceful in post war politics. From 1947 to 1967, between 7,000 and 10,000 children were sent to Australia and more than 500 to New Zealand. Some were orphans from Dr Barnados' Homes and some were Borstal boys or juvenile delinquents being sent to work on farms. There were many stories of abuse over the years, particularly in earlier times in Canada, and organizations have been established since to reunite children with relatives and to make reparations. During the voyage out however, the boys, like me, were enjoying the freedom of the decks and we would gather at the stern railing, where some of them smoked and I learned quite a lot of bad language and some interesting details about the facts of life.

Also on board were some refugees from Europe, a sad beautiful Jewish woman who wore her fur coat every day, even through the tropics, as it must have been her only remaining possession from a tragic wartime experience of dislocation and loss. There was a Jewish boy of about 14, perhaps her son, who played his violin on deck early in the mornings, but never spoke, either because he had no English or because he was too traumatized by his war experience. I admired him from a distance, but he never acknowledged my presence.

We stopped for a day in Curacao, with its Dutch architecture and strong smell of oil from the huge refinery in the Willemstad harbor. My sister and I were hosted by some Girl Guides and their mothers who took us swimming at a beach club along the coast. They mistook the boarding time for the ship and returned us to the wharf just in time – anxious parents and ship's officers were pacing at the bottom of the remaining gangway. I would have been happy to have been marooned there if my sister had not been with me.

We made our way through the locks of the Panama Canal, with the intense green of tropical forest on both sides and a strange stillness as the ship's engines were idling. We had a few hours in Cristobal, hot and crowded, and my most vivid memory was of shops filled with colorful flamenco dresses and puffs of tulle and sequins that must have been folkloric costumes. I yearned for one and nearly lost the family in the crowd as I lingered, enchanted and wistful.

Crossing the Line was always a feature on cruise ships and the Rangitata's crew started preparing soon after we left Panama. The ceremony is at least 400 years old and observes a sailor's evolution from Pollywog, a seaman who has not crossed the equator, to Shellback. It was a way for sailors to be tested for their seaworthiness and on cruise ships it included passengers as well. Ribald jokes, sailors dressed as mermaids and ducking in the swimming pool were all part of the initiation which we children enjoyed as spectators, happy to get a certificate later to prove we had crossed the Equator.

Pitcairn Island was our next stop, anchoring at sea while the islanders came out to us in small boats. My mother was excited. Her maiden name was Christian and family tradition said that we were descended from the respectable Christians who remained in England and had nothing to do with Fletcher Christian the mutineer. But there was a family link and as children, we were delighted to be considered descendants of the renegade who defied authority and became a folk hero, in Hollywood versions anyway. I watched fascinated as the islanders came aboard, carrying woven fans, carvings, and baskets to sell, and speaking in a strange mixture of Tahitian and old Devon accented English. I hung back as my mother introduced herself to a group of women and was taken aback when they hugged her and shouted out to the others to come meet Cousin Cecilia. They crowded round and discussed genealogies, while I kept away, not entirely happy to be included as family by these strange, roughly spoken barefoot people.

My mother's father, Frederick William Christian had kept his distance also, too much of a gentleman to be associated with descendants of mutineers. He came out to the Pacific in the 1890's to study and compare the different languages, settling in Samoa for three years on a property next to Robert Louis Stevenson's home. My grandfather evidently had not given up his undergraduate habit of drinking too much – a story from his days at Oxford recounts that he rented a bear on a chain from a gypsy encampment and paraded it drunkenly around the college until it climbed a lamppost and would not come down. In a letter to a friend, Stevenson wrote of meeting "young Frederick" on a path in the moonlight – very drunk and weeping – but he obviously forgave him as they exchanged dinner invitations and became friendly neighbors.

Another letter from Stevenson to my grandfather, I discovered many years later in the Huntington Library in California, acknowledged receiving some poetry that Frederick had written, wanting Stevenson's opinion. Stevenson wrote that while it might turn the head of a young lady on a moonlit beach, his poetry "failed to startle," suggesting that Stevenson was a kind critic as well as a great writer.

We arrived in Auckland in November, and my father had to go straight on to Fiji while we stayed on in New Zealand for the rest of the long summer holiday, visiting aunts in the North and the South Islands and getting to know cousins for the first time. I found it strange to meet family who were also strangers and while our parents assumed we would all get along immediately, I failed to make connections with any of them. Their lack of curiosity about our travels was off-putting and as we had no shared experiences, I felt adrift and wistful about other people's close families. I took refuge in books, a voracious reader for several years already but now hungry for the classics. Reading Dickens' *Great Expectations* helped to lay that ghost and end my nightmares about the convict in the graveyard. At last, just before my fourteenth birthday, I was beginning to feel liberated from the tyranny of my big sister.

Our life back in Fiji was now in Suva, the capital city, where my father had been promoted to be Acting Director of Agriculture. My brother was settled in boarding school in Auckland and my sister and I resumed our schooling at the Suva Girls Grammar School, where it was difficult to feel at home because of our year away. Many friends were now away in boarding schools in England, Australia or New Zealand and the classes shrank each year until there were only four of us in the Sixth Form or final year. I passed the University Entrance exam in 1956 when I was 15, too young to go to University. and was sent back to New Zealand for a year of boarding school at the Epsom Girls Grammar School. I had achieved the highest grade in the whole of Fiji that year and was eligible for the Fiji Scholarship which would have paid most of my expenses at University in Auckland. It was awarded instead to the next highest student, a boy, on the grounds that girls get married and never return to Fiji, whereas boys would come back and be an asset to the country. Ironically, I came back to Fiji and the boy who took the scholarship money to Sydney University gave up after a year and went off to study art in Italy.

My father had a similar attitude as there was only money enough to pay for my young brother's boarding school and university expenses. He argued that we girls would only get married and waste our degrees, failing to see that that was our only alternative, especially without a home base in New Zealand.

I had had a miserable time living in the school hostel in Suva, when my mother, with my little sister Juliet, went to New Zealand to settle my sister Jane in Teachers Training College. Jane had rebelled and instead got herself a job as cub reporter on the New Zealand Herald. My mother was so put out by the family turmoil that she could not cope and sent for my father who took early leave and left me alone in Fiji. I hated the experience. I did my homework each night in a music room with bars on the windows, the piano smelling of dead mice. Because I was Head Girl and disciplinarian, I was remote from the younger hostel girls and also from the day girls as they had their freedom after school and weekends. I had more in common with the two young resident teachers than I did with my fellow students.

The brightest memory of that year was my English teacher, Gabrielle Garland, new to the school, attractive, enthusiastic and whose love of poetry and literature was infectious. She opened my mind to a whole new world of books, and I was devastated when she fell out with the headmistress and returned to New Zealand after just a few months. None of the other teachers had shown such an interest in my work and the rest of the year was like a prison sentence.

Because of my interest in biology, I had spent some Saturday mornings with the doctor husband of my teacher. He was researching the cause of nephritis among Indian women, and I was happy to help him prepare slides and spend time examining them under the microscope. It inspired me to want to study medicine, which seemed a rather impossible dream.

The school year ended just before my sixteenth birthday. I was to go back to New Zealand for a year of boarding school at the Epsom Girls Grammar School I returned alone on the Matua, the friendly little ship that made two trips a month between Suva and Auckland in the days before air travel became more usual. I stood at the stern each night watching the phosphorescence of the wake, not knowing what lay ahead but overwhelmed with the enormity of the possibilities.

5. New Zealand 1957

Sometimes we haven't had the time to understand ourselves, yet we've already found the object of our love. When we realize that all our hopes and expectations of course can't be fulfilled by that person, we continue to feel empty.   Thich Nhat Hanh (from Brain Pickings)

My year at boarding school at Epsom Girls Grammar ended prematurely. I soon realized I had no chance of catching up in the subjects I needed for medical school as I was four years behind in Latin and Math. I took advantage of all a big school had to offer; I learned to play field hockey, improved my tennis, sang in the choir, used the library a lot and joined the debating club. But I was restless and out of place, eager for Sundays when I had permission to leave the hostel and attend the Methodist Church, which I had chosen only because it was close to my sister's apartment. She tolerated me turning up for an hour or so to listen to her latest records – Carmen Jones and Elvis Presley – and begging to try her cast-off makeup.

The two-week Spring school holiday created a problem of what to do with me while the school hostel was closed, and it was decided that I should visit my aunt and uncle in Christchurch. I was delighted as Aunty Judy had always been my favorite aunt. She had taught ballet and had trunks full of costumes which she allowed me to play with. Uncle Peter was South African and had been a champion wrestler in his youth and had huge silver embossed trophy belts on display. They were much more exotic than my rather prosaic parents and I looked forward to seeing them again. I set off by train from Auckland for the trip to the South Island, stopping over in the town of Levin on the way to have lunch with my grandmother.

I remembered when Jane and I had once stayed with her, years ago without our parents, I believe in her apartment in the Prime Minister's house where she was housekeeper. Gangan as we called her wore rustling black dresses and had a bunch of keys at her waist which I found intimidating. Jane was her favorite and over some dispute I was found guilty as usual and was shut in a small dark room for what seemed like an eternity. When I was finally released and allowed outside to play, I ran out to the garden to the top of a small hill and rolled and slid down a bank of soft autumn leaves. Unfortunately, I cut my elbow rather deeply on a sharp stone, which bled copiously, requiring a trip to the local hospital for stitches, and I managed to annoy my grandmother again when I fainted during the procedure.

She was as stout as ever, and her second husband Edward had a girth to match and the two of them carved and served Sunday dinner of roast lamb and vegetables, with enthusiasm. Our conversation was stilted, and they took me back to the station to catch the boat train to Wellington, without much sentimentality or affection on either side.

I sat by the window, and was joined by a man in naval uniform, who immediately started to talk to me, and as the journey went on, became increasingly attentive. He was good looking and much older than I and I found him easy to talk to about his travels and mine. He draped his coat over my knees to keep me warm he said, but then his hand started exploring up my skirt. I was excited and alarmed but stayed beside him instead of moving away, shutting my eyes and my mind to everything but the moment. We arrived in Wellington and boarded the night ferry with him close behind me. I found my assigned six - berth cabin and opened the door. Five nuns looked up as I walked in and to my enormous relief, I was able to shrug my shoulders, give him a rueful smile and shut the door in his face.

I had a warm welcome from Aunty Judy, and I loved being in their house with their two cocker spaniels, Prince and Princess, and the player piano which I was encouraged to play as much as I liked. My cousin John had been invited to join us as he was on Spring break too and my aunt thought it would be good for me to have company my own age. John was freckle-faced and friendly and already had his driving license, so we were allowed to take my aunt's Morris Minor for a drive one night. John decided we should go up to the Cashmere Hills to see the city lights at a distance.

When we stopped, I realized from the other parked cars that it was a favorite lovers' meeting place and when John attempted to kiss me, I was outraged. I think I probably said something about preferring older men which made him angry. He drove back down the winding gravel road far too fast, going from one long skid into another until we drove into the bank, turning the car over on its side. We climbed out, unhurt, and I told John to turn the engine off and put on the handbrake before we managed to push it over on its four wheels again. We drove home in shocked silence, and I was amazed by my calm presence of mind. It was not until we were sitting round the kitchen table explaining ourselves that I began to shake uncontrollably in a delayed reaction. "Give the girl a brandy," said Uncle Peter and I remember vividly the warm glow that filled my being and the sense of comfort it brought.

Before the school year ended I found an opportunity to work and train in a medical laboratory just over the road from Auckland University, and telling both the school and my parents that each had given me permission to leave, I tossed aside my navy gym tunic and school tie and became a working adult just before my 17th birthday.

I could not stay with my sister – she had already married under fraught family circumstances. Not yet eighteen, she needed parental consent, and my father flatly refused to give it on the grounds that the man was ten years older, a Catholic and had been adopted, of unknown parentage. Truth is, I do not think he could abide the thought of his blonde blue-eyed baby girl leaving him so soon. Jane took his angry letters to a magistrate and got legal permission, citing my father's unreasonable objections.

I was torn between loyalties and could not refuse when Jane asked me to be her bridesmaid. My parents stayed in Fiji for the wedding, disowning us both. I remember spending a week's wages on a set of brightly colored kitchen china as a wedding gift and being dismayed some months later to find it greatly depleted – "We throw it at each other," was Jane's airy reply. From then on I was always a little afraid of her husband Bernie because of his intensity and short temper.

Photo of me by Bernie Hill, my sister's husband

I had stayed with my widowed aunt for a few months after leaving school, catching the bus each day to the laboratory and going to classes at the University in the evening. It was not a success – Aunt Betty worried about me and did not like the responsibility for me in my parents' absence. I was feeling lost and alone and longed for life to happen but was unsure about what to do next. I had my freedom, but it was not worth much yet. I was trying new experiences with a reckless courage but without much moral underpinning and certainly no adult guidance.

I hated the weekends – shops were closed on Saturdays and Sundays and I had little money for going to the movies. I decided to get an evening job as a waitress in a local Chinese restaurant but that lasted only a few weeks. The manager said I was too lady-like and was not friendly enough to the bikers and Maoris who came to the take-out window.

I loved my work at the laboratory however – the precision of interpreting results, examining blood samples, making detailed analyses – and my colleagues were encouraging and patient as I learned the routines of the different departments. I particularly enjoyed the Bacteriology Department, growing cultures on agar petri dishes and testing the bacteria for their response to different antibiotics. I should have given up my evening classes in French and Anthropology and concentrated on getting a Medical Technician's certificate, but I was having too much fun at university.

I had become friendly with Raewyn, one of the lab technicians, and went with her and some other girls to a beach cottage for the Easter break. The weather was cold and gray most of the time and becoming bored on Sunday with the girls' chatter I went for a walk by myself on the beach. The wind and spray were exhilarating, and I walked along the hard, wet sand, avoiding the incoming waves, reveling in being the only person on the beach. In the distance however, I saw two figures in black wet suits, and as I got closer could see that they had been surfing. I stopped and watched. The young men came up to me and we started to talk. They were both German and the taller, blue-eyed one said his name was Otto and that he was with the German Consulate in Auckland.

I asked why he was not feeling the cold and he had explained his Buddhist training enabled him to resist it. I was deeply impressed, and with his candor and friendly questioning, both of us appreciating that we had more cosmopolitan backgrounds with experience of living overseas. We parted eventually with Otto promising to be in touch when we returned to Auckland, but as I had not given him my address or phone number, but only told him where I worked, I did not expect to hear from him. I felt a little wistful but also aware that he was about ten years older than me and thought he was just being charming.

A few days later I was completely embarrassed when a dozen red roses were delivered for me at the medical laboratory, and I was teased at morning coffee break by colleagues who had seen a message for me in the Personal column of the daily paper. "Susan from the beach, call me, Otto." I do not know why I lacked the courage to call the

German Consulate and ask for him. I was confused for days afterwards and wondered how my life might have changed if I had done so.

I had moved into a flat with three other girls and was beginning to enjoy student life in the evenings after class. I had got to know some reporter friends of my sister, Jim the sports reporter who took me to my first national tennis tournament and stock car racing wearing a borrowed Press badge, and Robert who took me out on the harbor in his small sailboat. My sister would say in later years that I stole her boyfriends. I replied that in fact I had inherited her cast-offs. I loved being with Robert as he was like a big brother, and he gave me space to grow a little. We sailed one day through the middle of an 18-footer race which caused much ribald comment from the racing crews, and our dinghy slowly started to fill with water as we tried to maneuver back to land. We then spent weekends scraping down and re-caulking the leaks in the clinker-built dinghy, with Robert taking me home on the back of his motor bike. Robert later went off to explore the world as crew on an ocean-going yacht and many years later I met him in London. He was as attractive as ever, and I was tempted to exchange the puppy love I had once felt for him to something more. But I was on my way to Greece with my daughter to meet someone else, so we had an awkward and nostalgic parting.

While technically still a student, I had given up on lectures and became pretty much a party girl, a follower of a group of students involved in writing and producing the annual Student revue. I was ostensibly working backstage but mainly I learned to play poker and drink beer with a bunch of wild young men, including Peter, the secretary of the Young Socialists. Peter and I became close and I learned to appreciate classical music because of him and to expand my horizons in politics and literature. I wanted so much to be "in love" and was frustrated by his lack of ambition and lack of money. I bought myself a little amethyst ring when we decided to become "engaged" but I increasingly started to find fault with him and became more confused and unhappy myself.

I had been in New Zealand for about eighteen months and probably due to too many late nights and parties during Student Rag Week, I was feeling stressed trying to manage my life. A laddered stocking reduced me to tears, I never had enough time or money and I hated the New Zealand winters. I was sick of student parties and warm beer – the only sophisticated night life in Auckland was restricted to just three licensed restaurants, otherwise you had to take your own wine in a brown paper bag and pay corkage. This did not seem like the adult freedom I was yearning for.

So when my mother wrote begging me to consider returning to Fiji, saying she needed me and all was forgiven, I decided on impulse to return.

6. Fiji 1958-60

In lying to others we end up lying to ourselves. We deny the importance of an event, or a person, and thus deprive ourselves of a part of our lives. Or we use one piece of the past or present to screen out another. Thus we lose faith even within our own lives.   Adrienne Rich *(from Brain Pickings)*

I sailed on the Matua again after a tearful farewell with Peter on the wharf. I stood at the rail watching him recede and wondered why I had taken this step, not knowing if he genuinely cared or whether I was feeling remorse or relief. Certainly, I felt a rush of fear and excitement about the unknown ahead of me. A friendly man joined me at the rail, and we talked. He was a teacher on his way to Fiji on assignment from the New Zealand government and must have been experienced in counseling confused teenagers. I remember his kindness at the time, and he gave me advice and courage to enjoy the three days on board. One grey, rough day when most people were confined to their cabins, I ventured into one of the lounges where three older ladies were sitting at a card table. They welcomed me effusively as they needed a fourth person and over the next few days taught me to play bridge, one of them reaching into her knitting bag for a bottle and offering me sips of blackberry wine at any signs of seasickness.

I soon realized that my mother's motive in welcoming me home was not out of any great affection for me. My father was drinking heavily, and she wanted an ally. Cocktail hour began early in the tropics and my father graduated from beer to whisky as the evening progressed. He would pontificate at length about the state of agriculture in Fiji and the inadequacies of the Department and was particularly bitter about being supplanted by a new Director of Agriculture from the Colonial Civil Service in Africa. Merryn Watson was a slightly eccentric elderly Englishman, due for retirement after this posting and his droll jokes in his upper-class accent about elephants in the elephant grass offended my father's sense of egalitarian pragmatism. I was delighted to be big sister to five-year-old Juliet, however, and set about finding a job as soon as I could.

Fiji was changing fast, having emerged from the war years to a new prosperity and as more Australians and New Zealanders had money to travel, the tourist industry was thriving. Suva was becoming a little more cosmopolitan and I started meeting government bachelors at the Tennis Club and Yacht Club. I applied for a position at the Fiji Broadcasting Commission where my mother was running the Women's Programs and I became a trainee announcer, a job I really was not capable of doing. I found it stressful as I was terrified of making a mistake on air, which probably made it inevitable. One morning, the duty technician went on a bathroom break leaving me alone at the controls — a long silence after the BBC news got me flustered and I started to read the weather news over the recorded announcement. I was mortified. I was more than happy to be in the backroom from then on, writing 50-word commercials and researching and preparing programs.

Fiji was still a Crown Colony, and the Governor would show up in his white uniform and plumed topee on ceremonial occasions. The annual Garden Party at Government House was a big social occasion for the English residents, but increasingly, Australians and New Zealanders were staffing government departments and were less sentimental about England as Home. Fiji had changed a lot since we had first arrived, as resentment grew about its status as a Crown Colony. I overheard one of my father's colleagues saying bitterly, "When I first came the Fijians would step off the sidewalk for you, now you're lucky if they don't push you off."

There was also continuing underlying friction between the two ethnic groups, the native Fijians retaining title to their land while the Indians were tenant farmers. With more education and more contacts with trends overseas, the labor force was getting restless, and there was an ugly demonstration one day that reminded us all that Fiji was no longer an untroubled island paradise. No one was killed, but cars driven by white men were stoned and for weeks afterwards, European residents armed with billy clubs patrolled the residential areas at night.

One afternoon, I was at the front desk at the radio station while the usual receptionist was on holiday. I was listening to our reporter giving a live commentary from the huge meeting at the nearby park called by a labor union organizer from Australia. I could hear the roars of approval from my desk and sat there in some trepidation when the rally ended, and a stream of people poured along the road towards the corner of our building. I sat there like a goldfish in a bowl, wondering if the men upstairs would come down to see if I was alright. For a moment I imagined they were going to take over the station, but the thirsty crowds were only helping themselves to water from our outdoor tap.

The usual sight when I returned from work each day was my mother's back as she sat typing at her desk and my father sitting with a drink, smoking his pipe and eager for my company. I would play with my little sister Juliet and get dinner on the table and I was grateful to my father for teaching me to drive and for letting me take his car in the evenings. I began to spend more and more time at the Royal Suva Yacht Club, sailing in the weekends and escaping to the bar from evenings at home, often returning to find my mother in tears and wanting to confide her unhappiness and complaints about my father. Increasingly I felt as if I was being erased as a person, acting roles to satisfy other people's expectations of me and losing touch with my own self. I knew it was childish to say to myself – It's not fair - but I felt powerless and unable to rise above the circumstances I had chosen by leaving New Zealand.

One awful night, when all three of us were shouting at each other, with Juliet crying in the background, I grabbed the car keys and left for the Club. Only the old-timers were there drinking at the bar and I felt totally out of place. When I returned home, I found that my mother had thrown all my clothes and possessions out onto the lawn, and was standing at the door, arms akimbo. My father had retired to their bedroom and I felt completely betrayed. The bottom dropped out of my world and in a moment of black despair, I went into the kitchen and slashed my wrist with a carving knife.

I sat on the kitchen floor and in a moment of clarity, I realized I would never be the same again. I had literally cut away my childhood and I looked in horror at the bloody mess I had made. I had not even done that properly and was stitched up later by our disapproving family doctor. Weeks followed with guilt on both sides, tiptoeing around each other and with me feeling stunned and in a fog of unknowing. I would wake in the night with my thumb in my mouth again, rocking myself to sleep in misery. We never spoke of it again, except that my mother dismissed it as "an attention -getting device", but at least she stopped running into my room at night seeking refuge from my father.

My job at the radio station was my lifeline and I had decided that I would pursue a career in radio journalism and go to England to seek my fortune and hopefully, get a job at the BBC. I started saving for my fare on the Johan Van Oldenbarnevelt, a Dutch liner that had brought many immigrants from Europe to Australia after the war , returning to Europe with young Antipodeans seeking adventure and opportunity in a wider world. It was the cheapest way to get to England and as I got closer to having the full amount for the ticket, I was feeling uncomfortable again, torn between fear of the unknown and reckless courage. I also felt scarred and remote, and unable to process what I had done to myself.

It was a relief when I was asked to help with sailing a new dinghy built by George, a Government architect whose wife was my father's secretary. He had never sailed before, and he was charming and good looking, and we sailed the Toucan together around the harbor, without much expertise but with increasing confidence. I was flattered by his attention and wanted him to consider me more than just a young kid helping him to sail but I think I put him off by my eagerness to be seduced by an older man. The situation was also confused by the fact that his red-headed wife was my father's secretary and I think she may have had more than just an office relationship with my father.

I then met Ken, an older man at the Yacht Club who had bought the Moonfleet, a romantic old yacht that he intended to sail back to New Zealand. We spent time together and I agreed to cook and crew for him. Some of the yachties at the Club heard about this and went over the Moonfleet, looking at its log and decided it was unsafe for me to sail in. Evidently there were three entries recording that the rudder had been carried away in bad weather and the skipper had had to jury rig a rudder to survive. I was flattered that the boys were concerned for me and forgetting Ken and the Moonfleet, I started crewing in the weekends on the Talei, one of the 18 footers owned by a group of Colonial Sugar Refinery employees.

The Talei and its sister yacht the Tarua had featured in the Pacific 18-footer championships earlier that year. I had gone out to watch them race past the New Zealand Air Force base at Laucala Bay, and excited by the speed and beauty of the tall sails and skimming hulls, I was reminded of all those years ago when I had watched the Pamir sail home. It was fun to be the only girl sailing with four or five young men and though I did not do much beyond shift myself from one side to the other under the boom, I was useful for opening and distributing beer cans. We capsized in the harbor once when trying to out-race the Tarua and we sat in the sail, waiting for the duty launch to come rescue us, trying not to speculate about sharks' ability to bite through canvas.

One of the Talei's crew was John, my future husband, and his work as an agronomist with the Colonial Sugar Refining Company had the approval of my father. Flattered perhaps that his daughter had chosen a man in the same profession, he had someone to drink with when John came to call, and both my parents encouraged me to become engaged.

John was then posted round to the other side of the island, so I saw little of him for some months leading up to our wedding day.

I spent that time torn between opting for the safety of marriage and wanting more from life than being a Company wife. I had seen the sugar mill compounds with their ugly wooden houses, built Queensland style with wide verandahs and corrugated iron roofs, the golf course, tennis courts and clubhouse, and anticipated correctly that the community would be more stifling than that of the Civil Service community in Suva. But my parents were urging me to marry, as they had planned a trip to England with my brother and little sister, there would not be room for me and it would be more convenient and cheaper for them if I were married off.

It did not stop my mother however, from saying nastily after several sherries that I would not be happy with John as "he is not your intellectual equal." She also made a great fuss when my father bought me a set of stainless-steel copper-bottomed saucepans for a wedding present. She had always wanted some and was angry with both me and my father. I took out the money I had put down as a deposit on my fare to England and paid for the wedding dress and cocktail reception at our house and drove off into the rainy night with John, all my possessions in the back of his car. I had just had my 19th birthday.

My wedding day in 1960 with my father about to give me away.

7. Fiji 1960 - 68

The problem, I now know, is that no one ever really feels wise, least of all those who actually have it in themselves to be so. The Older Self of our imagination never quite folds itself into the older self we actually become. Instead, it hovers in the perpetual distance like a highway mirage.   Meghan Daum (from Brain Pickings)

We took a small open boat across a bay to reach our honeymoon cottage in pouring rain. At the last minute, my mother had given me a brown paper bag full of eggs and as the paper soon disintegrated, I had to hold them in my skirt. The hurricane lamp on the bow attracted a fairly big fish which leapt out of the water into my lap, breaking some of the eggs, which caused the friendly boatman some amusement, telling me I would have to clean the fish and cook it for breakfast. And so I did.

It was not an ideal honeymoon. I spent a miserable few days, mostly on my own with stress-related menstrual cramps, while John swam and snorkeled in the bay. I went for long walks along the beach, trying not to think "Is this all?" The beaches in Fiji are mainly white coral sand and in those days, you could pick up hundreds of small cowrie shells on the beaches and find beautiful live shells amongst the coral. We would bury them in sand and allow the ants to eat the decayed flesh, leaving them clean and shiny for display.

Today, after years of tourists doing the same thing, shells are now rare, and the reefs have been spoiled by pollution and souvenir hunters.

Our new home was miles from the sea however, in the Colonial Sugar Refining Company mill compound of Rarawai. The house was huge, with dark screened rooms and wide verandahs, and even when I unpacked my few belongings, it still looked rather desolate. I had my copper-bottomed saucepans though, and set to work to become a wife, cook and homemaker.

I found it strange that nobody came to call. I thought at first that my neighbors were giving us some privacy as newlyweds, and then I became irritated thinking they were ignoring me as I was not a typical Australian CSR wife but came from a civil service family in Suva. Either way, the first few weeks were long and lonely, with John off to work at 7am, home briefly for lunch and off again till 4 pm.

Our social life was based on the Club with its bar, library, and tennis courts just over the road from our house. Increasingly I would see John's Land Rover parked there on his way home, and instead of waiting with dinner drying up in the oven, I would walk across the lawn and join him. There were sometimes a few other women there, but I found the men's conversation more interesting and often joined them at the bar, which I suppose did not make me popular with their wives. I was certainly looked at askance when I started teaching at two Indian High Schools.

The Arya Sumaj movement was a form of reformed orthodox Hinduism and schools were founded in India and wherever Hindus lived. I taught a British curriculum of English Language and Literature at the two schools in the township of Ba, the boys' school at one end of town and the girls' school at the other. The boys' class was preparing for the Senior Cambridge exam, which was equivalent to a High School diploma and was needed for entry to most professions in the Colony or for higher education overseas. Some of the boys were close to my own age and it was a little intimidating being a teacher, without any formal training and only just having left school myself.

My pupils were wonderful, however. Polite, attentive, and mostly responsive, there was never a discipline problem. I helped them through the required books that year, which were Shakespeare's *Twelfth Night* and Dickens' *Tale of Two Cities*. We got to grips with Shakespeare by translating the play into modern English and performing it for parents and the rest of the school with improvised costumes and scenery. I watched the performance with a mixture of pride and dismay, as we mangled Shakespeare's poetry and turned it into a riotous Bollywood production. But all the boys did well in that section of the exam, so my effort paid off.

At this time there was growing unrest amongst the cane farmers about policies and prices mandated by the Colonial Sugar Refining Company. The word "colonial" was becoming increasingly despised and the company changed its name to South Pacific Sugar Mills. The government in Suva was becoming concerned about unrest in the cane-growing areas as well as the urban population in Suva. Setting the CSR cane fields on fire was a popular form of protest and disruptive because the cane then had to be harvested within three days or the crop would spoil. Often a farmer would have grudge against a neighbor and would set his crop alight out of spite. Cane fires at night were dramatic and alarming if they were close to our houses. One burned right up to our fence line on a hot, windy night and we were lucky that no embers drifted beyond our lawn.

One day I received a phone call from a government officer asking for a meeting with me. I was mystified when he announced he was from military intelligence in Suva and wanted to know if I had knowledge of any treasonous conversations about communism among the teachers at the Arya Sumaj schools. He also knew that I had been teaching English to a group of Chinese women, wives and family of the Chinese bakers and shopkeepers in town. I laughed rather rudely and said that if anyone was to blame, it was the British authorities whose set books for the schools – Dickens and Shakespeare - were about class, poverty, inequality and overcoming injustice.

I wondered who had told him to interview me. I was genuinely concerned about the way Fijians and Indians were treated by the Company and other local Europeans. Living conditions in the Company Labor Lines, as their housing was termed, were appalling and I had spoken to the government District Officer about what could be done. He had recently married one of the teachers who had supervised me at the Suva Girls Grammar School hostel, so it was a pleasure to meet up with her again. We worked together to collect and distribute clothing to destitute Indian women. I wished I could have done more.

John was spending months away from home, doing a soil survey of cane land in the Sigatoka Valley and again a three-month study trip to New Zealand. When he was back, his Land Rover was more often at the Club than the garage at home. I was restless and lonely and often depressed for days on end. I toyed with the idea of running for the Town Council and John was told in no uncertain terms to keep his wife in check - "Company wives do not get involved in local politics." I did a little work for the Fiji Broadcasting Commission as a news reporter, carrying a heavy tape recorder to events such as the local heat of the Miss Fiji competition. It was hilarious – the emcee of the evening, our local butcher, was drunk, the girls were too shy to talk into the microphone and the electricity failed the moment the band started to play.

I was delighted then when I discovered I was pregnant. We had been married for two years and after the first few months I knew that my mother had been right. I had thought to change John's tastes from beer and jazz to wine and classical music, but I soon learned of his deep distrust and resentment of people with university degrees and his pride in being a practical agriculturalist. I had admired him because he was nearly ten years older and had lived and worked in Australia for the national research organization. But the cheerful camaraderie at the Club bar dominated his life and he would come home late most nights just to eat and sleep. I would lie awake, his beery snoring beside me, too proud to admit I had made a mistake.

The thought of a baby filled me with the misguided hope that this would rescue our marriage. As the months went by, the local doctor became alarmed by my blood sugar reading and decided I had pregnancy related diabetes and needed to be close to better medical facilities. To my dismay, it was decided that I should go back to New Zealand and live with my parents for the duration. I was deeply hurt that John agreed to this so readily as I felt he was abrogating his responsibility as he knew how ambivalent I felt about my parents. But it was decided for me and I left Fiji again, this time by Air New Zealand from the airport at Nadi.

My father had retired from the Colonial Service and my parents and little sister Juliet were living in Auckland while my father tried his hand at teaching science at a local high school. He complained every evening about the lack of respect shown by young people these days and said that he felt more like an entertainer than a teacher. He finished the year and moved on to become Liaison Officer at an agricultural research station near Hamilton which suited him much better. The months I was with them passed slowly – I wrote long letters to John hoping to create a better bond and eager to receive his replies from the friendly postman who never failed to greet me with "Still in one piece?" We played Scrabble each night after dinner and watched television while I sewed, and my parents drank Dalmatian sherry and beer.

My younger brother Robert turned up unexpectedly one weekend to talk to our parents. A law student at the University of Wellington, he was in great distress. His girlfriend was pregnant. Her parents were horrified as they had a social position to protect in the Hawkes Bay wealthy farming society. It was too late for an abortion and Rob was distraught because it had been decided that the baby would be adopted, and the matter hushed up. I was deeply outraged by my parents' acquiescence in this plan. Pregnant with a wanted child, I was appalled that a baby could be considered an unwelcome nuisance to be disposed of for social niceties. I offered to take the baby back to Fiji with my own child but was ignored. I completely lost faith in my parents and my brother as the discussion ranged back and forth and it seemed that money and appearances were more important.

I was even more disappointed in them all when Rob and his girlfriend were married the following year with a society wedding which my parents attended. My isolation from my family was complete.

Our son was born, nearly three weeks overdue, at the Wakefield private hospital, in Auckland. John's mother came up to see me, all the way from Napier by bus, with a shoebox full of freesias from her garden. She also brought some first of the season strawberries which I ate, and immediately brought out the baby in a rash, making me feel so guilty that breast-feeding became an issue. I had become unreasonably upset when my mother was allowed into the delivery room and got to hold my baby boy before I could. I was reluctant to take him back to my parents' house and was able to stay for two weeks in a facility for new mothers where there was professional assistance with new-born babies. I was able to go out during the day and have the baby in the nursery at night so I could get some sleep, a wonderful provision by the Karitane Association which had pioneered baby care in New Zealand.

I just wanted to take my baby and get out of New Zealand and back to Fiji as soon as I could, which according to airline regulations was when he was at least four weeks old. I landed in Nadi finally, excited to be home and looked eagerly for John to show him his new son. He was not there in the Arrivals hall. I waited. And waited. I tried to call our home but there was no reply. I waited for over two hours, feeling more and more distressed as airport staff were leaving for the night and people kept asking if they could help. John eventually turned up, explaining that he had had two punctures, and had to get a ride to a garage to repair the spare and there had been no phone where he could leave a message. I heard later that he had been drinking at the Club with the local Fire Chief and had left much later than he should.

The homecoming was even more of an anti-climax when he explained that the Fijian house girl had left the kettle on when the electricity went off, a common occurrence. The power came on again after she had left for the day, the electric kettle boiled dry and by the time John came home from work the kitchen had caught fire and been extinguished by neighbors and the local fire brigade. So I had to deal with noise and confusion as workmen repaired the damage, leaving me with no kitchen, no privacy, and a crying colicky baby as I had to switch to formula to feed him. I was bitterly and probably unfairly disappointed with John. I wished I had never left New Zealand.

As the months passed however, I delighted in my baby, completely absorbed in his care and grateful for my friendship with Jill, another young mother with whom to share Dr Spock's advice. I cooked and gardened and sewed, and in a burst of creativity, I wrote an article for Redbook magazine in their series called Why Young Mothers Feel Trapped. I was taken aback when it was accepted and I was paid $US 500, a small fortune in those days. Surprised by the fan mail I received, I was intrigued about being a public person but was upset and stifled by John's reaction. "Great," he said, "Do this every week and I can retire." I did not try to write for publication again as I wanted it that part of my life to be mine, not John's.

It was a relief when John was transferred to the next bigger town of Lautoka, to a much nicer house on a hill overlooking the sea and with so much more to do that I did not miss the solitary work of writing. There was a British Council Library, a government High School, a community Club with a swimming pool and a much bigger presence of government and businesspeople instead of just the sugar mill community. John's work was mainly in pasture development on the Company cattle station many miles from town, so he was often away all day.

I resumed working for Radio Fiji as their news reporter in the North-West, which included doing a memorable live broadcast by phone from my living room window during a hurricane, as I described a sugar ship being blown from the harbor onto the nearby reef. I made new friends and became absorbed in working with the YWCA in establishing Fiji's first multi-racial kindergarten. I started teaching dancing to local children and that venture grew to nearly 70 pupils and a lot of work putting on plays and recitals. I taught English part-time at the local government high school and worked with the Fiji Arts Council to bring visiting artists to perform in Lautoka. We had performances by an American jazz quartet, the Kathakali Indian Dance Troupe, and a small company of Shakespearean actors from England, and I was kept busy doing publicity and ticket sales, all of which I loved.

Occasionally we would hire a boat and go fishing, staying overnight on one of the outlying islands in a Fijian village in their guest bure, or thatched hut. But more often we would drive down the coast to where a group of investors were building Fiji's first big, glamorous hotel resort. John was advising them on establishing a golf course and landscaping in return for free accommodation and it was fun to watch the resort take shape and to party on the beach with the Irish and American developers. We met Paddy and Nuala, an Irish brother and sister and Americans Pete and his artist wife. We also got to know Captain Oscar, a colorful character who ran cruises out to the beautiful and then unspoilt outer islands and his American wife Connie. Suddenly my horizons were expanding beyond Fiji and I was restless for something more than my identity as wife and mother with part time interests, fulfilling as they may have been.

Christian's third birthday was spent in the Company holiday cottage compound at Cuvu, a beautiful bay near the small town of Sigatoka. John was doing a soil survey of the area, so we lived there for about six weeks. One evening he decided to use the repair facilities at the nearby rail yard to check underneath our Volkswagen Beetle. He emerged in agony, having slipped a disc and from then on, our life was dominated by his constant pain, his refusal to see a doctor, and his self-medicating with alcohol and painkillers. I was lonelier than ever, knowing that our relationship had shifted, any intimacy was out of the question and I was to be the caregiver now instead of being cared for. I felt I no longer had the right to complain when he spent too long at the Club at the end of the day, but it did not make me feel any happier about being alone.

Fiji was moving towards independence by the mid-60s. The island group had been ceded to Queen Victoria in 1870 by Fiji's paramount chief, King Cakobau, with the land to be held in trust for its native owners. One hundred years later, this had become a serious fault line in race relations as descendants of the original East Indian indentured laborers could only lease but never buy land. As they were the hard-working entrepreneurs and professionals of the community, this bred resentment, especially as the Indians were by now in the majority. The Colonial Government decreed that Fiji had come of age and deserved its independence in 1970, leaving future conflict to be resolved by the new administration. Independence also meant that European residents would have to decide on leaving or staying on as Fiji nationals, which in our case, meant renouncing our New Zealand nationality.

While we were worrying about our future, the Company solved the problem in 1967 by sending John to the University of Hawaii for a year in their graduate School of Agriculture. This was a major change in our lives, a great opportunity for John to grow professionally and for me to leave the parochial world of Lautoka for new horizons. We sold the VW Beetle, packed, and stored possessions and put my beloved dog Chloe to sleep as she was old and suffering from heartworm despite regular treatments over the years. I wept for hours – she had been my only companion for countless lonely days since I had married John. I felt so guilty about this necessary rite of passage but it meant the beginning of a new world for me.

8. Hawaii 1968

Most of the time we fail to see the big wide real world at all because we are blinded by obsession, anxiety, envy, resentment, fear. We make a small personal world in which we remain enclosed. Iris Murdoch (from Brain Pickings)

I had not really been prepared for living in Honolulu on John's salary which had been fine in Fiji with free housing. But paying rent in a student apartment complex meant we could not afford a car and we also could not afford much of the wonderful array of products in the supermarkets. I felt like a country bumpkin, wistfully exploring the variety and choices unheard of in Lautoka. I had never seen coin-operated laundry machines either and colored television with all its different stations was amazing. Our son Christian was enrolled in the Ala Moana Elementary School kindergarten class and with John catching the bus each morning to the University, I was left alone to explore this wonderful new world.

I soon found the short route to Waikiki beach to swim and sunbathe among the tourists at the many resorts along the coast. I loved window shopping along the Ala Moana mall with its cheeky mynah birds wolf-whistling at passers-by and the familiar tropical plants made me feel less like a stranger in a strange country. Frangipani flowers were called plumerias, salusalus were called leis and bula shirts were called aloha shirts, but the heat and humidity were the same and palm trees and hibiscus shrubs flourished here as well as they did in Fiji.

The biggest difference however, which impressed me deeply, was the influence of Asian culture on the landscaping, art and architecture, and the food, blending with the culture of the islands into something exotic after the pragmatic Britishness of Fiji. We were invited to Thanksgiving Dinner by the head of the agricultural science faculty which was rather an alarming experience as the guests were all much older than me, and the house was the most elegant I had ever been in. There seemed to be acres of white carpet and all eyes were on Christian as he carried his plate of blueberry pie carefully -and successfully-back to his seat. More used to the stereotype of poorly paid British academics, I was impressed by the status and comfort enjoyed by American academics.

Our hostess arranged for me to speak at a meeting of the Honolulu League of Women Voters. I prepared a passionate request for help for the kindergarten I had started in Lautoka, explaining how the Colony of Fiji was becoming independent and multi-racial but that funding was so limited we had to make our own jigsaw puzzles. When I stopped and was considering asking directly for donations, a woman raised her hand, and said, "Please don't stop talking. We just love your accent." I was deflated and wondered if they had even heard what I said.

John discouraged me from accompanying him to the University campus, but I went ahead anyway on my own to enquire about enrolling as a student. I learned about entrance requirements and was given a sample of the test paper with bubbles to be filled in and questions that seemed either simplistic or illogical. Disappointed that they did not recognize my New Zealand University Entrance qualifications, I set to and passed the test despite not understanding some of the math problems at all. I was too late however for enrollment in the Anthropology course that I wanted and instead spent time at the library of the Bishop Museum.

When I introduced myself to the librarian and asked her help in finding material about my grandfather, she welcomed me warmly and took me under her wing. "So you are the granddaughter of Frederick William Christian, "she said, taking me to meet others on the staff. I was given a wealth of references and started with his book, *The Caroline Islands: Travel in the Sea of Little Lands* which he wrote in 1899. He had been a gentleman explorer and amateur ethnologist until the First World War, when he lost his inheritance and income because it was invested in Germany. He had spent some time in Hawaii, working on his comparative studies and dictionaries of the approximately 40 Pacific Island languages; my mother's second name is Kapiolani, after the much-loved Hawaiian Queen who died in 1899.

His book, *The Caroline Islands*, afforded the only glimpse I could get into his character and personality. A grainy black and white photo of him is too small to see much more than his slight figure in a tropical linen suit, under a white straw hat. Most of his book is a detailed account of language variants from island to island but there were occasional insights into his personality. For example, on the voyage from Sydney to Hong Kong in 1895, he writes in overblown Victorian prose.

"Our dear old captain Hugh Craig is the life and soul of our merry bachelor party. Day after day we creep northward, gliding over a glassy sea, our Lotus eaters' monotony only broken by sumptuous meals served by noiseless and discreet Celestials in airy attire. Evening after evening, many a noble rubber of whist is played out on deck with the Southern Cross and the myriad lamps of the sky gleaming overhead; with the kindly breezes of starry-kirtled night playing softly around us, as with rhythmic beat of clanging machinery, the great boat marches on with a fiery train of phosphorescent sparkles in her train".

I am not sure if my grandfather's description of Thursday Island betrays his upper-class prejudices or perhaps was a journalistic exaggeration to capture the attention of his readers.

"The island is a barren sandy spot, and the township a miserable collection of tumbledown shanties and stores faced

with shaky verandahs and roofed with corrugated iron, which with the fiery heat beating down overhead makes the interior a positive furnace, creating a hell-like heat and thirst, which many of the settlers appropriately quench with huge draughts of spirits that might have come out of Beelzebub's own private still. Here indeed is a wonderful mixture of races for poet, painter or artist of an unhealthy turn of mind. Crapulous unwashed white men with low foreheads and cunning shifty eyes, Cingalese, Malays, Papuans, Chinamen, Portuguese, African and Australian niggers, and half-castes of all sorts of lovely dissolving shades of white, dirty brown, sooty black and sickly yellow, pullulating together like vermin in the mud-honey of drink, opium and filth…"

The man who wrote the introduction to *The Caroline Islands* at my grandfather's invitation, Admiral Sir Cyprian Bridge, took exception to this description of Thursday Island, and while admitting that there was "*a noisy quarter in which there is much debauchery,*" he went on to say, "*Whilst nothing would induce me to walk across a London Park after 10 pm, I would readily walk from one end of Thursday Island to the other at any hour.*"

The Admiral's opinions were quite enlightened for the times – he was aware, as was my grandfather, of the diminishing of native populations due to modern diseases such as measles and smallpox. But the existence of the stone ruins in the Caroline Islands, as described by my grandfather, he felt could assuage white guilt.

"That the native population is diminishing – equally under conditions of coddling or neglect – is certain. There is, however, nothing to show that the actual rate of decrease is greater than, or even as great as, that of former ages. Indeed, it is reasonable to suppose that the natives had been rapidly moving towards extinction before the white man ever appeared on the scene. If the great ruins were the work of a pre-existing people, it would strengthen the belief ......that the dying-out is really independent of the white man's action. Consequently, we may console ourselves with the refection that however sorely we may have sinned against them, we are not responsible for the extinction of the island races of the Pacific."

He is also ready to defend the influence of missionaries and notes that, *"The civilization of the islanders – Europeanisation would be more accurate – has not been the work of the missionaries alone. The white trader has had no insignificant share in it."*

My grandfather spent the years 1890 to 1893 in Samoa, and *"deeming idleness a thing unrighteous"*, he cultivated economic plants, *"mostly of the Eucalyptus order, for distribution among the natives."* He wrote, *"Supplies of seeds for this purpose were regularly sent to me by the Forest Department of New South Wales, in return for which I consigned seed-packets of native trees and plants."*

His interest in philology dated from his college days and was encouraged by *"the sympathetic counsels of the late Master of Balliol"* and by Robert Louis Stevenson, his neighbor at Vailima. After becoming a corresponding member of the Polynesian Society of New Zealand, he sold his land to Stevenson and set out for Eastern Polynesia, Tahiti and the Marquesas to study and record their language, customs, and legends. On his return to Sydney, he met the well-known write Louis Becke who told him about the mysterious ruins in the Caroline Islands of Micronesia, which had already been explored by a German J.S Kubary. Kubary gave my grandfather his plans of the Metalanim ruins shortly before his death in 1896 and paid tribute to him in the preface to his book; "All honor to German scientists for their work in Pacific waters. And shall we, the English, sit by and dream, while others are up and doing?"

When he could no longer travel with his retinue of hired photographer, boatmen and porters, he returned to England with crates of artifacts that he had acquired from the ruins in the Carolines. He gave lectures at Royal Geographical Society gatherings and made time for visits to Covent Garden in London where he met my grandmother. She was a lay volunteer for a city mission which did good works for the poor, and I imagine, tried to reform the prostitutes who frequented Covent Garden. They married and lived in Essex, then in Lymington in Hampshire for some years, where my grandfather wrote another book titled *Eastern Pacific Lands;*

Tahiti and the Marquesas Islands (1910). The First World War and the loss of his investments in Germany meant that my grandfather was forced to earn a living. My mother was 12 years old when Frederick and Lillian left England with their six children and went out to the Cook Islands as teachers with the London Missionary Society.

They lived on Mangaia, the southernmost of the Cook Islands where the London Missionary Society had been established in 1824. The next hundred years had seen the usual tragic story of changes to the Mangaian culture and way of life. The old gods were destroyed, and the missionaries' puritanical rules outlawed traditional dance, drama, and music. At the same time, the native population was ravaged by measles, mumps and chickenpox and more recent research indicates that Pacific cultures did not succumb passively to missionary domination as their many records state.

By the time the Christian family arrived and took up residence in the schoolmaster's house, the people of Mangaia had "lost a certain amount of their individuality, self-respect and pride of race" and consequently, the people began doubting the value of their old ways and beliefs. This was according to the New Zealand Maori anthropologist Sir Peter Buck who described in 1933 how Christianity had replaced Mangaia's indigenous values with an inferiority complex. I wonder if my grandparents contributed to this mindset or whether they had the grace and imagination to compensate if they could with a more enlightened viewpoint. I will never know.

My grandfather's books reveal a somewhat Victorian and paternalistic attitude towards the natives he encountered on his earlier travels, but family tradition has it that he had taken a Tahitian princess to Sydney with him, where she died of influenza, according to my grandmother *"because she wouldn't keep her knickers on."* My grandmother burned all my grandfather's papers and manuscripts after his death.

9. Iraq 1969-70

*If everything is ahead then nothing is behind. You have no
ballast. You have no tailwinds either. You hardly ever know
what to do, because you've hardly done anything. Meghan
Daum. (from Brain Pickings)*

Our year in Hawaii came to an end. My husband had
been offered a job with the Hawaiian Ranch Company to
improve their tropical pastures with the legume strain that he
had developed, phaseolus atropurpureus. He was proud of his
work in Fiji establishing a plant nursery for different strains of
pasture grass and alfalfa to find out the best varieties for
tropical climates. He had come home one night after checking
his experiment to tell me that the cattle had broken down the
fence and trampled his entire research plots. But instead of it
being a disaster, they had eaten the Phaseolus down to the
ground and ignored most of the other plants, proving,
fortunately, that that was the strain to retain and develop. He
gave several seminars on his work at the University of Hawaii
and had immediately received job offers.

We had visited the ranch on the Big Island of Hawaii
and spent a couple of nights with the manager and his wife in
their lovely home. They were very welcoming and took us to
see the nearest town of Naalehu, the southernmost town in

the whole of the USA, where Christian would go to school. We also saw the sloping tract of land where our new house would be built with its wide view of the ocean and ample room for me to establish a garden. We visited some of the tourist attractions in the area including the painted churches and the renowned Halemaumau National Park, with its enormous deep crater – "the world's only drive-in volcano." The park ranger explained that the crater was cold and dead now, but could erupt at any time and sure enough, our excited hostess woke us early the next morning to say there had been an earthquake during the night and the eruption had begun.

We drove to the crater rim just as a van load of nuns arrived, their black robes billowing in the strange hot wind as they walked towards us. Christian clutched my leg as he looked at them and then into the fiery pit of the crater. "Is this Hell? "he whispered to me. Close enough, I thought, but hastened to reassure him as we stood and marveled at the awesome sight, while more and more people were arriving on special flights from Honolulu and the mainland. A Hawaiian priestess, garlanded with leis, came to chant prayers to Pele, goddess of the volcano, while we were being showered with "Pele's tears," little drops of molten glass being tossed up by the roiling winds from the crater. It was a profoundly moving experience and one that filled me with excitement about our future on the Big Island with the constant backdrop of elemental nature to add significance to our life.

Back in Honolulu, we checked with the Immigration Service regarding my visa status, as John's student visa would be changed to a Green Card to reflect his employment. We explained that I was returning to Fiji to pack up our stored belongings and then on to New Zealand before returning to be with my husband. No problem, we were told. Just check in with the American Consulate in Auckland. We were naïve to accept this vague information and in retrospect, we heard what we wanted to hear without questioning more closely. As I found out later, it was a mistake to leave US territory as I was no longer protected by John's student visa status and had to apply as an individual and be prepared to wait my turn in the allotted quota for New Zealand immigrants. This could take at least eighteen months I was told by the unsympathetic American Consul.

So I was back in New Zealand again with my parents in Hamilton for an indefinite period. John assured me that the company was doing its best to resolve the situation by enlisting the help of Congressman Daniel Inouye to enable me to get a preferential Green Card. My parents made space for me and Christian, and we enrolled him in the local school around the corner while we waited for news. The weeks turned into months.

Juliet, Jane, my father and mother, Robert and me in Hamilton,

August 1969

I became more and more despondent as time passed and John's letters were full of the new friends he was making, the new car he had bought, a Ford Mustang, and I began to suspect him of being unfaithful to me as his letters were becoming more and more impersonal. After five months, my relationship with my parents was becoming strained. My mother was a martyr to my father's drinking, and she often indulged in a sherry too many, making the evenings either sentimental or acrimonious. I also felt it was time my little sister Juliet had her bedroom back to herself, so I decided to move up to Auckland to be closer to my older sister Jane.

I negotiated a long-term rate in a motel unit with a small kitchen that was an easy walk to my sister's house and the elementary school her children attended. Each morning I walked up through the little shopping center with Christian who attracted attention in his smart Sears clothes and cowboy boots. Sometimes I stopped in for coffee with Jane, who had suffered a terrible loss when her husband had been killed in a car accident, leaving her with four children and a high-powered job as editor of a women's magazine. I had hoped we would perhaps become closer as a result, but she was as judgmental as ever and scornful of our American destiny as she and her new husband were planning to move to Europe.

My loneliness increased and I spent my days reading and knitting a sweater for my father, while waiting for school to be out and for the postman to bring news from Hawaii. I did not feel like initiating anything as I expected news any day that I would be able to leave New Zealand. But the Green Card never happened. As a solution, John was eventually offered a job with Hawaiian Agronomics International, a company that was setting up a sugar industry in southern Iraq. It was a great opportunity for him to get international experience and after nearly a year apart, we were finally to be a family again.

We decided it would be a good idea for us to meet in Fiji for a few days, as we had been apart for nearly a year and the flight from Hawaii stopped there anyway. My mother looked after Chris and I flew to Nadi airport full of anticipation about a new start, an exciting future, and a renewed hope for a closer relationship with John. I could not believe it when once again, he was not at the airport to meet me. I got a taxi to the Mocambo Hotel and sure enough, there he was at the bar "talking story" as the Hawaiians put it, regaling strangers with anecdotes, obviously many beers later. He had forgotten our plan to meet at the airport and insisted I join him for a drink, announcing that he was dying for a good hot Indian curry. By the time we were seated in the café, his voice was loud and abrasive as he demanded a really hot curry, "none of your tourist muck." The dignified waiter brought him a curry so hot that his eyes watered, his face went red and he could hardly speak, and I must admit I felt he deserved what he got. It was not the reunion I had anticipated.

I should have taken the next plane back to Auckland. Like many unhappy marriages, it was a "death by a thousand cuts" – as there was never one definitive moment where it was clear that it was over. It was not that I forgave him, but I continued to ignore his behavior and lower my expectations, while becoming acutely aware that I was living in a state of "bad faith." I had understood enough of my reading of Jean-Paul Sartre to know that bad faith or inauthenticity is a state of mind where a person refuses to accept that they have the freedom to change and continues with the mistaken belief that "I can't do anything about it." Any introspection on my part led to self-pity rather than courage to change the things I could, and I hated myself for it.

However, we flew back to New Zealand the following day and on the two-and-a-half-hour flight, I was able to learn something about Hawaiian Agronomics International, the job and the place where we were to spend the next two years. It would be a new beginning, which was always hopeful. Once Chris and I had the required visas and vaccinations, it was time to pack again. My parents and John's father visited us at the motel to say farewell and wish us luck on our way to an unknown country and an uncertain future.

Travel arrangements had been made for us and I was delighted that we had an overnight stopover in Teheran at the Hilton hotel before going on to Baghdad. It was luxury that I had never experienced before and that night I leaned on our balcony railing watching a wedding party below in the hotel grounds. "Come and see how the rich folk live," I called to John, but he was already fast asleep. A fairytale marquee of flowers and lights framed a glittering assembly of elegant, jeweled women with elaborate sculpted hairdos and shimmering embroidered gowns. The buffet was laid out on Persian carpets with ice towers at intervals, hollowed out with lights inside to feature large bowls of caviar; traditional music and the perfume of exotic spices wafted up to where I watched, a completely enchanted and wistful country bumpkin.

Breakfast with a background of the snow-capped Alborz mountains included iced melon with a sweetness that far outdid our usual papaya and delicious flat breads and coffee with a hint of cardamom. I could have stayed forever, completely entranced with this new world of color and romantic history. But we only had time for a quick tour of the suq with its enticing carpets, brass and copperwork before our flight to Iraq.

We were coming to a turbulent country, as Iraq had just experienced a bloodless coup in July of 1968, led by General Ahmed Hassan al-Bakr. The socialist Baath party was in power and Saddam Hussein, a major participant in the coup, was al-Bakr's deputy. The regime was anti- Israeli and anti-American, so we were viewed with suspicion the moment we landed. Our suitcases were searched thoroughly, and we happened to have a couple of Frank Sinatra cassettes with us. These were confiscated on the grounds that Sinatra had recently given a concert in New York to raise funds for Israel. I found this almost laughably naïve of the Customs officer but when airport officials are unsmiling soldiers with businesslike rifles, I restrained myself. It was something I never got used to, having grown up in British countries where the police were unarmed, and it was disconcerting to feel vulnerable to armed men in uniform who do not speak your language. I had a lot to learn about living in a military dictatorship. It certainly was a universe away from the Big Island of Hawaii.

After a night at the Hotel Baghdad, which was nowhere near as glamorous as the Teheran Hilton, we set off for the long drive to the Amarah Sugar Project, some 230 miles south. The heat was extremely uncomfortable as the car's air conditioning was not working and the desert air was like an oven. It was not a great introduction and it was even worse when we stopped in the town of Kut as Chris and I needed a bathroom break. I could not believe the state of the women's restroom – a foul hole in the ground with barely a clean space for my feet as I squatted. The stench made me dizzy and my heart sank as I realized how completely we had left civilization behind.

By the time we arrived in Amarah, both Chris and I were quite distressed by the heat. The Project was a compound of brick houses within a barbed wire perimeter, with armed guards at the gate, not so much to keep the Americans safe but to prevent us from leaving without a pass. We unpacked in a small, temporary house with swamp coolers to ease the stifling heat and a view of endless, dusty, flat land stretching off to the village of Mujar-al-Kabir in the distance. Our new bigger house with proper air-conditioning was not ready for us yet, and we had few belongings anyway, as we had to wait some months for our sea freight to arrive. I wished many times that I had had a proper briefing on what to expect and what to bring, instead of John's airy expectation that I would adapt to circumstances with British stoicism.

We were welcomed by the Project residents – mostly Americans from Hawaii but also some Australians and other nationalities. I was pleased to find there were some women close to my age, but most were older and without children. There was a small school for the Project children and Chris would fit in right away, but it would take me a while to adjust to the ugliness of the compound – trees and lawns had only just been planted and the new brick houses were the same color as the bare dusty brown soil. The only green was the new sugar cane fields being established in the distance.

While the land was being levelled and drained, ready for planting the cane, the sugar processing factory was being completed by an Italian company, Impianti, and we got to know some of the Italian construction workers and their Irish foreman. It was a strange community, in the middle of nowhere, and unfortunately when people need a leader in such a situation, the Project Manager, Cedric Weight was already quite ill with cancer. He was needed for frequent trips to Baghdad to negotiate terms for our continued residence, but we all wished he would go back to the States for medical treatment.

As it was, in the following months, we gradually lost some basic privileges; we could not have our own company American doctor on the Project and had to accept a locally trained man instead, we could no longer get imported goods for our commissary and the Project was being integrated with Iraqi families moving in. The swimming pool became impossible for American women as the Iraqi men were lascivious and pushy, so we had to sit there fully dressed while our children enjoyed the water.

It was impressive however, to drive around the cane fields with John on occasions to see how the Hawaiian agronomists had made the desert flower. Centuries of neglect of ancient irrigation systems had caused the land to become poisoned by an accretion of salt. The Americans levelled the ground, laid tile drains some feet underground then flooded the fields for up to 40 days with water from the nearby Tigris

River. The salt was washed down to the tile drains and back into the river. Cane that took about two years to mature in Hawaii took only nine months in the leached and now very fertile soil, leading some to suggest that the Amarah Project was a second Garden of Eden. Archaeologists claim the biblical garden of Eden was probably at the confluence of the Tigris and Euphrates rivers some distance south of Amarah and it always amused us to see the primitive sign on the road to Basra, marking a few date palms and rusted barbed wire as the site of the original Garden.

Most of us had kitchen gardens and I grew the biggest cauliflowers I had ever seen – others had phenomenal broccoli plants and we shared our crops and recipes as we struggled to live off what we could grow or buy at the local market. We made our own bread and pizza and my Australian friend Jill showed me how to make blender mayonnaise using peanut oil. But the biggest lack was books – I had not realized how dependent I was on reading until I had no access to a library. Fortunately, some of the Project residents had brought books with them and I am ever grateful to Evan, a Greek American who lent me some books on Iraqi history.

I became fascinated by the history of the Kurdish people and their age-old struggle for autonomy despite constant betrayals by the Great Powers of Britain and France, then Turkey and more recently, the Americans. They had their own religions, ancient sects such as the Yazidis, who worshipped a Peacock Angel and the Zoroastrians who worshipped fire. Persecuted over the centuries, the Kurds suffered terribly under Sadaam Hussein who gassed the townspeople of Halajdah in Northern Iraq in 1988, an act of genocide denounced internationally. Then again in 2014 Hussein tried to eliminate the Yazidis by forcibly relocating them from their historical villages which would then be destroyed. The world witnessed the tragic trek over the mountains of thousands of still defiant Yazidi women and children as international relief agencies struggled to aid them.

During our time in Amarah however, the Kurds still had some freedom and the newly appointed Liaison Officer was a charming Kurd, Roshan, who spoke good English and enjoyed a party, of which there were many to relieve the boredom. He had been a bodyguard to the Iraqi King Faisal the Second, who was assassinated in 1958 as he and his family were trying to escape from the palace. "So where was the bodyguard?" I asked Roshan, who cheerfully admitted that he had been hiding behind a pillar. He was very diplomatic when we questioned him about the regime, and openly warned us that he was required to report back on conversations he overheard while socializing with us. The Mukhabarat or secret police were everywhere, he said, and we should keep a low profile.

Some months after our arrival, the Israeli Air Force had bombed an Iraqi installation near the Jordanian border and as a result the Iraqi regime became even more virulently anti-Israeli. The authorities began arresting alleged conspirators in a so-called "American-Israeli spy-ring." In a shockingly barbaric action, in January 1968, the prisoners were hanged, and their bodies were strung up on lamp posts on display in one of Baghdad's busiest squares. Our friend Nina, the Project schoolteacher happened to be in Baghdad that day for a dentist appointment and was shocked when her taxi driver insisted that they drive past to see what happens to "enemies of our beloved country." Baghdad Radio had invited citizens to Liberation Square to "come and enjoy the feast." 500,000 people reportedly attended the hangings and danced and celebrated before the corpses. Nina told me that she had heard of another recent execution of an Egyptian dressmaker, a woman who naturally had many contacts in the international community and was deemed therefore to be an Israeli spy. I was appalled to hear of the random nature of the regime's repression. I began counting the days until we could leave.

Our lives on the Project were fairly remote from Baghdad politics however, and sometimes I felt our biggest problem was how to get regular supplies of alcohol and cigarettes from the many smugglers in the area who went back and forth between Iraq and the more liberal Iran. Seeing they supplied Iraqi police and soldiers as well as the Mukhabarat, a little extra bribery from time to time kept the black market an acceptable practice.

Friday, the Muslim day of prayer, was our "weekend" and there were occasional events organized, such as barbeques or basketball games, usually with plenty of alcohol involved. A memorable outing was a trip to the Marshes in a boat hired for the occasion. I had read *The Marsh Arabs* by British traveler and writer, Wilfred Thesiger, and was delighted to see the strange world of the marshes for myself. Long a refuge for escaped slaves, tax-dodgers, and dissidents, it was a series of villages with houses built of reeds on floating islands, with primitive canoes and water buffaloes, and exotic bird life. Our boat nosed through narrow canals, reeds touching on each side and then into open lakes to small villages with children running alongside, shouting, and throwing what turned out to be dried buffalo dung at us. We stopped at a village and were shown the schoolhouse, with its mud floor and one ancient chalkboard. I regretted that I had not thought about the level of poverty we would encounter – I could at least have brought them some of Christian's old books.

One Friday, when some of the Project wives and I were going into Amarah to the local market in the small company van, eager to get there and back as quickly as possible because of the dust and smells and flies, we had to stop and wait for a religious procession to pass by. The Iraqis in the south were mainly Shia and celebrate the first month of the Islamic year, Muharram, by mourning the death of the martyred grandson of the Prophet Mohammed. We were appalled to see the men in the procession flagellating themselves with chains and wires as they shuffled along, chanting prayers hypnotically, almost as if drugged. Quite young boys were there too, lashing themselves with intensity and seemingly oblivious to the busload of startled white women, looking on with horror.

The high point of our first year in Iraq came during one of the longer religious holidays, the Eid al-Fitr at the end of Ramadan, when we were able to get passes and visas to go to Iran. We drove the 125 miles down to Basra, an ancient seaport made famous by Sinbad the sailor, but now a rather desolate and scruffy town. We hired an open boat to cross the Shat-al-Arab, the confluence of the Tigris and Euphrates Rivers which separates Iraq and Iran, landing at Abadan, an oil port. We were greeted by Iranian officials with smiles. *"Welcome, welcome Americans! You must be happy to leave Iraq and come to our beautiful country!"*

It was an auspicious start to our vacation, which included a visit to Persepolis, the ancient ceremonial capital that was set on fire by Alexander the Great in about 330 BC. It is not clear if the fire was an accident or a deliberate act of revenge for the burning of the Acropolis of Athens during the second Persian invasion of Greece. The ruins were still impressive however and I found it a deeply moving experience. I thought of Shelley's great poem *Ozymandias,*

Look on my Works, ye Mighty, and despair!

Nothing beside remains. Round the decay

Of that colossal Wreck, boundless and bare

The lone and level sands stretch far away."

We stayed a night in Shiraz, a beautiful city of mosques and roses, and the comfortable hotel featured Iranian musicians to entertain us at cocktail hour. Our son Christian was fascinated and sat cross-legged on the ground in front of the musicians, totally absorbed in their hypnotic music, somewhat like Romanian gypsy music. John and our friends were in the bar however, deep in conversation with a Russian who they said later was "pretending to be a tourist, but we think he is a spy." He was probably working for oil interests and was charming company, and I enjoyed his conversation later that evening after the endless discussions about sugar cane.

Both Iraq and Iran were dependent on oil at this time and most of the political turmoil was based on nationalized oil companies and the jockeying for power that went along with the new ownership. Iran's oil had been nationalized in 1951, when production came to a virtual standstill as British technicians left the country and Britain imposed a worldwide embargo on the purchase of Iranian oil. Twenty years later in 1972, Sadaam Hussein had nationalized the powerful Iraq Petroleum Company, with the help of the Soviet Union. The huge oil terminal at Abadan on the Gulf was a reminder of the importance of oil in this part of the world and contrasted vividly with the culture and beauty remaining from ancient Persia. I was eager to see as much as possible because I knew that we would probably never be back in Iran again.

We visited Isfahan, the most beautiful Iranian city with its ornate and majestic mosques, tiled and sculpted and illumined by the unique blue of Iranian art. Its suq was another fascinating world of artists and artisans, producing crafts of great beauty and precision, the copper smiths fascinating us as they tapped and chiseled their intricate designs. I was so proud of six-year-old Christian on this trip as he responded with interest and sensitivity to not only the musicians but the craftsmen too, and naturally he was impressed by the young children weavers in the carpet section. Some of our friends bought carpets but our prize was a copper and pewter inlaid tray which was quite a challenge to transport home on the small boat across the Shat-al-Arab again.

As Western tourists we were sheltered from the real issues of the country then under the autocratic rule of the Shah. "We are happy with our beloved Shah," proclaimed our taxi driver in Shiraz, but that evening when we ventured out from the hotel to find a local café, we passed a street where a prisoner was being moved. Shackled in chains, he was picked up by two burly policemen and thrown into the back of a Land Rover as if he was a side of beef. I was troubled by this, but John rationalized that it was inevitable when keeping order in such a vast country of many religions and tribes. We both agreed it was certainly not as bad as in Iraq, where Saddam Hussein was jockeying for power and the Baath Party was eliminating rivals and dissidents at an alarming rate. During our time in Iraq, there were so many Minsters of Agriculture denounced, imprisoned, or found floating in the Euphrates that our manager was constantly having to go up to Baghdad to renegotiate with the new authority.

The weather in Amarah was awful –hot and dusty in the summer months, cold and rainy in winter. We made our own social life, parties with home-made alcohol, pasta dinners with the Italians at the sugar factory, and bridge with other bored wives. I was glad that I had learned to be self-sufficient in Fiji but many times I felt defeated and depressed. I remember sweeping the floor one day after a sandstorm, with the music of Lucia de Lammermoor playing at top volume as I wept along with Maria Callas, her glorious voice expressing the despair I was feeling.

I was finally able to escape – I became pregnant and company policy decreed that it was out of the question to remain in Amarah or even Baghdad where the hospitals were presumably more westernized. The Project management arranged for me to have an apartment in Zurich, where they had a subsidiary office, and as I had no intention of going back to New Zealand, I was happy to go to Switzerland as the nearest safe, clean country.

John's first year was up in June and he was due for some leave in Europe, so we flew to England first, where he settled us in a basement apartment in a hotel in London, before returning to Iraq. Christian and I enjoyed the summer weather in London and went sight-seeing as much as I could being seven months pregnant. We walked to the museums in South Kensington where our favorite exhibit was the Tipoo Tiger, a mechanical figure, commissioned by a Rajah, of a tiger devouring an official of the East India Company. We visited the Tower of London and the British Museum and fed the pigeons in Trafalgar Square. The high point, however, was sitting in front of our black and white television set in the hotel, watching the landing on the moon. Years later, Chris was to remind me," I didn't get to see it all because you had me holding the antenna for a better picture!"

I had arranged that Chris and I would meet my Australian friend Jill from the Amarah Project and her three children in Austria. Instead of flying or taking a train, I decided to go on a bus tour through France and Belgium and into the Tyrol before meeting Jill in Wolfgangsee, a lake resort near Salzburg. I loved it – the friendly tour guide Maurice kept offering me Belgian chocolates, people carried my bags and were so kind to Christian. Every time we went over a bump,

Maurice called out, "Still in one piece?" I loved the countryside with the French farmhouses where women were still wearing wooden clogs, the houses in Austria with a riot of colorful hanging baskets and window boxes. Even the cows, such gentle golden beasts with huge bells round their neck, were more beautiful than those in New Zealand.

I was thankful to have Jill's company in the pensione by the lake as it rained a lot and Jill had the energy to rent a little rowboat to take our children for small excursions. Then we discovered that for a modest sum, we could put the kids on the daily ferry boat, under the reluctant but watchful eye of its captain, and they were returned safely after a round trip of delivering milk and mail. One sunny day we all went into Salzburg and were enchanted by music everywhere. It was a few days before the Salzburg Mozart Festival, and it seemed that wherever we went there were soloists, quartets, and full orchestras rehearsing. It was glorious and I think even the children enjoyed Mozart that day, or perhaps it was Mozart and ice creams.

The time came for Jill and her children to return to Iraq and for Christian and me to carry on to Zurich. "Give my regards to the Project," I said, "and of course to John." I had accumulated a lot of luggage by this time and it was quite an undertaking getting on and off trains, but with a little help from kind strangers, we made our way to the apartment in Kloten, a Zurich suburb near the airport. It was the beginning of September and Switzerland was particularly beautiful at that time of year, with leaves just beginning to turn to their autumn colors. Everything was tidy, clean, and ordered. I was grateful to Fritz and Lotti from the Zurich office of Hawaiian Agronomics International who made sure I was settled and comfortable and had offered to look after Chris while I was in hospital with the baby. I was booked into the Frauenklinik and checked in with a friendly doctor who assured me all was well and that the baby was due in about three weeks.

My first major purchase was a sturdy folding pram with a bed that lifted out and could be carried on and off trains and planes. Chris was enrolled at the International School in Zurich and was picked up by bus and returned each day, so there was little to do, once we unpacked, but knit and wait. I could walk to the local supermarket but found it difficult to carry groceries back again and decided one morning to do a lot of shopping and call for a taxi. This became complicated when I discovered that the public phone was down a flight of stairs and I had to leave my shopping cart unattended. I was momentarily at a loss and called out to a friendly looking woman who was heading for the parking lot. "Do you speak English?" which was rather silly because most people Switzerland do. It is only Americans who are so bad at foreign languages. "Of course, "she said, taking in my predicament, "Can I help?" She turned out to be a minister in a local Lutheran church and she kindly drove me home. I went to church with her the following Sunday and loved the elegance of the unadorned whitewashed walls and the simple wooden cross, after the rococo splendor of Austrian churches with their ornate gold and marble.

Sophie Talei was born on a glorious September morning, after I had seen Chris off to school and had called for a taxi to cross the city to the hospital. I remembered to take the book I was reading, Arthur Koestler's *Darkness at Noon*, and as most of the staff were German speaking I kept it with me as a distraction right to the last moment when Herr Professor Dr. Held said, "It's time to put your book down Madame as your baby is nearly here." When he announced, "It's a girl," I could not believe it at first, having had so many disappointments in my life. I was overwhelmed to be getting exactly what I wanted for a change.

One of the German-speaking nurses was named Sophie and she was pleased that I had chosen that name for the baby, and I did not want to spoil her pleasure by explaining it had been chosen months ago, with Talei as a middle name, a Fijian name meaning "something precious." Later that day when I was holding my little girl and looking out at the Zurich skyline, all the bells started to ring from ancient cathedrals and churches, startling the last swallows of summer in the golden evening light. I felt a rush of pure happiness and optimism, sure in my bones that all was well, and that "all manner of things" would be well, as Eliot reiterated in his poem "Little Gidding."

The weeks that followed were somewhat difficult as I had decided to use formula right from the start as I knew that the lack of privacy would be an issue when returning to John. Remembering the bathroom in the hotel in Kut, I could not bear the thought of trying to feed my baby there. The baby threw up a lot and laundry was a problem as the apartment building had strict rules about the use of the washer and dryer downstairs. A roster of once every two weeks was no use to me with my limited amount of clothes and linen and despite appeals to the Hausmeister in broken German/French, I had to use the bathtub and drape wet laundry around the apartment to dry.

I was able to do a little shopping and sightseeing in Zurich before returning to the desert. I loved the feeling of order and solidity in this German-speaking part of Switzerland, especially the area of big banks near the station. I discovered the Café Sprungli on Banhofstrasse where the daily newspapers were stacked on wooden rollers by the door for patrons to borrow. I always looked for the International Herald Tribune to read while enjoying the wonderful coffee and cakes. I lingered in the parks with their great spreading established trees, knowing I would miss them when I returned to the bleak land of Southern Iraq, where the only trees were sparse dusty thorn bushes and date palms alongside the Tigris and Euphrates Rivers.

The Swiss pediatrician insisted that Sophie needed a TB vaccination before we returned and that it could not be done until she was at least six weeks old. By the time we were packed and almost ready to leave, my visitor's visa had expired and one morning there was a knock at the door and two Swiss policemen were there to admonish me. "Madame, you are here illegally," the older gendarme said. I showed them my half-filled suitcases and the plane tickets, but they were unsmiling and told me I should have contacted the police station to let them know. I was impressed by their efficiency and had been somewhat disappointed when I learned that Sophie was not automatically a Swiss citizen through birth. Unlike the USA, citizenship had to be earned by birth plus at least ten years' residence.

The day of our departure, I awoke early and was taken aback to see snowflakes falling gently past my window. At first I thought it was the neighbor upstairs shaking out her feather duvets until I realized that winter had come. I was nervous about flying when it was snowing, but the taxi driver laughed off my fears, saying "If Swissair pilots could not fly in this weather, we wouldn't have a national airline."

The flight to Baghdad was uneventful and I felt some trepidation as we landed, wondering how life would be back in Amarah with a new baby. John was there this time to meet me and his new child, but I was really upset to find he was not alone. It was obvious that he had been drinking at the airport bar with a colleague from the Project that I did not particularly care for. Both men were loud and cheerful, completely ruining the tender and emotional reunion I had envisaged after four months on my own. We drove down to Amarah, John up front with the driver and us in the back seat, with me staring at the back of John's head for over 200 miles, wondering what the next year would bring.

10. Spain and Rome 1971

Human beings are works in progress that mistakenly think they're finished. The person you are right now is as transient, as fleeting and as temporary as all the people you've ever been. The one constant in our lives is change.   Dan Gilbert (from Brain Pickings)

The situation at the Project had become more tense during my absence as more of our privileges were taken away and passes to leave the compound had become more difficult to obtain. The Commissary rarely had adequate supplies of fresh meat or vegetables and more Iraqi families had moved into the smaller houses, as the Americans were training their counterparts to take over eventually. They viewed us with suspicion and sometimes downright hostility. My baby was a novelty in our small community and people got used to seeing me wheeling the Swiss pram around the neighborhood when the weather allowed it. But I was uneasy, wondering what I would do if she became ill so far from an English-speaking doctor. I was becoming increasingly weary of the drinking and infidelities that were so common amongst expatriates on the Project. I was pleased then when we decided that I would return to Europe with the baby in May before the summer took hold, to wait for John's contract to finish in September. Chris would stay with John and finish out his school year. I knew he would be fine as he spent most of his time with my friend Jill and her children.

I decided on Spain instead of Switzerland and found an affordable apartment in the village of Arroyo de la Miel on the Costa del Sol, not far from the growing tourist center of Torremolinos. Once again, I was setting up another temporary home on my own in another foreign country, this time with a baby to care for. I had tried to learn a little Spanish from a Peruvian woman who lived on the Amarah Project but soon discovered that the Andalusian pronunciation was quite different from hers. Trying to get some hot water to heat the baby's bottle at 4 am the night I arrived was a challenge – a sleepy youth delivered a bowl of fruit instead. The local people were very friendly however, and I got by with a dictionary and a lot of laughter. The local doctor was helpful and for the first time helped me understand that Sophie was probably lactose intolerant and from then on, she began to thrive on Spanish orange juice instead of milk.

The restaurant on the ground floor of the apartment building was owned by Manuel who had lived for some years in England and thus was a valuable translator and source of local information. I would carry Sophie down in her Swiss carry cot each night for dinner and wine with a view of the ocean sunsets. Manuel introduced me to other English-speaking patrons, including Kay and Cahal, an older Irish couple who lived nearby. Cahal was blind and they both loved cheap Spanish brandy, and many nights I worried about them getting home safely, with Cahal lurching through the dark holding Kay's hand and singing Irish songs or declaiming poetry at the top of his voice.

I met Annette, an attractive Danish girl and her handsome Spanish boyfriend Chimo, who wrote poetry and played the guitar. We spent happy hours at the beach together, lying in the sun listening to Chimo's music and drowsing after a lunch of fish and salad at the beach kiosks. Annette showed me how to steal a little olive oil from the café tables to use as suntan lotion and I was careful to keep Sophie under a beach umbrella. She was everybody's darling, as she was such a friendly baby and loved being greeted by tourists passing on the beach.

I also met an American couple when I was in Torremolinos one day, heading for the newsagent that sold English books and newspapers. We were two young mothers passing each other with our babies in prams on a narrow street. I was trying to think of how to say," I'm sorry, I think our wheels are stuck," in Spanish, when she laughed, and we discovered we both spoke English. Irene and Phil had been teachers in California before they decided to leave the rat race and move to Spain where Phil owned and ran a bar. Irene became a good friend and as her little boy was about the same age as Sophie, we had much in common.

The months went by with enough diversion to keep me from feeling completely adrift. I was grateful for my new friends who took me in their car to the nearby towns of

Mijas and Ronda, where I fell in love with the whitewashed villages perched on the mountainsides, the arroyos brilliant with flowering oleanders and the sky a perennial blue. Sometimes I would go down to the local bar for a grilled ham and cheese sandwich as an excuse to sit and watch bullfights on Spanish television, alternately repelled and fascinated by the spectacle and ritual of la corrida de toros or bullfight. The leading matador in Andalusia at the time was known as El Cordobes, and he was renowned for his unorthodox theatrical style and breathtaking courage in the bullring. I had read his biography, *Or I'll Dress You in Mourning*, by Larry Collins and Dominique Lapierre, published in 1968, and I became intrigued by his story and wished I could see him fight. His boyish good looks and reckless arrogance made him an idol first in Spain and then internationally after he had starred in several movies.

I was excited then when I heard from Manuel that El Cordobes was going to fight in Torremolinos and I was able to get a ticket. The crowd's enthusiasm overwhelmed the repugnance I had about watching a live animal be killed. The grace, the courage, the color, and ritual of the matadors made it an experience I will never forget and while it hardly seemed to belong in the 20th century, it seemed appropriate to the darker side of Spain's history of the Inquisition and the Civil War.

That year, 1969, was the year of the My Lai massacre, Woodstock and sex, drugs and rock and roll, yet in Spain, American culture seemed remote. Spain was still dominated by the Franco regime but was undergoing an economic renaissance after years of depression in the late 1940s and early 1950s. The Costa del Sol on the southern coast was being developed for sun-worshipping Europeans from England, Scandinavia, and Germany, and while bikinis were still banned on the beaches, liberal ideas were beginning to take hold. General Franco began showing symptoms of Parkinson's disease in the 1960s and his dictatorship was beginning to relax its grip on the country. By 1973, Franco had resigned as Prime Minister and he died in 1975.

My Californian friends, Phil and Irene, were students of Spanish culture and history and I learned a lot from them, spending siesta time with them in their bar by the beach, drinking Lumumbas, iced chocolate milk with Spanish brandy named after the African dictator, while our babies slept or played in their carry cots. I envied their life and freedom, but also sensed that it was not all easy, with seasonal trade and restrictive local laws making their income insecure.

John's contract in Iraq was due to end in September but he wrote to say he was coming to Spain earlier. Things had become so bad on the Project that people had

had no fresh meat for many weeks, so John and a colleague decided to buy a young steer which they killed and butchered and shared with grateful families. Obviously, they had not performed the correct Halal ritual before they killed the animal, and as there was always someone watching the Americans, John was reported to the local Mukhabarat. He was ordered to leave Iraq immediately.

We had no idea what he was going to do next as we could not return to Hawaii with our visa status in limbo. So, we were carefree tourists for a few weeks and explored the nearby cities of Cordoba and Granada. It was wonderful to have Chris with me again after two months and he quickly made friends with some local Spanish boys, visiting the beach and the local feria with them. Late summer was fiesta time and the towns on the Costa del Sol seemed full of flamenco music and color. We visited a World Bank contact of John's in Seville and were enchanted by the architecture and history of the lovely old city and the fiesta costumes and carriages parading in the evenings along the avenues. I loved the countryside too, and each time I saw a picturesque, white-washed farmhouse, surrounded by olive and orange trees and fields of brilliant sunflowers, I wished we could buy one and stay there forever.

John needed to earn some money however and accepted a three-month assignment with a Belgium based American company in Ghana, so he planned to leave us again almost immediately. We flew to Brussels and while John was settling details of his new assignment, the children and I explored the old town, photographed the Mannequin Pis of course, and spent time in the Africa Museum. That night after dinner we were surprised and delighted by a firework display over the city rooftops for National Day. Dinner had already been memorable for the children as at the next table, an elegantly dressed older woman was sitting with her poodle in a chair opposite, with a place setting for the dog's meal as well.

We needed a cheaper place than Belgium for me and the children to stay and found an affordable apartment above a shop in the little Swiss village of St Cergue. I was happy to return to Switzerland for the rest of the summer. My Danish friend Annette joined us as she had become pregnant and her relationship with her Spanish boyfriend Chimo had become unraveled as a result. I was happy to offer her a temporary home while she agonized about her future, with long tearful phone calls to her mother in Denmark and to Chimo in Spain. In the end her mother arrived and took her home. Annette sent me letters and photos of her little girl for a while, and then we lost touch. I often thought of her over the years and hoped she found happiness.

St Cergue was up in the mountains – reached first by rail from Geneva to Lausanne, then up the mountain by a smaller train, then by rack railway to the village which was surrounded by alpine meadows and flower-bedecked chalets and farms. It was delightful, and as it was in the French speaking part of Switzerland, it was much easier to communicate with my schoolgirl French instead of non-existent German. The last day in August was Swiss National Day and the villagers went up the mountainside with their fireworks to celebrate. I had bought some rockets and took an empty wine bottle with me to launch them. Christian was delighted when our rocket ignited, the bottle fell over and the firework whizzed past the head of the local gendarme. He was unhurt but unhappy. I kept saying "scusi" instead of "pardonnez -moi." I could see he was unimpressed with my poor attempt at an apology.

John returned from Ghana, with tales to tell of life there which confirmed that our future lay elsewhere. He had applied for a job with the United Nations Food and Agriculture Organization, so we set off to the headquarters in Rome. He hired a van, which was needed by now for our accumulated belongings and we drove over the Alps to Italy and on towards Rome through the

September countryside. We arrived in Florence to find that every hotel it seemed was full because of conventions. We were finally offered a room in the home of a friendly hotel concierge, where the paint on the bathroom floor was still wet, causing much voluble Italian and some laughter.

I could have stayed in Tuscany for much longer. We only had time for a cursory visit to the Uffizi Gallery and the obligatory photo of the statue of the naked David, and I wished we could have explored some of the walled towns and villages we drove past on our way south. It seemed every road we took was picture-postcard worthy, with elegant Italian cypresses framing spectacular views as if designed on purpose. The food at little village restaurants was a wonderful discovery. I thought of how we used to eat canned spaghetti, with strands of soft pasta and artificial red sauce. Pasta would be al dente from now on.

In Rome, we needed somewhere affordable to stay and found a cheap pensione by the main railway station. Every day John went off to the headquarters for the seemingly endless bureaucratic process of signing on to a position with the United Nations Development Program, while I explored Rome with Chris and Sophie in her stroller. The days were getting colder, and I was pleased to find some fashionable midi skirts, boots, and sweaters at a street market. We loved to visit the Torre Argentina, a plaza where there were hordes of stray cats, fed daily by old ladies with leftovers from the local restaurants. The site is most famous for being the place where Julius Caesar was stabbed to death on the Ides of March in 44 BCE, but Chris and little Sophie were impressed more by the cats than history. Chris would often say, "Who knew that cats love spaghetti!"

We visited the Trevi Fountain, the Forum, and the Vatican as I insisted that we see the Sistine Chapel. While we were gazing up at the marvelous ceiling frescoes, I became aware that a small crowd had gathered around little Sophie in her stroller. She too had tipped her head back and was looking intently at the ceiling, making a charming subject for tourists' cameras. I will never know if she was simply copying the adults all around her or whether it showed her artistic nature as she certainly had talent which developed in future years.

Most evenings we ate at a little ristorante where the owner's elderly mother made a great fuss over the baby and Christian's blond hair. Chris got to know a young couple who lived on the same floor in the building across the street. Often, we would hear their music drifting across between our open windows – *The Age of Aquarius* was a favorite -and several times they took their guitar and Chris with them to the Borghese Gardens while they busked for lira. Chris was a great help, they explained, as people stopped when they saw his blond hair and blue eyes and were more generous than usual when he held out the hat for donations. We were also stopped in the street one day by an American movie maker who wanted Chris as an extra in a crowd scene. I sat and watched the "lights, camera, action" process from a sidewalk café and we were "paid' in cake and coffee.

It was a strange time again - in another limbo of waiting for John's next job to be finalized and wondering where it was going to be. I really had no desire to go to another Arab country and I dreamed about going to South America perhaps, where friends had worked for FAO in Bariloche in Argentina, a lovely part of the world. To my dismay, John came back from work one day in early November and announced we were going to the Sudan.

11. Sudan 1971-1972

*The stories we tell ourselves about our private pasts shape how we come to see our personhood and who we ultimately become. The **thin line between agency and victimhood** is drawn in how we tell those stories.*
Rebecca Solnit (from Brain Pickings)

As we landed in Khartoum, John looked at the rows of agricultural vehicles and equipment lined up beside the hangars, obviously foreign aid from some country. "My God", he said, "Look at the graders. They're not for road building, they are old snow ploughs!" A gift from Russia, we found out later, it was typical of the sometimes haphazard nature of development funding and we assumed that the United Nations would do better. Sudan was a country in transition after gaining its independence from Britain in 1956. Just before we arrived in in November 1970, the Sudanese government had nationalized all the banks and our assigned house had formerly been the residence of a Barclays Bank manager. We were happy to move into the pleasant bungalow, with its shady trees and lawn, with servant's quarters in the back.

We hired a houseboy who cooked and cleaned and an Ethiopian nanny for Sophie who had just started to walk. Hidat, the nanny, lived with us and because her second language was Italian, Sophie's first words were "mama mia." We got to meet the expatriate community at the British Club, a lovely old colonial building in extensive grounds with a pool and several tennis courts. The Government would sequester it a year later and turn it into the Ministry for Youth, and the British community had to move to an alternative much smaller site for our Friday gatherings for cold beers and a curry lunch. We also became members of the Blue Nile Sailing Club, and I was intrigued by the fact that the clubhouse was the old gun boat, the Melik, dating back to 1896 after the fall of Khartoum and the death of General Gordon.

The popular image of Gordon was as the solitary hero taking on a vast horde of fanatical Muslims. But like the misguided general in the infamous siege of Kut in Iraq, it was his pride that led to a disastrous siege in 1884 with both the garrison and the population of Khartoum starving to death; it was said that there were no horses, donkeys, cats, or dogs left in Khartoum as the people had eaten them all. In the hours following Gordon's death an estimated 10,000 civilians and members of the garrison were killed in by the victorious Mahdi and his Muslim followers.

The French later hoped to gain control of the Sudan but to prevent that Britain sent General Kitchener to

Khartoum in 1898 to destroy the Mahdi and his army, an imperial power grab and not solely to avenge General Gordon's death. The final and bloodiest battle of the campaign was the Battle of Omdurman in September 1898.

"The Khalifa's army of about 55,000 men suffered over 11,000 killed and unknown numbers of wounded, as compared to trifling Anglo-Egyptian casualties of a few dozen killed and wounded – most of these being sustained in the famous and, it must be said, foolhardy charge of the 21st Lancers, in which Winston Churchill took part."

Gunboats had bombarded the enemy in Omdurman, destroying the Mahdi's tomb, which made the British even more unpopular, and the Melik later transported Kitchener and his staff across the Nile from Omdurman to the ruined Governor's Palace in Khartoum. In 1926 the Melik became the clubhouse of the Blue Nile Sailing Club and remained as such for about sixty years until she was swept up onto the riverbank by an exceptionally high flood. It seemed at first to be almost a sacrilege to be using the historical vessel for an expatriates' clubhouse but that was soon forgotten during my many happy evenings there, dancing with new friends on the deck and drinking sundowners while the sun set over the river, framed by date palms and distant minarets.   I learned to water ski on the Nile, staying up straight away mainly through fear of what lurked in the water – crocodiles of course, but also bilharzia, a parasite which was a serious health hazard.

Rabies was also relatively common, and one awful afternoon, Chris came home from playing with school friends to say he had been bitten by a stray dog. If we had been able to catch the dog, we would have had it tested first, but it was long gone. So Chris had to undergo the painful treatment of daily anti-rabies injections for several weeks. To reward his courage, I bought him one day an ice-cream from the Greek grocer – which created another problem as it gave him food poisoning. He attended the small international school which only went up to Grade Four, and after that he would have to go overseas to boarding school.

But in the meantime, we settled into our new life, with John on frequent long absences from the city, "on safari", as his work entailed advising wheat farmers on dry land irrigation techniques. The desert land beyond the Nile depended on the sparse rainfall each year and traditional land ownership meant that sons inherited narrow strips of land, allowing each son a fair share of better land at the bottom of a hill, ranging up to the dryer, less fertile land at the top. John's job was to teach them the wisdom of combining the strips into one holding and planting their wheat and sorghum on the contour, so that maximum use was made of the rainfall being held by the furrows instead of running downhill. It was a cultural shift for the farmers, but results were spectacular, with yields more than doubling with little investment apart from a surveyor's level.

Life was very pleasant for our first year in Khartoum, apart from the heat in summer and the days when the *haboob* winds covered everything in sand and dust. I played bridge again and enjoyed the social life at the different Embassies and clubs, with Mohammed the cook and Hidat the nanny to take care of domestic duties. I took up tennis again and it was at the old British Club tennis courts that I met Alan, a Scottish bachelor who became an important part of my life for the next ten years. He was a good tennis coach and dance partner and with John's constant absences, it was inevitable that our relationship developed as it did.

Alan was born and raised in Alexandria, Egypt, then went home to Scotland when he was 12, after the death of his father. He had spent some time living in Bangkok and had a sophisticated and experienced approach to his relationships with women, to which I responded immediately. He ended the loneliness, the lack of connection and the physical emptiness of my life and with a reckless lack of concern for John and the wider community, I became his constant companion.

Over the months I spent more and more time with Alan at his house, in his swimming pool with Chris and Sophie, or on the river, sailing his boat or water-skiing and while it may have seemed scandalous to some in the community, my behavior was condoned by a small circle of understanding friends and also by John, who I think at this stage understood that he had lost me. We continued to live as friendly but remote colleagues, maintaining the home for the sake of the children.

Our tranquility was short-lived however, when in July of 1971, a short-lived communist-backed coup, led by Major Hashem al Atta, took place against the government of President Nimeiry. As soon as I heard the news, I drove home from Alan's house across the bridge, where army checkpoints were already being set up, and feeling very afraid, saw the first tanks rumbling down our street. Hidat and Sophie were safely indoors, and John was out in the neighborhood looking for Chris who had gone to play with his friend, the son of a government architect. The more John banged on their door, the more terrified our friends were and refused to let him in until they recognized his voice at last and let him retrieve Chris and take him home via the back streets.

It was a tense time until we realized that we expatriates were not the target. I was awakened the next morning by the nanny shouting in the garden and ran out, fearing the worst. Sure enough, there were armed soldiers behind the trees in our front garden, aiming at other soldiers in the house across the road. Hidat was telling them to go and fight somewhere else as she did not want them to wake the baby. The coup and countercoup certainly had a surreal quality with all offices closed, work at a standstill and a curfew imposed. Most of us had packed essentials and loaded our cars in case we needed to make a swift retreat to the airport. After a lull of a few days, tensions rose again as Nimeiry loyalists launched a countercoup, freeing Nimeiry and toppling the short-lived rebel government. Tanks rolled down the streets again and we stayed indoors and kept our heads down.

The coup brought major changes in Sudan's foreign and domestic policies. Because Russia had inspired the coup, Nimeiry became very anti-communist and ordered the execution of leading members of the Sudanese Communist Party. The British and Americans were relieved that we had not been in the crosshairs this time. We carried on playing tennis, sailing, and making occasional trips on religious holidays to places like Omdurman, where we saw the strange and exotic sight of whirling dervishes. This Sufi sect originated in the 13th century as followers of the poet and Muslim mystic, Rumi. Their mesmerized spinning enables them to reach a state of nirvana and they silently whirl round with one hand pointed upward to heaven and the other hand pointed toward the ground. We watched six expressionless men wearing conical hats and long full white skirts which belled out as they whirled around in active meditation or self-hypnosis. I was fascinated and wished I knew more about Sufism and Rumi. It was so different from the barbarism of the Shia self-flagellations of Muharram that I had witnessed in Iraq, and a reminder of the huge differences between the many sects of Islam, just as exist in Christianity and other world religions.

After eighteen months, we were due for overseas leave. John and I would spend a few weeks in Europe, and I would stay on to get Christian established in the international boarding school we had found in Gstaad in Switzerland. We would have to leave our house and find another on our return as the UN was not prepared to pay rent for an empty house while we were away. So it was time to pack and store our belongings again and head for the airport once more.

12. Khartoum and Cyprus 1973

Misguided lovers all too frequently take the intensity of the infatuation for proof of the intensity of their love, while it may only prove the degree of their preceding loneliness.   Eric Fromm (from Brain Pickings)

John returned to Khartoum at the end of our leave and the children and I went on to Switzerland. I hated having to leave Chris in his new boarding school, the John F. Kennedy International School in Gstaad. It was built in Swiss chalet style and had recently been taken over by a dynamic American staff whose principal assured me that Chris would find friends immediately among the international students. The uniform was relaxed, with students able to choose from combinations of red or navy pants and sweaters, and Chris brightened when he saw photos on the wall of students skiing and playing ice hockey. He was only ten years old and I wept as I drove back to my hotel room with Sophie, knowing it was for the best but having to convince myself that he would be happy there. Alan joined me the next day and I was deeply grateful to have his company to ease my distress about leaving Chris. We drove slowly back to England through France in glorious late summer weather. Sophie was an easy traveler, and we stopped for memorable meals and wine as we crossed France. We visited

Chartres Cathedral on our way to Paris. The cathedral could be seen at a distance as we drove towards it through golden wheat fields and I imagined the thousands of pious pilgrims who had made their way towards it over the centuries. Sunlight was streaming through the famous stained glass rose window and a choir was practicing as we walked in, the boy soprano voices soaring into the ancient stone arches. I felt that this was as close to heaven as I was ever going to achieve. I felt humbled and fulfilled at the same time, a complexity of emotions that typified my life with Alan at the time and later would cause me much grief.

With Alan in London

While in London, we went to Wimbledon which was especially exciting as Alan was able to talk our way into some spare seats in the Press Section, right in the front row of a match between the current stars, Ilya Nastase and Jimmy

O'Connor. What I had not realized from watching tennis on television was the amount of bad language you can hear on the court as an actual spectator. At one stage in the match Nastase walked across to where we were sitting and for a moment I thought he was going to speak to me, but he reached out and took a bite from an apple offered by a very pretty girl sitting close by, to delighted applause from the audience.

London with Alan was a different city. It was exciting and reassuring being with him as he always knew where we were going and how to get there. We were restricted by Sophie, but the hotel provided babysitters and we went to the theatre and enjoyed some excellent dinners. We shopped for tennis gear at Lillywhites, the famous London sports store, and wandered along Carnaby Street, enjoying the fashion and the music. I was reluctant to return to Khartoum, but Alan's life and work were there and as a pragmatic Scotsman he was not going to do anything rash or romantic like taking me away from my unhappy situation. I was alternately thankful to have him in my life and disappointed with him that that were limits to his sense of responsibility for me. Time and again, I was reminded that only I was responsible for my own happiness, but I kept on wanting someone else to take charge.

John had found a spacious apartment for us on the edge of New Khartoum, overlooking a large square where Sudanese children played soccer and the occasional goat could be seen eating trash that had blown in the wind. I missed the house but there was still room for Hidat the nanny, so our routine had hardly changed. There was tennis and lazing by the pool, I joined a yoga class run by the wife of the Swiss Ambassador and I started giving dance classes for children at the International School.

We had a little excitement with the royal visit to Khartoum of Princess Anne in February of 1973. The British expatriates were in a flutter of excitement as the women dug out their gloves and hats for the reception at the Ambassador's residence. Mr. Etherington-Smith was reportedly in quite a dither over the visit and inevitably the royal princess arrived late by which time the guests and our host had enjoyed rather too many cocktails. The Ambassador strode forward to greet Princess Anne at the entrance, forgetting in the excitement of the moment the shallow pond in the foyer. With great British aplomb he waded through the water and out the other side, hand outstretched for a formal greeting, with both the Princess and the Ambassador ignoring the puddle round his feet.

My friends and I found it difficult to restrain our giggles and the reception continued with an undertone of mild hysteria. People started leaving while they were still upright, and we just managed to restrain one of the guests from peeing in the plants in the lobby.

While John was away for weeks at a time, Alan and I played a lot of tennis despite the heat. Our regular partners were Mawia and Marion, an English nurse with the World Health Organization, who told me horrific anecdotes about genital mutilation of very young patients. I found it difficult to comprehend how this was countenanced by a religion like Islam, which apart from its jihadi teaching, is supposedly based on universal principles similar to Christianity. We did not discuss religion or politics with Mawia, a handsome young Sudanese playboy and a good tennis player. Marion his girlfriend, would playfully rub his hair and call him "my golliwog" which shocked me at first, but Mawia seemed to ignore political correctness and accepted it with a cheerful grin. We were also friendly with Kamal and his English wife Vera, married happily for years, unlike many mixed marriages in Sudan. The British Embassy was used to helping naïve young women who had met handsome Sudanese students at English universities and married them, only to find out that life was impossible in a home shared with mother-in-law and several other non- English speaking wives.

Beyond the "bubble" of our insular international community there were constant reminders of a complex and primitive world. The existence of Arabic speaking tribes in the north and the mostly Christian Nilotic tribes in the south was a recipe for continuing civil war. Those early British map-makers had caused lasting problems when they drew their national boundaries to encompass such disparate peoples.

One of the most interesting cultures was that of the nomadic cattle herders or Baggara. In addition to taking sides in the long civil war between north and south, conflict between nomadic tribes in Sudan would break out over scarce resources such as grazing land, cattle and drinking water. John accompanied our friend Alistair on safari once to advise on pastoral practices among some semi-settled nomads. Alistair was a veterinarian with the United Nations Development Program, and his mission was to persuade the nomads to stay in one place long enough for their cattle to be inoculated against the many diseases prevalent among livestock in Africa. He and John discussed this one evening on returning to Khartoum and I was dismayed to hear Alistair say,

"The only way for them to want to settle in one place is to convert them to a consumer culture. If we provide them with shiny things like trade goods and transistor radios, they will see the need for jobs and money and then they will stay long enough to benefit from schools and clinics."

It seemed a cynical way of looking at a way of life that had lasted for thousands of years without Western intrusion. I thought of other native people, like the American Indians and Aboriginals in Australia, who had been seduced first by blankets, axes and beads and then corrupted by guns and alcohol, all in the name of civilization. If the nomads were encouraged to live in villages, they could only survive if pastures were adequate for their numerous cattle and with Africa's cycles of drought and locust plagues, I felt this would be impossible. John and Alistair laughed at my concerns as they drank on into the night, planning a caravan of shops on wheels to follow the nomad routes and entice them to buy trade goods. As usual, I would leave them to it and go to bed alone, disillusioned once more with the whole premise of "development" in a developing country.

Little remained in Sudan of its ancient history as mud bricks do not withstand the ravages of wind and sandstorms over the centuries. An exception was the ancient Nubian kingdom of Meroë which was the southernmost city along the Nile during the time of the Egyptian pharaohs. About 150 miles north of Khartoum, over forty queens and kings were buried there in small stone pyramids, long since plundered in ancient times, and more recently in the 1830s by an Italian explorer Giuseppe Ferlini, who raided and demolished many of the pyramids in his search for treasure.. I was happy to join a group of families who set off in Land Rovers one religious holiday weekend to visit the site, along with an English archeologist who told us a little of Meroë's history. It was depressing to see that the pyramids had all been vandalized and plundered and while we could marvel at the civilization that built them, there was little left to remind us of the people who had once lived there. There were a few pottery shards to be picked up and examined, but we were careful to leave them there in case they were meaningful to future archeologists. I couldn't help sharing Chris's disappointment when we got back into the Land Rover for the trip home again. "Is that all? "he said.

There were few wild animals to see around Khartoum but sometimes the birdlife was spectacular. I loved going out on the river with Alan and one early morning we decided to go up the Nile to watch the sun rise. We slowly made our way past the mud brick village of Omdurman, and as the sky lightened, we heard the muezzin calls from mosques beside the river. People were stirring and coming down to fetch water, staring at us curiously but also occasionally giving us a friendly wave. We passed irrigated fields of cotton and date palm plantations, still cool in the early morning air and as we rounded a curve, we reached our destination. On a low sandbank stretching into the distance were hundreds, maybe thousands of white ibis, feeding and preening, with the strange music of their birdcalls that we could hear over the sound of the boat's motor. Then to my delight and dismay, they rose into the air, the scarlet sunrise turning their wings a soft pink as they flew past us upriver, creating a momentary breeze from thousands of wings that brushed my cheek. I almost wept for the beauty of it and was glad to be sitting there in silence beside Alan, imprinting a memory that needed no words.

Another moment of breath-catching beauty we shared was when we were finishing dinner one night at his house, listening to music, when his cook Osman, came in and spoke urgently to Alan in Arabic. Alan grabbed my hand and we walked quickly down his drive to the main road. It was past midnight, but the moon was nearly full, creating an almost

unearthly light. Alan hushed my questions and said," Listen!"
Then we could hear them coming, a muted jingling of harness,
the thud of hooves on the sandy roadside, the grunts and
rumbles of a seemingly endless caravan of hundreds of
camels, ghostly in the moonlight as they swayed past us, close
enough to smell them, close enough to see the white flash of a
smile from the camel drivers as they passed by. They were
heading for an annual camel market, Osman had explained,
and we had been lucky to see them pass by. It may have been
ten minutes before the last of them lurched by in the
moonlight, incongruous in the 20th century, and seemingly an
apparition once the night was still again.

One awful Friday in March 1973, we were shocked by
the news that eight masked Palestinian gunmen belonging to
the Black September group had burst into the Saudi embassy
where a formal reception was being held for foreign
diplomats. They took the Americans hostage as well as Guy
Eid, a Belgian attaché, and the boyfriend of DeDe, my Scottish
friend. As our apartment overlooked the Saudi Embassy across
the square, we had a succession of visitors that day who came
to look across at the building through binoculars, watching
masked gunmen who patrolled the roof at intervals while they
waited for the US government to agree to their ransom
demands. John and colleagues from the UNDP sat around
that day with many beers, deploring the situation and talking
nonsense about how they were going to rescue the hostages.
I was disgusted with them, unreasonably so because they

could do nothing, but I felt they were behaving irresponsibly when a human tragedy was taking place within sight of our home. When President Nixon refused to negotiate, the gunmen killed the two Americans and Guy. DeDe and I sat together staring across at the Embassy in shock when we heard the news. Suddenly Khartoum no longer seemed to be a safe place for us to live and I could hardly wait to leave.

Fortunately, John's second 18-month contract was coming to an end and we left with Sophie to meet Chris in Switzerland for the school holidays in June. I wanted to stop over in Israel on our way to England as I had a great curiosity about the country, having read so much about its history. The novels of Leon Uris had filled me with indignation about the way Britain and the US had treated Jewish refugees from Hitler's Germany and accounts of the Holocaust had filled me with grief and horror. What little I had seen in the Middle East so far had shown that barbarism was just under the surface in Muslim countries with civilized mores having only a tenuous hold. Beleaguered Israel was the only democracy in the Middle East and its principles of equality, and the kibbutz movement had my deep respect. Israel had impressed John also, as they were achieving miracles with innovations in agriculture, using best practices with their limited water supplies. One method of irrigating orange trees in the desert was particularly impressive; strips of asphalt were laid down with holes punched at intervals for the orange seedlings, each with its little hose dripping water in measured amounts, prevented from evaporation by the stable asphalt.

When we went through immigration at Tel Aviv airport, we were given visitors' visas on a separate piece of paper, as Arab countries would probably refuse us entry in the future if they saw Israeli stamps in our passports. I privately thought that would be an excellent idea and offered my passport, which was refused with a smile by the Israeli official. We left our luggage at our hotel and immediately hired a taxi to take us to the Holocaust Memorial of Yad Vashem on the slope of the Mount of Remembrance near Jerusalem. On the forty-mile drive, we passed a burned-out tank on the side of the road, a reminder of the Six Day War in 1967 and the precarious nature of Israel's existence, surrounded by enemy nations. I was profoundly moved by Yad Vashem and our quick visit to the Wailing Wall in Jerusalem, the whole experience heightened by exhaustion after the long flight and a powerful sense of Israel's tragic history.

We had changed our travel arrangements to include the stopover in Israel and were infinitely thankful that we had done so. We heard later that the TWA flight we were originally booked on from Athens to London had been destroyed by a terrorist bomb and all 88 passengers were lost. I was profoundly grateful to Israel for being the inspiration for my insistence that we stop over for 24 hours.

We stayed a week in a resort on the Greek island of Spetses, avoiding Athens as there was a lot of unrest in the city, with demonstrations and strikes protesting the repressive government of the Colonels. The far-right Greek military junta had ruled Greece for seven years, ending in July 1974 under the pressure of the Turkish invasion of Cyprus. We befriended some Greek university students who were working the summer at our hotel, and I left John to babysit one night while I went with them to listen to a band playing songs that were banned by the regime. We drank ouzo and though I understood nothing of the words, the atmosphere of revolutionary hope and optimism was infectious. As in Jerusalem, I felt connected momentarily with something so much larger than myself, thought-provoking and exhilarating at the same time.

I wanted to spend the rest of the summer in a Mediterranean climate rather than return to a New Zealand winter and had decided on Cyprus. I had read *Bitter Lemons* by Lawrence Durrell, describing his time there during the Enosis movement in the 1950s, when Greek Cypriots were fighting for freedom from British rule. His descriptions of Crusader castles and ruined abbeys had intrigued me, and once John had left for Rome to find out his next assignment, the children and I found an apartment overlooking the harbor in Kyrenia, a picturesque town on the northern coast.

Each morning, the tinkle of goat bells under our windows meant that young Martin the goatherd and his flock were passing by, a signal for Chris to run downstairs and join him. During the day we were entertained by the sight of the pirate ship with red-striped sails that set out from the Crusader castle on the harbor, with realistic puffs of smoke as they fired the cannons. It was being filmed for a movie called *Ghosts in the Noonday Sun,* starring British actor Peter Sellars, which was evidently so bad that it was almost not released. The movie crew filled the tavernas along the harbor in the evenings and the beach during the day was filled with blond, blue-eyed Finnish soldiers, the UN forces keeping the peace between Greeks and Turks. To go shopping in Nicosia, I was meant to go in the UN convoy for safety, but several times I took the local bus instead. I loved being with the older women who were heading off to market - they would talk to me in voluble Greek, offering me almonds and patting my hand, smiling at our attempts to understand each other.

I found a little nursery school for Sophie that was run by an English woman and most mornings we would walk up through the Turkish part of town, passing old men playing dominoes and women in black sitting in the sun, making lace. The men wore red fezzes and baggy black pants, and time seemed to have stood still in this idyllic part of the world. I wanted so much to belong there as I found the mythology, the history, and the scenic beauty captivating.

One night, there was a knock on my door and an American woman stood there, "Hi, I'm your neighbor upstairs, and I'm hoping you want company!" Her husband was a professor at the American University in Beirut, and she was having a break from the tensions there. She went back to her apartment and returned with a bottle of ouzo and a pack of Tarot cards and we had several amusing evenings together. She talked of the time when life was much more dangerous in Kyrenia when the rebel, Grivas, was hiding in the mountains nearby and she and her husband helped his supporters with food and money. I missed her when she returned to Beirut, but Alan was able to join me for a week and I was happy to have him with me again, even briefly.

He rented a car, so we were able to explore more of the country. We spent a day in the capital Nicosia after driving through the mountains in the UN convoy, passing the ruined castle named for an obscure saint Hilarion who was said to have fled to Cyprus after the Arab conquest of the Holy Land. Perched high up on a rocky cliff, the castle was further fortified in the 11th century against Arab pirates raiding the coast. Although mostly ruined today, the upper floor has an elegant carved window, known as the Queen's Window, which has a spectacular scenic view of the northern coast of Cyprus.

That week Alan and I also visited the place I loved most -the ruined abbey of Bellapais, a few miles from Kyrenia. Founded in the early 13th century by Augustinian friars who had been evicted from the city of Jerusalem by Saladin, the monastery of Bellapais has drawn pilgrims to the island of Cyprus ever since medieval times. The writer Laurence Durrell had lived in the little village surrounding the abbey, making it famous in his book *Bitter Lemons*. I had spent hours there while Sophie was at her nursery school, immersed in a timeless sense of the past, with thousands of friendly ghosts joining me under the ruined arches.

I was upset to say goodbye to Alan when he returned to Khartoum and Chris flew back to school in Switzerland. I drove back alone in tears after leaving them both at the airport, while the car radio was playing the song, with the chorus, "I can't live, if living is without you", by Harry Nilsson, a song that ever since has never failed to bring a sentimental lump to my throat. I felt deserted and desolate and was again reminded that I had unrealistic expectations of what Alan felt for me. I was left with Sophie, and the needlepoint cushion that I was working on, waiting to hear from John about his next assignment.

Hoping that this time it would be South America, I was very taken aback when he called and said it was to be Saigon. He would go there first and get our housing sorted out and I would follow in early December. I was frustrated that I had no choice, no one to turn to, nowhere else to go and felt life was spinning out of control again. Vietnam as far as I was concerned was still a country at war. But once again, I was expected to pack and follow. And once again, I naively told myself that after all, a new country meant a fresh start and maybe an opportunity to forget Alan and build a better relationship with John.

13. Vietnam 1973 -74

We deceive ourselves about love — about who; and how; and when; and whether. We also discover and correct our self-deceptions. The forces making for both deception and unmasking here are various and powerful: the unsurpassed danger, the urgent need for protection and self-sufficiency, the opposite and equal need for joy and communication and connection.   Martha Nussbaum (from Brain Pickings)

Vietnam was in a state of uneasy peace. In August 1972, the last US combat troops had left Vietnam but there was still a large American presence of about 7,000 U.S. Department of Defense civilian employees remaining behind to aid South Vietnam in the ongoing war with communist North Vietnam.

Vietnam was effectively one country with two governments, one in the south led by President Thieu, and North Vietnam led by the Viet Cong. But with the signing of the Paris Accords, peace had been declared, Kissinger had his Nobel Peace Prize and the United Nations was moving experts in to help reconstruct the war-torn country. International peace-keeping troops from four countries, the International Commission of Control and Supervision or ICCS, came to supervise the cease-fire, the withdrawal of troops, and the dismantling of military bases.

But it was hardly reassuring as the plane approached Tan San Nhut airport in Saigon and I saw from the window a huge plume of black smoke on the outskirts of the city. I learned later that the Viet Cong had destroyed 18 million gallons of fuel that day and gas prices skyrocketed as a result, skewing the local economy drastically. There was certainly tension in the air, and I was not reassured by John's breezy assurance that the Viet Cong were not after UN personnel as they wanted our financial aid and expertise. Everywhere we went, there were men in uniform, tanks guarding ministries and government buildings and the city was choked with humanity, refugees from the north and the countryside, together with residents trying to make a living, all crowding the streets on their little motorbikes weaving in and out of the exhaust-fumed and often gridlocked traffic.

We stayed in a hotel for a week, waiting for a house to become available as a UN doctor was taking his family back to the US and wanted us to house sit while he was away. I explored downtown somewhat tentatively on my own, holding Sophie's hand tightly, and discovered a shop that offered the most exquisite embroidery done by Vietnamese nuns, and we also found the pet market with cages full of puppies and Siamese kittens for sale. I wondered grimly how many of the pups would be fattened and eaten and wished I could rescue them all. John would return to us in the late afternoons, for several beers together on the terrace of the nearby Continental Hotel, complaining when the local brew called 33 was served with ice in it. Sophie and I would enjoy citron presse instead, freshly made lemonade. The hotel bar was usually full of journalists, and the terrace faced the square where a Buddhist monk had set himself on fire, a powerful and tragic protest against the continued war. I felt a palpable atmosphere of anxiety and fear, or maybe it was just my imagination.

South Vietnamese troops were endeavoring to hold onto their territory but inexorably were being pushed south while the government in Saigon was becoming more and more ineffectual. Over two million Vietnamese soldiers and civilians had been killed and that was really brought home to me when we later visited the cemetery at Bien Hoa and saw the endless rows of white crosses, stretching into the distance. So many lives lost and so little gained.

The Christmas vacation meant that Chris would fly out from Switzerland to join us for a few weeks and we did our best to provide a normal family background for him. We went to the Cercle Sportif to swim and play tennis and had some memorable meals in restaurants by the river and out in the countryside where venison was on the menu. Evidently it was supplied to the chef by American helicopter pilots who machine-gunned the deer and flew the carcasses back to the city. We were able to use the Commissary at the American base at Tan San Nhut, which made shopping much easier when we were setting up our home once we had found a suitable house to rent. Owned by a South Vietnamese Army Major, there was a delay of nearly two weeks before we were able to sign the lease and move in. My new friend MyCo explained that the Major was waiting for an auspicious day and that he would have consulted the fortune-tellers daily at the Buddhist temple until the timing was right.

Our landlord's respect for tradition was a reminder of the pervasive culture of Buddhism and folk superstitions that gave the people an aura of calm acceptance of the fate of their country. We inherited three young sisters from the American doctor's house – a cook, a maid, and an extra hand with the third sister who was a college student, being supported by her two older sisters. It was a happy arrangement, and most mornings I would find Sophie, sitting on her knees on the lawn by a tree, where the girls, graceful in their white ao dais, would be praying silently before a candle, a flower, and an offering of food. They ran our house better than I could, and we added to the household two puppies for watchdogs and a Siamese cat for Sophie.

I was asked if I was interested in teaching as there was a great need at the Ngyen Noch Linh International School where we had enrolled Sophie in the kindergarten class. I agreed and each day we both went by cab to school, me to my classroom and Sophie to hers, while I learned fast how to engage 30 young minds in learning English and elementary math, with limited resources. All the children were part-American, part Vietnamese, and all were hoping for visas to join their American fathers who by now were back in the US.

We got to know people at the Cercle Sportif and at social events at the various embassies. Richard and MyCo became our friends, Richard a rather mysterious Englishman, as he seemed unattached to an embassy or mission and was evasive when questioned. We decided he must have been with the British Secret Service. MyCo, his Vietnamese girlfriend we assumed, was a reporter on the Vietnamese newspaper Dai Tan Toc, which was always being shut down by the repressive government for its honest and therefore inflammatory reporting. MyCo had been briefly married to an Italian American journalist who had been killed in a car accident on their honeymoon in the Italian Alps. She was very reticent about her loss and dignified, and I admired her gentle resilience as it must have been difficult for her, being only partially accepted in both worlds.

She turned up to our house one day and offered to take Sophie to a picnic. I was hesitant, thinking of her on the back of MyCo's Lambretta, heading off into Saigon traffic but it seemed such a normal thing to do and Sophie was so excited that I forgot my misgivings and waved them off. I found out later that the picnic was a garden party reception at the Presidential Palace and that my little Sophie had been introduced to generals, ministers, and ambassadors, as needless to say, she certainly stood out in the crowd.

While we were in Saigon, my parents had been in Taiwan for a year where my father was consulting on agricultural programs being subsidized by the New Zealand government. They came to visit us for a few days on their way back to New Zealand. It had been about six years since I had seen them, and I assumed we had all grown up a lot since those unhappy days in Fiji. I took time off school and I got the maids spring cleaning and shopping for some great meals and was really looking forward to the reunion.

I don't know why I expected anything different, but John and my father immediately settled down over a bottle of whisky to talk about agriculture and my mother seemed to talk of nothing but frivolous memories of Taiwan and the parties they had attended, telling me how they had once driven past a huge municipal rubbish dump where dozens of children were picking through trash for a livelihood.

"But they were smiling and happy, Sue dear," my mother recounted, unable to see or understand my distaste for her sentimental interpretation of such abject poverty. As the evening drew on, Mother decided to show us her imitation of Charlie Chaplin that had been such a hit at a party in Taiwan. I was mortified when I caught sight of our maids' bemused expressions as they cleared the table.

I was both sad and pleased when they left. I wished I had had more time to talk with my mother about the rest of the family. My father at least gave me a long hug and said that we would probably never see each other again. I said, "Nonsense, we will be back in New Zealand for a visit someday," but he seemed serious. I remembered that moment later and guessed that he had already been diagnosed with a heart condition. My parents' behavior had seemed so inappropriate in a country on the brink of disintegration. Instead of being the wise mentors I wanted them to be, they were parochial New Zealanders at heart despite their experience of living overseas. As T.S Eliot said, in his poem, *The Dry Salvages* they "had the experience but missed the meaning." I was very aware that we too, were leading superficial lives while Vietnam was going through death throes as a nation, and John was almost enjoying the drama of it all.

During this time, he was as usual, spending more time in the countryside as his work involved farmers, not city officials, and the UN project was primarily helping to relocate wetland rice farmers from the Mekong Delta. He was teaching them how to plant rice on the contour on hillsides, and the bulldozers and tractors used to clear the land had to be armor-plated underneath as they were constantly setting off land mines. John gravitated to the clubs and bars run by the ICCS when he was in Phan Thiet province and I will never know what else he did after work while he was away for weeks at a time. He occasionally had to drive back to Saigon by a different route because the Viet Cong had blown up a road bridge, and said he sometimes saw men in Viet Cong black uniforms stepping off the road into the trees when he drove by. The big blue UN rondel on the doors and roof of his Land Rover was his protection, although he had had a somewhat disconcerting conversation with a North Vietnamese general at an Embassy party. Both slightly drunk, John had asked the general to tell his men not to fire at him while he was in the countryside. The general promised but added wistfully that the big blue rondel on the vehicle door would make a lovely target.

I had met the wife of the New Zealand ambassador and we had similar concerns. She told me about a state banquet she had attended, where there were about twenty courses, including a soup which was a great delicacy with a tiny whole bird in it, its beak hanging over the edge of the bowl. She managed not to throw up, she said, and then caught a glimpse through a partly ajar door of a crowd of street children who had been begging for food and were being beaten off by kitchen staff with long sticks. She picked me up one day in her chauffeur driven Mercedes and we visited an orphanage that had been funded by donations at a time when everyone had responded generously to the plight of Vietnamese orphans. Now, because donor fatigue had set in or because the war was officially over, the funding had dried up.

I was saddened to see the children listlessly sitting on their beds, no books or toys in sight and wearing an odd collection of clothing, probably originating in the US from donations to Goodwill. I took notes as I had promised to write an article for publication in New Zealand newspapers, hoping to stir interest in resuming funding again for these neglected children. I wrote it and sent it off but received no acknowledgement from either of the two major papers. I will never know if the articles even passed the censors at the Saigon Post Office and I realized later that I should have sent them out through the diplomatic pouch. Normal procedures like mailing something and expecting it to get there were no longer functioning in a country on the edge of chaos.

Another day, when MyCo's newspaper office had been closed again by the government, she came and asked me if I wanted to go with her to a fortune-teller. "She is famous in Saigon for knowing the future," MyCo explained, "and is more of a seer and a psychic than a mere palm-reader." I was ready for a new experience but was a little taken aback when I realized the fortune teller was Indian and could speak no English and had only limited French. With MyCo translating, I was told that I was very unhappy, which I already knew and that there were three important men in my life; I laughed it off, and said I knew only two and the third must be my son or my father. "No, no", the psychic said, "there is still a third man in your life you will love in the future." I did not think of it again until I met my second husband, many years later. She did sense something about me after all, a restless need that required no language.

I met an American couple, also John and Sue, who became good friends. John worked for the World Health Organization and Sue had small children and was as distressed as I was about the situation. Together, with the blessing if the UNDP Director, we started a newsletter for UN personnel, which we named *UNique,* acknowledging the bi-lingual nature of the community. We intended it to improve morale amongst international residents as so much of our lives were based on rumor and propaganda, but increasingly the cheerful directives we were forced to print seemed more and more insincere. The Communists were coming, and we all knew it.

I became disenchanted with the UN leadership when I heard that instead of being altruistic peacekeepers, many were profiting from the situation by buying gold and precious Buddhas, looted from temples as the South Vietnamese soldiers were deserting or being forced south. MyCo introduced us to a friend of hers, a diamond merchant, who wanted us to move into his beautiful villa and fly a UN flag, in the hope that the Communists would leave his property intact. I was horrified that John even entertained the thought, although years later, I was wistful that we did not have a handful of diamonds for our retirement fund.

Our second Christmas in Saigon came, and Chris flew out from Switzerland again as an unaccompanied minor. We expected his plane around 6pm and I was resting after a morning at school, when there was a knock at the door and there was Chris. He had changed his flight in Bangkok to an earlier one as he did not see the point of waiting an extra six hours. On arriving at the airport and seeing that we of course were not there to meet him, he got a taxi and directed the driver in French to our former house, where the Vietnamese staff were able to send the taxi on to our current home. I was deeply impressed by his resourcefulness once I was over the surprise and never really worried again about his future travel arrangements seeing that he had proved himself so capable at the age of 12.

John took some time off and we went to stay at the beach resort of Vung Tau, now almost deserted after being a thriving R and R destination for American troops. We sheltered from a spectacular thunderstorm at a beach café where I tasted salt and pepper crab claws for the first time, fresh and delicious and never as good again when I ordered it in other cafes in other countries. We also went to Dalat, a mountain resort that had originated in French Colonial times for residents to escape the monsoon humidity of Saigon. Now, like Vung Tau, it was nearly deserted but oddly charming with its holiday chalets and villas nestling among the tropical flowering trees.

We visited the market in Saigon several times as Chris and Sophie both loved to see the bird and pet markets with little monkeys and exotic snakes but I found the experience depressing and even alarming as the alleys were becoming so crowded with displaced refugees and disabled soldiers begging; the crush was premeditated by pickpockets as I found out when momentarily stopped by a soldier on crutches. Once I was able to pass by and catch up to John and the children, I found that my purse had been expertly sliced open and my wallet removed without me knowing.

One morning Sophie woke us to ask why there were bottles of beer lined up on the lawn by the wall. We were confused until we realized that thieves must have climbed into our yard and discovered the easiest thing to steal was the crate of beer in the back of John's Land Rover. Intending to throw the bottles over the wall one by one, they must have been disturbed by our dogs and decided to try their luck elsewhere. The desperation of the local people was getting a little too close for comfort.

Another alarming event was when a friend had been walking along a busy street and a daring thief on a motorbike had grabbed her purse, riding off with her hanging on to it as long as she could until she fell and let go. Saigon was becoming too unnerving and I was thankful when the UN office agreed that I could leave with the children that December.

Now Chris was 12, he was finished with the elementary school in Gstaad and we needed to find an English-speaking high school somewhere for him. Cyprus would have been my first choice but sadly, it was out of the question. Turkey had invaded Cyprus in July of 1974, six months after I had left for Vietnam, and I was very distressed to read that they had bombed the castle on Kyrenia Harbor, changed the name from Kyrenia to Girne and occupied a large portion of Northern Cyprus including Famagusta. The Turks had launched their invasion following a coup d'état in Nicosia, when the Greek Army in Cyprus ousted President Makarios and replaced him with a pro-Enosis nationalist, hoping to ally Cyprus with Greece to the detriment of the Turkish Cypriot community. The Greek Cypriots wanted enosis, integration with Greece, while Turkish Cypriots wanted taksim, partition between Greece and Turkey. The uneasy peace was over.

So I opted for the nearest Mediterranean island where English was spoken and made plans to take the children to the tiny British colony of Malta. Once again, I packed and started off for a new life on my own, in a new country. This time, I decided I would have to be more resilient, and rescue some of my own hopes and dreams and turn them into reality if I could. Above all, I wanted to start writing again.

14. Malta 1974

The Journey

One day you finally knew
what you had to do, and
began,
though the voices around you
kept shouting
their bad advice --
though the whole house
began to tremble
and you felt the old tug
at your ankles.
"Mend my life!"
each voice cried.
But you didn't stop.
You knew what you had to do,
though the wind pried
with its stiff fingers
at the very foundations,
though their melancholy
was terrible.
It was already late

enough, and a wild night,

and the road full of fallen

branches and stones.

But little by little,

as you left their voice behind,

the stars began to burn

through the sheets of clouds,

and there was a new voice

which you slowly

recognized as your own,

that kept you company

as you strode deeper and

deeper

into the world,

determined to do

the only thing you could do --

determined to save

the only life that you could

save.

Mary Oliver

"Yells, bells and smells." That was how the English poet Lord Byron described Malta on his visit in 1809, when he was forced to spend twenty days quarantined there because of an outbreak of yellow fever. I agreed with Byron - Malta certainly was noisy, especially on Sundays when church bells seemed to ring out continually, and again on the frequent Saints' Days when there were processions, street bands and noisy rockets being fired up into the night sky. The Maltese people were voluble and excitable, their normal conversations sounding like heated arguments in their unique language, a hybrid of Italian, Arabic, and a medley of other Mediterranean languages. Because the island had been British for a time everyone spoke English of a sort, and there was a lot that was familiar so it would feel like home for a while.

I found an apartment in a blue and white tourist apartment complex near the marina of Ta X'Biex and was able to get Chris into a Christian Brothers School, a bus trip away. I had few possessions as we just arrived with suitcases and the children and I settled in to wait for the situation in Vietnam to be resolved one way or the other.

I made friends immediately with Jill upstairs, an attractive divorced English woman with a Maltese boyfriend. Jill had lived with her doctor husband in a lovely villa by the sea and was unhappy being on her own in an apartment, her Catholic boyfriend being unwilling to marry a divorced woman. She, like me, felt that her life was on hold, and we consoled each other over glasses of wine as the sun went down and the children played outside, getting to know the local children and their dogs.

"I couldn't live with my husband's infidelities and now I can't live with my own," she said. "I am madly in love with a much younger man and I know it will end badly." Jill was amusing company, and a good cook but we were not particularly good about giving each other useful advice. But she did teach me a lot about Malta which was helpful.

The island of Malta was quite different from Cyprus as there were very few trees and the landscape was mostly of creamy yellow limestone, the same material used to build the churches and houses of the old cities of Valletta and Medina. Malta had been invaded many times over the centuries by Romans, Arabs, Normans, Spanish and French until it became British in 1800. The main city, Valletta, was a maze of narrow alleys, with steps on the steepest streets, and buildings that dated back to the Knights Templar and the days of the Crusades. It was remarkable that it had survived for so long as there was no water apart from the huge underground aquifer, which was gradually being depleted and infiltrated by salt water from the ocean, making it barely palatable. Malta had been a British naval base since the Napoleonic Wars and during the Second World War, it was an important supply base and therefore suffered from heavy bombardment from German aircraft. The courage of the Maltese was acknowledged by King George V who awarded the whole population of Malta the George Cross for valor.

Chris settled down in his new school, and I had to remind him not to tell the priests that he had never been christened. The Christian brothers were enlightened enough to accept a Protestant, but they may not have been so generous to a heathen. I met a New Zealander, also named Sue, married to a Maltese lawyer, who told me about a little nursery school that her daughter attended. I tried to get Sophie to go on the bus with her, but she cried and clung to me. "You'll have fun and make new friends," I tried to persuade her. But I did not have the heart to insist. After all, we were only going to be here for a few months.

Our days were sunny and uneventful. My new friend Sue took me shopping and introduced me to the street fairs which were noisy, colorful, and useful for buying remnants of fabrics, cut in lengths known as fents. Sophie and I would go down to the nearest beach most days where she would play with an English spaniel named Bonkers. Once a week the vegetable seller came round in his truck and I would buy the local spinach for "green soup", fortunately a family favorite. I would also buy fresh sardines and monkfish from the local fishermen when they came in to the jetty along the coast from Tigne Beach. They would unload their catch and beat the octopi against the concrete, whether to tenderize them or finally kill them I was not sure. I bought one once and put it on to cook, without realizing that it needed minimal cooking and once it had toughened it would take hours to soften up again. Every time I lifted the lid to poke it, a baleful eye stared back, and in the end I lost my nerve and threw it out.

The weeks turned into months of watching the news each night on television, disturbing me deeply with reports of the loss of life, and with the fall of Saigon becoming more inevitable each day. As usual, I got little information from John, and I wondered where he was and when I would see him again. To remain in Malta, the children and I had to leave the country and reapply for another three-month visitor visa. England was close and the fare affordable, so it was easy to go to London for a week of shopping, dentist, and a little sight-seeing before coming back to wait again.

By now, I had become quite depressed and lonely, unable to settle to writing, and I spent a lot of time lying in the sun, with a book and a bottle of wine close by. I was restless without a role to play – neither a wife nor a lover. I played a little tennis with a young woman I had met, also on her own as she was waiting for her divorce to be finalized, a lengthy business in Catholic Malta. Shirley was fun, and one night on an impulse we dressed up and went to the local casino, leaving Chris in charge of Sophie. We played the tables and flirted a little with strangers and were flattered when we were approached by a man who said his master wanted to meet us. His master turned out to be a wealthy Libyan sheikh, who wanted to be seen with Western women, but when we went over to meet him, we discovered he was totally blind. It was rather bizarre, but we spoke courteously with him for about five minutes and managed a dignified exit.

The months went by and every night the BBC news showed the imminent fall of Saigon, with no word at all from John, until finally the city fell on April 30th. The iconic footage of helicopters lifting off from the roof of the American

Embassy, with desperate people trying to get aboard at the last minute, made me concerned for John's safety and for the future for me and the children. I found out later I was right to be concerned for John. He had been trapped up country with the North Vietnamese army between him and Saigon and had been asked at the last minute to go pick up an American priest who had stubbornly refused to leave his village mission. John set off in his UN Land Rover and found the priest preparing to defend his parishioners single-handed with a small arsenal of weapons he had acquired from departing soldiers. John was able to persuade him that the villagers would be better off without him, and they drove off at some speed, hoping they had not missed the last plane out of Danang. As it was, they caught the last helicopter out, which dropped them off on the deck of an Australian aircraft carrier which was evacuating refugees to Singapore.

John flew straight to Rome to find out where his next assignment would be while I continued to wait in Malta. By now I was feeling really dislocated. The school holidays had begun, and Chris had gone on a school cruise of the Mediterranean. I was still living like a tourist as our ocean freight had still not reached me, the removal company in Vietnam having assumed that I lived in Malta, Ohio instead of Malta, the island in the Mediterranean. I had had to buy bed linen and basic kitchen ware, but after six months I was really missing my own belongings, my blender, my sewing machine, my typewriter. I tried doing a writing course by mail but found it very unsatisfactory and gave it up. I was very tired of floating, of drifting, of being unanchored. Also, I was very tired of being alone.

I called Alan in tears one night and he arranged to come out for a week with me. He was based in London now that his time in Khartoum had ended. I had met a young Australian woman with three little girls who was also on her own, waiting for her husband to finish a tour of duty in Libya, which while not as turbulent as Vietnam, was still not a happy country for Western women and children. Our little girls played happily together at the beach and when she offered to have Sophie for the week, we were both delighted. Sophie would have friends her own age and I could finally spend time with Alan, and hopefully come to some resolution about my marriage.

It was wonderful to see him again. We had a warm and loving reunion and the next morning, he rented a car and we drove to the end of the main island and crossed by ferry to the resort hotel on the little island of Camino. I was starved for connection, for intimacy and for emotional support and it was probably my over-eagerness that created a distance between us straight away. All Alan wanted to do was sit in the sun, read his English newspaper, and drink beer. It was his well-earned holiday and he did not want to be burdened by my untidy emotions. I was hurt and angry and on the fourth day I had had enough. I left the hotel without telling him, got the ferry and a taxi and returned on my own to my apartment at Ta'X Biex.

My friend Jill was in London and Shirley was in Italy, so I was totally alone. I remember pacing back and forth, angry, self-pitying, rebellious, tearful until finally I remembered Alan's bottle of duty-free whisky and found oblivion that night. Alan turned up the next day, somewhat contrite but also rather annoyed with me and he went back to London a few days later, without us achieving anything resembling the new understanding that I was hoping for. We had become just like any other unhappily married couple, only we were not married.

I was thankful to have Chris and Sophie back with me again to add some structure to my life.   And only a few weeks later, the ocean freight finally arrived, and the boxes were stacked in the garage for me to unpack and sort. I was still doing that when John arrived.

After the fall of Saigon, he had been taken to Singapore by the Australian navy and then flown to Rome to be debriefed and assigned to his next UNDP project. He had come to Malta for a few weeks before going out to Jordan, where he would find a house to rent, and the children and I would follow in time for the start of the next school term.

We were sorting out our possessions and throwing out the breakages when the phone rang. It was my brother in New Zealand to tell me that my father had had a massive heart attack and had died three days ago. He and my mother had been staying in a friend's beach cottage on the coast in Fiji, where a seasonal high tide had swept a lot of coral sand up onto the lawn. My father was shoveling it back onto the beach when he collapsed and died almost immediately. My mother had to take his body in a taxi to the nearest small rural hospital some twenty miles away as there was no ambulance available.

As I listened to Rob's voice, difficult with the static over a long-distance call, he said, "There will be no memorial service as Mother wanted to return to New Zealand as soon as possible".

So, there was no need for me to fly off to be with family, as there was to be no funeral, no service, nothing but the stark realization that my father was gone. He had been right when he told me in Saigon that we would never see each other again.

I was deeply upset. He had always been there in the background as a potential ally if my world had totally fallen apart, as a last resort if I could no longer cope with life. He would have been there to comfort me, to rationalize my distress, pour me a drink, while smoking his pipe and giving me one of his giant bear hugs. I was thankful that I had just unpacked a framed photo he had given me, inscribed, "To my very dear Susie." He was the only person I allowed to call me Susie, and now he was gone, I missed him terribly. John and the children left me alone in the garage, surrounded by half-unpacked boxes, some books, cassettes, china, our Iranian tray, now bent in transit, the tangibles of our restless lives. I wept not just for my father but for all the losses I had ever experienced, as if he were the catalyst and not the reason for my overwhelming sense of grief and loss.

I think the intensity of my emotion surprised John and probably alarmed the children and for several days they left me to myself, which instead of inspiring my gratitude, made me feel like a pariah, somehow, as the British would say, letting the side down by not being more stoical.

I was not sorry to finally leave Malta as I had always been uneasy there, never sure how long I was going to stay and, in the end, resenting the island as it had seemed like an enforced exile. But at the same time, it was hard for me to feel any enthusiasm about the move to Jordan as we repacked our belongings in preparation for the next country to be called home.

15. Jordan and England 1975-76

When will you begin that long journey into yourself?
Don't be satisfied with stories, how things have gone for
<u>*others.*</u> *Unfold your own myth.*   *Rumi (from Brain Pickings)*

We arrived in Amman at the end of summer, in time for Chris and Sophie to be enrolled in their respective international schools. Sophie was delighted to report that her classmates included the twin daughters of the King of Jordan and his English wife Muna, and she settled in happily from the start. Chris was restless with another change of school, and he did not react well to his new teachers apart from one, a Vietnam vet with an unorthodox teaching style. I visited the school for a parent-teacher conference and the exasperated Math teacher said, "Chris has perfected the art of sharpening pencils theatrically and insolently, to the great amusement of his fellow students." When challenged, Chris told me," They do not give me credit for what I know already, and they're all boring except for Mr. Elliot, who actually flew helicopters in Vietnam. He treats me with respect because I've been there too." Chris enjoyed the field trips with his new mentor, and we put up with his poor school reports as he would soon turn thirteen and be going to an English boarding school.

Our house was rented from a Palestinian landlord in the part of Amman known as Shmesani, home to many expatriates and UN colleagues. From the previous tenants, we inherited Jamil, an older man who was cook, cleaner and laundryman, and who walked to work each day for several miles in his dishdasha and rubber boots. He was cheerful old man, happy to have British people to cook for as he had been trained by an English woman. It gave me time to look around and I soon found work as a feature writer for the Jordan Times, the only English newspaper in the country.

I loved doing special assignments and remember my ambivalence when covering a fur fashion event attended by the wealthiest of Jordan's society, including Queen Muna and other members of the royal family. I had visited the refugee camps the previous week and been appalled by the poverty, apathy, and squalor of the camps, and now in stunning contrast I witnessed glamour, ostentatious wealth, and elegance. The furs and the models were Swedish and very lovely, but I was glad the photographer with me took lots of photos for the article as I really could not think of much to say.

Another assignment covered somewhat less obvious extravagance when I interviewed a Russian jeweler, a talented young woman whose specialty was creating jeweled covers for Korans. She was finding clients all over the Middle East prepared to pay generously for gold and silver filigree covers inlaid with precious gems, in opulent Byzantine designs. I admired the Russian girl's talent and initiative and she thanked me afterwards for my article, saying it had brought her several new commissions.

A quite different story I wrote involved driving many miles into the countryside to meet two elderly Englishwomen who had been farming in Jordan for over forty years. They had created a little bit of England in the middle of the Jordan Valley, and they were happy to reminisce as they poured tea from a teapot complete with a knitted tea cosy. They had lived unscathed through many political upheavals in an oasis of calm and practical common sense, teaching their farmhands all they knew about sheep and irrigation. One of them told me they knew they should go back to England now that they were ready to retire. "But where can we go? Jordan is our home and England is the foreign country now".

I was eager for more work with the paper but had to wait for the editor to call me with projects. I had made few friends this time, mainly because I was reluctant to drive our Mercedes; I had heard too many stories of reckless Arab drivers causing accidents. I spent much of the day on my own after Jamil left for the day, and evenings were spent with John and his colleagues, drinking, and talking agriculture. My job was to provide them with food and to open yet another bottle of beer or wine. Again, I felt suffocated by the tedium of my marriage, and feeling that I was playing an inauthentic role of mother, wife, and journalist. I lived in quiet despair. Alan and I had exchanged letters and phone calls since we had parted in Malta and as he had some leave due him from his job in London, we arranged to meet in Crete for a week of Mediterranean sunshine. John drove me to the airport, no doubt hoping I would come home a little happier after seeing Alan again.

Crete was welcoming and familiar – a little like Cyprus but without the Turkish population. It had been unified with mainland Greece in 1898 and the Muslim minority had been relocated to Turkey. Like Malta, Crete had been a strategic island in the Mediterranean during the Second World War, but after a fierce and bloody conflict it fell to the Germans in 1941. Resistance groups had soon formed in the Cretan mountains, with one notable British hero, the writer Patrick Leigh Fermor. He was one of a small number of British officers sent to help with the island's resistance to the occupation. Disguised as a shepherd, he lived for over two years in the mountains. I had first read about him in his friend Lawrence Durrell's book, *Bitter Lemons* (1957) which recounted how Leigh Fermor had visited Durrell's villa in Bellapais in Cyprus.

German officers exacted savage reprisals for resistance, killing Cretan civilians and destroying villages. As we drove around the island, we came across a memorial to the people killed in 1941 in the village of Kondomari, near the city of Chania. According to German records, a total of 23 men were killed but other sources put the total at about 60. It was very moving to read the names and reflect on how far-reaching the war had been, when our British culture naturally focused on how it had affected British countries.

I loved being in places where not only recent history was vivid and complex, but ancient myths and legends seemed alive and relevant. It was easy to imagine that the Minotaur existed in the palace of King Minos at Knossos, where Daedalus had built the labyrinth and where his son Icarus was kept captive. Icarus managed to escape by creating wings made of feathers and wax; however, he flew too close to the sun, the wax melted, and he fell to his doom. Flying too close to the sun was a metaphor that haunted me sometimes as I lay grounded on yet another beach chair, a cigarette in one hand, glass of wine in the other, wishing I could soar free in a world of my own making.

While Alan and I were in Heraklion, the capital of Crete, I insisted on finding the tomb of one of my favorite writers, Nikos Kazantzakis, and feeling a little self-conscious I laid a bunch of red carnations on his marble tomb. *Zorba the Greek* was the book that made him famous, but I had especially enjoyed *The Last Temptation of Christ*, which focused on the human nature of Jesus Christ and was why the Greek church excommunicated Kazantzakis. One of his quotes I liked was, "A person needs a little madness, or else they never dare cut the rope and be free". I am sure he was referring to political freedom, but I took it for myself to mean freedom from a loveless marriage.

We spent three days at a resort at Agios Nikolaos, where again Alan simply wanted to lie in the sun, with his English newspapers and a beer. I had long ago learned that he was not interested in history or literature, though he put up with me reading to him from guidebooks wherever we were. He was sometimes friendly when we went out in the evenings and we both enjoyed talking to local people. We had some excellent fish dinners in the little town a short walk away, with ouzo and bouzouki music adding to the atmosphere. One café was owned by a colorful Zorba the Greek look-alike, who was quite entertaining, if we paid for his ouzo, and we were befriended by an older man who turned out to be the local miller. He was insistent that we went home to his wonderful old stone windmill with him, although we had no Greek and he had no English. We visited with him and his toothless smiling wife who brought us more ouzo and a plate of local cheese and almonds as we all endeavored to communicate. We understood clearly that he was pleased we were British and not German, and we stumbled home happily in the dark after our unusual encounter.

I sometimes felt that my communication with Alan was like our visit to the miller and his wife – two of us speaking different emotional languages and never really coming together. I felt profoundly dissatisfied again, and wistful that we were no longer as happy together as we had been in Khartoum. So, Alan and I parted at yet another airport, and I returned to Jordan, pleased to see the children again but reluctant to resume a life with John based on drinking and agriculture. I welcomed some more assignments with the Jordan Times, but increasingly Sophie was causing us concern.

She would be sent home from school running a temperature, but often it had subsided by the time she got home. I stayed home with her more and more, missing out on a trip to Petra the fabled rose-red Nabatean city which was a disappointment. As Sophie's appetite was poor and she was losing weight, I took her to at least three Jordanian doctors over the next six weeks, who tested her for all sorts of maladies including TB, until finally, I had had enough.

I appealed to the wife of the UNDP Project Manager and asked that we go to England for medical treatment and to my grateful surprise, she made it happen almost immediately. I told John I no longer trusted the doctors in Jordan to find out what was wrong with our daughter and wanted to leave. He agreed once he found out that the UN would pay for all my travel and medical expenses. I called Alan and a friend from Fiji days who was now the Registrar of the London Hospital and two days later, we were on a plane to London.

It was February and bitterly cold, and when we were met by Alan at Heathrow, he had a warm rug ready in the car for little Sophie and was so calm and reassuring that I instantly forgave him any real or imagined shortcomings. It was such a relief to be welcomed and cared for and for Sophie to be treated so lovingly. I resolved to be more grateful in return, less demanding, less restless and more understanding. As we left Heathrow with Alan in charge, and our destiny in his capable hands, I knew I could never return to Jordan. My life without John had finally begun after sixteen years of trying and failing to find any hope of mutual integrity or respect.

16. England 1976

The need for attachment never lessens. Most human beings simply cannot tolerate being disengaged from others for any length of time. Anything is preferable to that godforsaken sense of irrelevance and alienation. One step further down on the ladder to self-oblivion is depersonalization — losing your sense of yourself.   Bessel Van der Kolk (from Brain Pickings)

Alan had rented an apartment in the suburb of Maida Vale and welcomed us with warmth and comfort and a fridge full of food and drink, so I slept well that first night, thankful that the stress of unknowing would soon be over. The next morning Alan drove us to Whitechapel to the London Hospital where we were taken immediately to an isolation room inside the children's ward, where Sophie could see what was going on behind her glass windows. I spent each day with her from then on, going over the road for a pub lunch where most of the doctors also ate. I discovered Ploughman's lunches with wonderful cheeses and pickles - fresh Stilton with celery became a favorite. After years of shopping in native markets, it was a relief to be able to buy good food in supermarkets again in great variety, knowing it was clean and fresh. Alan dropped me at the hospital most mornings on his way to work and I often met him somewhere in the West End for dinner at the end of each day.

Sophie underwent a tiresome period of blood tests, bone marrow studies and physical exams and was eventually diagnosed as having leishmaniasis or kala-azar as it is known in the Middle East. It is a serious parasitic disease – only malaria is more deadly. She had all the classic symptoms of irregular bouts of fever, weight loss, swelling of the spleen and liver, and anemia and I was angry that the doctors in Jordan had not identified it right away. It is endemic in the Middle East and is caused by a parasite that gets into the bloodstream from a sand-fly bite. The sand fly first bites an intermediate host, a dog, and then the human. I thought with dismay of our innocently happy afternoons at the beach in Malta, playing with Bonkers the dog, and often going home with itchy sand-fly bites.

Sophie became a little celebrity once she was diagnosed and enjoyed a stream of medical students visiting her, once it was established she had nothing infectious. The treatment, however, was extremely painful and everyone knew when poor Sophie was getting her daily intravenous shot of pentavalent antimony.

"I don't want an injection today", she would scream. "Take me back to the children's ward." "I promise you any treat you would like, if you are brave again today," I would try to bribe her because reasoning did not work." "May I have some garlic sausage again?" For some reason, this was her favorite food while she was ill, and it helped to have some on hand when it was treatment time again. Antimony is one of the old-fashioned poisons mentioned in some of Agatha Christie's murder mysteries, and her dosage was carefully calculated, with her heart rate monitored while it was being administered. After three weeks, we were able to leave the hospital and go in daily for the treatment for another three weeks before she was pronounced cured.

My mission in life was to get her eating and healthy again and we were fortunate that London was enjoying a hot, dry summer which meant we could spend time in local parks and playgrounds with picnic lunches while Alan was at work. I had visited the library at the Medical School attached to the hospital and had learned with horror that some of the side effects of the disease were disfiguring skin lesions, so I watched every freckle and blemish on her skin for months afterward. A side-effect of the treatment had been a certain amount of hair loss and her fingernails had turned a little grey, but she soon thrived and returned to her usual happy self, content to draw and color pictures for hours and delighting in the novelty of British children's television programs.

I had written to John making it clear that I was never going to return to him or any other third world country, and that Chris should join us and go to an English boarding school as soon as summer was over. I think he was relieved that he no longer had the responsibility for the children and could concentrate on his next career move which was to leave the United Nations Development Program and join the World Bank. As the long hot summer of 1976 persisted, I became more and more unsettled. Alan's company was sending him to Dublin, and it was time for me to find a home with or without Alan. I wanted to stay in England, and I set about finding a new home where Sophie could go to a good school and be close to her doctor if needed. So we said goodbye yet again.

I found the village of Windlesham, near the town of Woking in Surrey, not too far from London. I rented a house with a small garden and Sophie began school at a little private girls' school a short drive away. She was happy to have company her own age again after nearly nine months of hospital and grownups. She looked charming in her uniform of gingham dress, blue cape, and straw boater, and while she was a little behind in some subjects, she was way ahead in reading and general knowledge. Chris was enrolled at Dover College in Kent, an old public school with a growing international reputation. And by happy chance, around the corner from Sophie's school was the Tante Marie School of Cordon Bleu Cooking where I enrolled for the year's diploma course, thankful to have a clear objective at last and a way to earn a living once I graduated.

My sister Jane, her husband Jack and the four children were by now established in London and lived in a lovely old house in Chiswick. Jane was proud of the fact that it had been owned by a titled lady married to a famous writer – or maybe it was the other way round. I visited a couple of times but was never made to feel welcome, partly because Jane disapproved, quite rightly, of my smoking and always gave me the impression that she was afraid I would ask her for something she was not prepared to give. She and Jack were both successful and ambitious and busy with their careers in publishing and direct mail, and the children were all at prestigious private day schools in London. So, I tended to stay in Windlesham during the weekends, and if the weather allowed, Sophie and I would explore the countryside together.

Windlesham was a typical small English village with several pubs and a village green and I had rented a small furnished house with a year's lease to give myself time to decide about the rest of my life. A Cordon Bleu diploma would be an opening I thought for more opportunities to be self-sufficient, and it was certainly a pleasure to be working each day with young women who wanted to get good jobs in the world of haute cuisine. Most of them wanted to work in stately homes or in directors' dining rooms, and after our morning classes, we had lectures on food and wine and classes in making curtains and upholstery.

I remember making a Viennese gateau for one of my intermediate tests and was very pleased with the result – eight layers with caramel "wings" on top - and I decided to donate it to the village cake sale being held that weekend. It was received rather frostily by the Women's Institute ladies as it looked almost pretentious surrounded by plain Victoria sponges, rock cakes and scones. It was not an opportunity to make friends that day.

However, I got to know some of the mothers at Sophie's school and was happy to host a memorable seventh birthday party for her with plain cupcakes that the little guests had fun decorating with colored icing and a variety of sprinkles and sugar flowers. They also made their own party hats with pretty materials that I had prepared, and I heard later from mothers that the children enjoyed it much more than the standard birthday party entertainment of a hired magician.

After a few months, I heard from John that he was coming to England on his way to a new position in Indonesia. He turned up in England's early winter weather wearing his tropical suits and we promptly went into Woking to shop for sweaters and jackets. He was pleased with the way his career was progressing and our reunion was friendly enough until he took Sophie to the park the next morning while I was cooking. To my horror, he returned carrying Sophie in his arms — she had slipped and fallen from the top step of a slide and was slightly concussed. We put her on the sofa, covered her with warm blankets, watching her closely. When she threw up a dark substance, I thought it meant a ruptured spleen, and sent for a doctor in a panic, furious with John. I had not realized she had been eating black liquorice allsorts, a favorite English candy, and once she had been checked out and pronounced unharmed, I calmed down. However, I was unforgiving and could not believe John had been so careless the first time he had been with his daughter in nine months, especially after all

I had been through to get her well again since we had left Jordan.

John left for the US to sign on with the World Bank as Christmas was approaching. My friend DeDe from Khartoum had been in touch and was coming to spend a few days with me, then Alan called and said he would join us, so I would have a house full. I had to do a lot of food shopping and preparation as England in those days closed for ten days over Christmas and New Year. I remember being totally stressed as I was expected to provide Cordon Bleu meals for everyone without a lot of help, Alan and DeDe being happy to sit and drink and reminisce about Khartoum. I was in a mood to move on and think of the future, not the past, and I was quite pleased when the New Year came and I was alone again and back to the routine of school for me and Sophie. I was determined to take hold of my life and become emotionally independent and resilient. But that did not last long.

Mother had decided to come to England for another visit. She had stayed at first with Jane in London and it was not long before they fell out and Mother came to me in Windlesham. She had been a widow for two years now and I was prepared to be a more understanding and thoughtful daughter. But day after day, I would come home from the Tanta Marie classes and find her still in her housecoat, an ashtray full of cigarette butts and evidence of having had many cups of tea and glasses of sherry. She made little effort to get out on her own and was resentful of the time I was spending at cooking school and being with Sophie in the afternoons and evenings. She expected me to shop and cook the meals and even do the cleaning when I got home. I was disappointed as I wanted to help her but also would have welcomed a mother's caring support at a time when I was still unsure about my own future as a single mother.

When she first came to London, she had plans to find out more about her father's life and work and had contacted the son of the Admiral who wrote the introduction to my grandfather's book about the Caroline Islands. Sir Cyprian Bridge's son must have been a courteous old gentleman, as he invited Mother to visit his country home. My sister reported later that Mother probably drank all his sherry and became arch and flirtatious, so the Admiral's son politely suggested the next day that it was time she returned to London. She had another setback when she arranged to visit the British Museum to see the artifacts her father had brought back from the ruins he had explored in the 1890s. The young museum official who met her and took her down to the storage basement, reportedly said that my grandfather, like so many amateur Victorian explorers, was looked down upon by modern archeologists for removing trophies without a context and being little more than grave-robbers. Mother was deeply offended by this appraisal of her father, whom she had always revered as a gentleman and scholar.

She was also upset by how England had changed since the family was there in Coronation Year. I had never thought of my mother as racist, but she was quite upset by the number of West Indian bus conductors and shop assistants and thought they treated her with disrespect. She talked often about my father, whom she called Monty, saying how she missed him and how wonderful he was, doing everything for her, and insinuating it was her children's turn to care for her now she was alone. When I reminded her how she used to come crying to me at night, complaining about him and saying she wanted to leave him, she became indignant. I also reminded her that Monty had enjoyed his control of the family finances and had discouraged her from learning to drive, but she was free now to manage a cheque book herself and get some driving lessons. She became indignant again and said I was unfeeling and that she was going back to stay with Jane in London.

I was disappointed in her for being so sentimental and needy and similarly disappointed in myself for expecting her to have suddenly become a loving mother I could trust and respect. Her visit left me feeling uneasy, rattled, and self-reproachful and I had to cope as well with my sister haranguing me about not keeping her longer. Mother returned to New Zealand sooner than she had planned, where she moved to be closer to my young brother Robert, now a busy lawyer with four children and an unhappy wife. I suspect the wife was even unhappier when she realized that Robert would have to spend a lot of his spare time helping my mother with her finances and transportation.

Summer came and the end of the school year for the three of us. I was happy to have my Cordon Bleu diploma, Sophie had had a good year, was a healthy weight again and had easily caught up with her peers after missing out on so much school. Chris went off on an Outward Bound trip to France for a few weeks before coming home to me in Windlesham. He had settled well at Dover College after being initially rebellious but was now excelling at various school sports and enjoying the challenges of British public school life. The rest of the summer loomed however, the lease of the house was running out and I had some decisions to make.

17. Dublin 1977

"Our emotional life maps our incompleteness," philosopher Martha Nussbaum wrote. "A creature without any needs would never have reasons for fear, or grief, or hope, or anger." Anger, indeed, is one of the emotions we judge most harshly — in others, as well as in ourselves — and yet understanding anger is central to mapping out the landscape of our interior lives.   Maria Popova, Brain Pickings

Alan urged me to join him in Dublin, where he had rented a house near the beach at Dollymount and knowing that I could expect nothing from my mother or my sister, in the way of emotional support, I gave in. Instead of taking a courageous step to find a job and a new place to live, I loaded up my car and set off for Ireland. I knew it was a wrong decision and began to berate myself for acting like my mother, relying on a man's support instead of having enough pride to go it alone. As I drove through Wales to Holyhead to catch the ferry to Dun Laoghaire, I no longer felt the usual optimism about going to a new place and starting over but instead felt defeated and angry with myself. It was not a good start.

Dublin, like most cities, had two faces – the elegance of the Georgian squares and the dreary little pubs and markets off the main streets. Ireland was not yet part of the Common

Market and there was evidence of poverty everywhere. The farms were neglected, and it seemed that on every street corner in central Dublin, I would be accosted by a barefoot gypsy trying to sell me a sprig of heather. I was excited to be in James Joyce's Dublin however and read again the books I had loved when I was a student – *Ulysses* and *The Dubliners*. I walked a lot and discovered landmarks from Bloom's Dublin and visited the Martello tower in Sandycove, where Joyce spent six nights in 1904.

I had been told that I should live in Ireland to avoid paying British income tax on the allowance John sent me, but I needed to start earning some money as soon as I could. I had some friends to look up for advice and I first contacted the Irish couple I had met in Spain, only to learn that blind Cahal had died and Kay was on her own. She cooked corned beef and cabbage for me and became very sentimental over the many glasses of Jameson's whiskey which accompanied our meal. Sophie was uncomfortable and both of us found it difficult to understand Kay's Irish brogue, which became more unintelligible with every glass. I realized sadly that not all holiday acquaintances become lasting friends.

I had also got in touch with Nuala Doyle, the sister of the developer of the resort in Fiji where we had spent many idyllic weekends. Nuala had retired from her job of training air hostesses for Aer Lingus and for a hobby had a market stall where she sold china and silver that she had bought over the years during her travels. She persuaded me to join her and sell home-made soup and Irish soda bread, which seemed like a good idea, until sales did not cover the outlay and bad weather cancelled most market days as winter set in.

I applied for a job I saw in the paper and started cooking for an English language school in downtown Dublin which specialized in teaching technical English to medical students from Saudi Arabia. I had a tiny inconvenient kitchen to work in and cooked variants of spicy chicken, lamb, and rice for the students' lunches. It was totally unsatisfactory as I had to shop and cook and charge the students accordingly to make a profit. They soon discovered that they could eat more cheaply elsewhere, probably at Ireland's first McDonald's restaurant which had opened in May that year on Grafton Street. So, after working hard, with little reward, I gave it up, the decider being when I turned on the gas oven one morning, forgot to light it immediately and it went off with a bang. The whole experience was a useful lesson in cooking for the public – no matter how good the food might be, financial planning and pricing it right was everything.

I was very conscious of being Protestant in Catholic Southern Ireland. Nuala had warned me that I was unlikely to make friends as wives would distrust me and husbands would think me fair game. Ireland was still very Victorian in its attitude toward sex – abortion still forbidden, and tales abounded of pregnant girls who decided to take flight to London rather than endure the wrath of parents and Church.

I was concerned that there might be too much religious education at Sophie's school at Rathdown, but she was not overwhelmed with teaching about hell and sin and enjoyed her Gaelic lessons. I had quickly tired of the rented house in Dollymount and found a mews house in Ballsbridge, a more fashionable part of Dublin. Architect-designed, it had a scarlet spiral iron staircase leading up to Sophie's bedroom and lots of windows and whitewashed brick work.

I thought I could be happy there and started to look at more cooking opportunities. I had bought the book *A Taste of Ireland* by the writer Theodora Fitzgibbon and knowing she lived in Dublin, I fantasized about meeting her and maybe becoming her assistant. She intrigued me as she had travelled widely with her father in India, Europe, and the Middle East. It was said that she received cooking lessons from the former Queen Natalie of Serbia at a finishing school in Paris and had written a successful novel called *Flight of the Kingfisher.* But in the end, I lacked the courage to find her and introduce myself as I did not think she would be interested in someone who had nearly blown up a gas oven at an English language school. And I was not going to stay in Dublin much longer.

Alan's job in Dublin was short-lived. He had achieved the reorganization of the warehouse operation where the manager and his wife had been welcoming and invited us out to the family farm one long weekend. The countryside was lush and green, but there was little sign of active farming and while Sophie played with the farm cats, the grownups sat around playing cards and drinking the inevitable Jameson's. I was eager to explore the countryside but was overruled and we returned to Dublin after what I considered a wasted opportunity. But we did go home with Seamus, a black and white kitten for Sophie.

After Alan returned to England, I stayed on in Dublin until the year's lease was up on the mews house and Sophie's school year ended. We had a little time to explore the countryside then and I discovered Glendalough. About thirty miles from Dublin, it is one of the most important monastic sites in Ireland. It was founded in the 6th century and most of the surviving buildings date from the 10th through 12th centuries. We drove up on a misty grey morning, a light rain falling as it did so often in Ireland. We were the only people there, and as we walked among ruined churches, monasteries, and anchorites' retreats, I was overwhelmed with a sense of the past. I felt an almost mystical sense of awareness of the thousands of dead souls who belonged to that place, similar to the feeling I had in ancient cathedrals, "where prayer has been valid."

Ireland was a troubled country, about to be transformed by entry into the Common Market, but still in a time warp of ancient grudges and a dominant Church. I was thankful for the experience of Glendalough as I left Ireland at the end of that summer to meet Alan again, this time in Yorkshire. Harrogate was a different world, a prosperous town in Northern England on the edge of Bronte country and formerly a Georgian spa town where respectable gentry came to take the waters.   I had never felt comfortable in Ireland. Perhaps Harrogate would be better.

18. Harrogate and London 1978-1979

The human being ……. would indeed go mad if he did not find a frame of reference which permitted him to feel at home in the world in some form and to escape the experience of utter helplessness, disorientation, and uprootedness.   Erich Fromm (from Brain Pickings)

Alan had bought an apartment in a solid Victorian stone building, the second floor of what had been a small mansion in a respectable tree-lined avenue in Harrogate. He had finally had his furniture shipped to him and had unpacked his lovely Thai silver bowls, framed pictures of Thai dancers and carved teak furniture that he had acquired during his years in Bangkok. It all felt familiar and comforting from Khartoum days. I found a small boarding school for Sophie in the countryside on the road to York. Called Red House, it had previously been a prep school for boys but was in the process of becoming co-educational, a dynamic which I thought would be ideal. There were only eight little girls, ponies for riding lessons and the day started in the centuries-old chapel which I thought would do her no harm, so she was enrolled as a weekly boarder and I would pick her up each Friday afternoon and return her on Sunday evenings.

I found a job cooking at a directors' dining room in a village some ten miles away. It was for an international engineering company based in a lovely old manor house, surrounded by trees and lawns, with the eight directors having offices in the building and others coming and going. Finally using my Cordon Bleu diploma to advantage, I was employed to cook luncheons – sometimes for three or four, sometimes for ten or more and I started the job with enthusiasm as I had the idea of writing a cookbook about the experience. I had Linda to help in the kitchen, the daughter of the gardener of the former estate who still worked there and supplied me with fresh produce. Expense was no object and I was often there until late in the afternoon if there had been a large business lunch. They would drink wine with every course and often would send out for yet another bottle of port with their coffee. Several times I was asked for lobster or oysters which I ordered from London and had to pick up from the railway station early in the morning, and they also often requested traditional English dishes such as venison, pheasant, and hare.

The problem was that by the time I got home in the afternoons, I was too tired to sit down and write up recipes to be tested again later. I first had to shop and cook for Alan's dinner, which he expected on the table when he was ready, after several beers or whiskies with his newspaper. Once I put his slippers beside his chair and he took it as his due instead of realizing I was being ironic. It never crossed his mind to bring me my slippers after a day on my feet in the directors' kitchen.

I relished the weekends and enjoyed the drive to and from Red House through the Yorkshire countryside. One day, Sophie and I were delighted to drive past a re-enactment of a famous battle between Roundheads and Cavaliers. The Battle of Marston Moor was fought in 1644 during the First English Civil War. The English Parliamentarians or Roundheads under Lord Fairfax and their Scottish allies defeated the Royalists or Cavaliers commanded by Prince Rupert of the Rhine. It was quite disorienting for a moment to come across the battle raging on the broad meadow on a gray misty day and I stopped the car to watch, amused and impressed by the experience. On another cold grey day, we had stopped to watch a hunt streaming across the same fields, hounds sounding and huntsmen in their scarlet jackets in pursuit of some poor little fox. It was like a movie set and made my life seem humdrum in contrast.

The weekends were a welcome break from the drudgery of cooking and Sophie and I would go for long drives onto the moors and sometimes to nearby Castle Howard, one of England's finest stately homes open to the public. Made famous later as the background of the BBC TV series *Brideshead Revisited*, it was also where one of my former classmates from the Cordon Bleu School was working. Our reunion was brief however as she got a job cooking on a Greek millionaire's yacht in Nice. I day-dreamed about doing something similar but of course it was out of the question with Sophie to care for.

I met a local realtor in a pub one Sunday lunchtime who became a welcome friend. Anne was attractive, Jewish, unfaithful to her husband and on the verge of divorce. She like me, was restless and looking for diversion and companionship, and we would increasingly meet after work at our local pub for a glass of wine or two. Our friendship was more an attempt to assert my independence from the routine of cooking and a rebellion against being taken for granted night after night by Alan. It was fun for a while, until winter set in and that year in Harrogate it was a particularly vicious one.

Alan had the use of the garage for his car and mine had to be left outside in the snow. It got harder and harder to start the car in the cold, damp mornings and I was forever taking it in to the local mechanic for new spark plugs or whatever he said was needed. One morning I slipped and fell on the ice while trying to clear off my windscreen, and I could barely drive through the blizzard like conditions that day. I started to feel very resentful that things were so difficult. On top of it all, Alan's mother came to stay. I had never met her of course and was both curious and nervous as I rightly imagined her as a strait-laced Scottish lady who basically disapproved of me.

So I would get home from work with two people waiting for me to cook dinner for them and after several days of this, I suggested to Alan that he take his mother out for a meal as I was feeling exhausted. I could see this did not go down well with a frugal Scots lady who considered dining out an extravagance. Obviously, she was unaware that I was paying for our food while Alan dealt with the mortgage, and if I had not been so tired I may have been more understanding. I simply left the room and went to bed, leaving them to sort it out between them. I suppose I was looking for the last straw and this was it. The night Alan's mother left, I started to plan my escape.

I resigned from my cooking job and went to London for a few days to follow up on a house to rent I had seen advertised in the Daily Telegraph. I gave Alan strict instructions to water the pink azalea that I was so proud of, elegantly flourishing in its silver bowl. The young woman who owned the house was leaving for a job in Germany, having recently broken up with her boyfriend. We commiserated and although I was not entirely happy with the house's distance from Central London, the rent was affordable, there was room for the children during the school holidays and so I signed an agreement.

When I returned, the azalea was dead, and that really was the last straw. Suddenly all the resentments and the disappointments over the years came to the fore and I started to rant and shout at Alan, while he just sat there, pouring himself yet another whisky. I accused him of being uncaring, unethical in living off the allowance John sent me, neglectful, unimaginative, uncommunicative, betraying my trust in him, refusing to take responsibility for me or my happiness by not marrying me, taking me for granted as cook, cleaner and ironer of his shirts. I said he was just as bad as John, drinking too much and not having not the slightest interest in anything cultural or intellectual. I amazed myself as the pent up disappointment poured out in a tirade that I could not stop, even when the phone rang and our neighbor downstairs said she could hear every word, and sympathized, but she wanted to get some sleep.

The next week was awful, as I had packed and arranged to ship tea chests full of belongings to my new address, only to hear from my future landlady that she had reconciled with her boyfriend and was not going to Germany after all. She returned my deposit, but I was completely left in the lurch. I was in a cold panic as I did not want to stay a minute longer than necessary, so I arranged to rent an apartment, sight unseen, in Vauxhall in London. Sophie was happy to be leaving her school as the boys had bullied the few little girls, who instead of bonding, had been cliquey and catty. Both of us were relieved when I picked her up and after a final cold goodbye with Alan, we said farewell to Yorkshire and drove south with my little Fiat crammed to the roof for a new life alone again. It should have felt like an escape but illogically, I felt that Alan had abandoned me, and I felt no joy as the miles increased the distance between us as London became closer. I wanted to feel positive for Sophie's sake, but it all felt more like failure. But I had burned my bridges and was too proud to turn back. London was my future now, whatever that may bring.

19. London 1979-1980

Being a human means accepting promises from other people and trusting that other people will be good to you. When that is too much to bear, it is always possible to retreat into the thought, "I'll live for my own comfort, for my own revenge, for my own anger, and I just won't be a member of society anymore." That really means, "I won't be a human being anymore." Martha Nussbaum (from Brain Pickings)

I arrived in London in the co-called Winter of Discontent, an apt description of my situation but coined by journalists to describe the politics of the day. Britain was in recession with rising unemployment and there were many industrial disputes and strikes, the most visible of which was when uncollected black plastic bags of trash piled up on every street corner. Margaret Thatcher had just been elected Prime Minister, the first woman to hold that office, and she set about trying to dismantle many aspects of the welfare state. She was quickly dubbed Thatcher the Milk Snatcher for stopping free milk in the schools and earned the lasting nickname The Iron Lady for her uncompromising style and policies.

I found a job immediately as restaurant manager in a small private hotel, close to Victoria Station, which meant my apartment across the Vauxhall Bridge was only one stop away by Underground or a nice walk on a fine day. My landlord lived on the ground floor, and I rented the upstairs, which made me feel quite safe as the neighborhood was not the most respectable. It was in a row of red-brick terraced houses, within sight of the Battersea Power Station and I looked on it as only temporary until I could be earning more, unwilling to ask John for more than we had originally agreed.

I had found a promising boarding school for Sophie, the Royal Russell, just outside London, and hoped its international student body would mean a friendlier atmosphere for her after the Red House experience. Unfortunately, they operated on the usual public school system of exeats in mid-term, rather than allowing for weekly boarders, which meant she was there for six weeks at a time before she could have a visit home. I missed her terribly and determined to make the best use of the time by working weekends so that I could have time off when she was with me in London.

The private hotel was owned by an elderly English couple, the Tophams, who had turned Mrs. Topham's family home into a bed and breakfast during the war, when her brother who was in the Air Force brought home his friends who needed a place to stay when they were in London on leave. The hotel evolved from that beginning and it had a reputation amongst its faithful regulars for being charming, old-fashioned, and comfortable with an excellent dining room.

My job involved typing up the day's menus and consulting with the chef about anything he needed ordered for the day, making sure the waitresses were on time and being a gracious hostess in the dining room at breakfast and lunchtime. It was all a little stifling and I had little use for my Cordon Bleu Diploma as the chef resisted change at first, until I managed to win him over diplomatically. He allowed a few menu changes with my suggestions, but only after he had challenged me to a contest making choux pastry, with the kitchen staff to vote on the best result. I tried hard but of course the loyal assistant chefs voted for his pastry, and honor was satisfied, and the hierarchy left undisturbed. He was much friendlier from then on, and even teased me a little when I tried to establish a small herb garden outside my office window. I think we were both upset when it was smashed to shreds in an unseasonal hailstorm.

One morning the chef decided he needed some haricots verts, the fine French green beans that were in season and I willingly escaped from my office in the basement and went down the road to the greengrocer on the corner. To my astonishment I heard a familiar voice, "Sue Lamont! What on earth are you doing here?" It was June Knox-Mawer, my some-time mentor when I had been a trainee announcer at Fiji Broadcasting. I had always admired June because she had had a book published about her life in Aden, called *The Sultans Came to Tea*. She had started the Women's Programmes on Radio Fiji which my mother had continued.

I muttered something about a Cordon Bleu diploma and working as a restaurant manager, suddenly ashamed that that was all I could admit to. "What about your ambition to work for the BBC?" she asked. I did not know what to say. "Come and see me some time", she said kindly, as we exclaimed further about the coincidence of our meeting and finally said goodbye. I went back to the kitchen with my green beans, feeling a conflicting mix of shame and hope, remembering those early days when June and my other mentor from the BBC, Chris Venning, had taken an interest in me and my fledgling career in radio journalism. I would have to get out the hotel basement and get a real career.

I knew that there was no long-term future for me in this world of cuisine and restaurant management as cooking for a living was 90 percent drudgery and not at all well-paid. I had to get back to school and get a university qualification. I was disappointed that my New Zealand University Entrance was not recognized in the UK and I had to enroll in Adult Education classes at night to get A-levels before I could do a bachelor's degree course. I loved the English class right away and it was a joy to be reading Shakespeare again and being challenged by poetry that I had never read before. I remember being assigned to critique a poem by D.H Lawrence, the words and ideas flowing as I wrote, surprising myself with the real pleasure I got from the exercise. My tutor was very complimentary and urged me to carry on with my ambition to go to University, encouraging me all the way through the exams and entry process.

At the same time, I had noticed a non-credit class on offer on the philosopher Hannah Arendt, and I signed up for that also. Taught by a dynamic American woman living in London, it expanded my mind dramatically and I read late into the night when I got home after work and lectures. My early socialist leanings had been acquired from Peter, my first boyfriend, and it was exciting to have my ideas fully informed by Hannah Arendt's brilliant scholarship. She was best-known for her book about Eichmann, *The Banality of Evil*, because of the controversy it stirred among people who misread it and thought she was condoning Nazi atrocities. But it was her long and important work that impressed me most, *The Rise and Fall of Totalitarianism,* and I finally had an educated political conscience instead of my old half-baked ideas. I began reading The Guardian regularly but kept a sneaking loyalty for the more conservative Daily Telegraph because it had the only crossword I was able to finish.

I was home one night with a book and a bottle of wine when the phone rang. It was my sister Jane, announcing that Mother was coming to London again, this time with a woman friend and would I please put them up as she had no room for an extra person. I could only say yes, if it was while Sophie was at school, as there were two beds in the extra bedroom. They turned up with far too much luggage that I had to haul upstairs. Mother's friend had even brought an opera cloak with her, though how she would afford the £150 ticket to the Royal Opera House in Covent Garden I had no idea. I think they were both disappointed by my humble surroundings and that I had neither time, money nor a car to put at their disposal.

I did my best, but it was still disappointing to find them both waiting for me at the end of the day, sherry and cigarettes in hand, expecting me to cook a Cordon Bleu dinner. My mother had settled a little better into her role as grieving widow, and I found out from my sister Jane that my young brother had finally insisted that she learn to manage her cheque book and finances herself. Somewhat miffed at this, she had moved up to Auckland, where my little sister Juliet was living at the time. Juliet had finally found a niche working for an organic farming magazine and I was delighted to hear that she was much happier even though she was at Mother's beck and call.

The two ladies explored London during the day and inevitably fell out over sharing expenses as they were not prepared for the rise in the cost of living in Britain since Mother's last visit. The friend went to a bed and breakfast and Mother went to Jane's. I was finally able to give some thought and energy to my next job and my next move, both of which were an improvement on my present situation.

I was still a restaurant manager but this time for a merchant bank in Curzon Street with three in-house restaurants, for staff, middle management, and the directors. My new flat was in Maida Vale, still rather dreary but it was in a mansion block and had more privacy without a resident landlord downstairs. Jane and my mother came over one evening, ostensibly to help me settle in, but the unpacking was all done, so they proceeded to drink all my wine. Mother as usual became skittish and Jane argumentative, until Mother turned to me and said, "You know Sue, I've never really liked you."

I had always known this, but it really cut to the quick to hear her say it aloud. It gave Jane some satisfaction which also hurt. I could hardly wait to see them out the door and vowed that I would never let them get to me again. People call it "pressing my buttons" but it felt more like probing the tender spots with a knife. Once again I was angry with myself for wanting to trust and hoping to find a supportive family. It was the same feeling I had so many years ago when we were coming home in the school bus and Jane had offered me a colored gumball which I accepted, innocently surprised by her gesture. When I put it my mouth, she and her friends shrieked with laughter. "We found it on the floor, you are eating germs and dirt!" I was humiliated and do not know why I ever trusted her again.

The one good thing that Mother did for me before she went back to New Zealand, was to introduce me to the principal of a liberal co-ed boarding school in Surrey. A friend of a friend, he had been the sole survivor of a small plane crash and instead of entering the priesthood as he had intended, he decided instead to spend his life teaching. He and his wife were exceptional people, and when we talked about Sophie and her experiences at her different schools, he said, "You know, I don't make a habit of poaching pupils from other schools but I know your daughter would be really happy at Frensham Heights." We arranged for me to visit, and I knew immediately that he was right.

I moved her from the Royal Russell to Frensham Heights at the end of the term, happy that she would be a weekly boarder again and feeling relieved that the school leadership was based on spiritual integrity. I was pleased also that Chris was doing so well at Dover College, was active in most sports and had been appointed a prefect in his House. There was no reason for me to fret about the children anymore and I was free to move ahead with my life, unencumbered by regrets over Alan, my mother, or my sister.

At least, that it what I tried to tell myself, when I came home each night to an empty flat, tired and dispirited after a long day at the bank and turning to a bottle of wine instead of bothering to cook a meal. I had to find a way of going back to University and earning a living at the same time but felt unable to see a means of achieving that. I made inquiries about enrolling in Open University, but the workload would have proved overwhelming on top of a full-time job. I really did not enjoy my work, stuck in a small office in the basement of the Bank building, with an unfriendly chef and a kitchen staff I suspected of stealing supplies. I had to try and balance the inventory every week which I found impossible but at least I had the key to the wine cellar, where I could finish off the partly empty bottles returned after the directors' lunch.

John visited us briefly for Christmas that year, on his way to a posting with the World Bank in Washington DC. He was bluff and hearty with the children, taking them to Greenwich for an outing but mostly sitting around drinking, complaining of the cold, and offering me no further financial help. We discussed plans for the school holidays, and it was arranged that Sophie would join him in for the summer and that Chris would do another Outward Bound course which he loved. He had been mountaineering in Scotland and canoeing in the Ardeche in France and had also been to France illicitly one exeat weekend, with three friends who decided to cross on the ferry without getting parental or school permission. I admired his spirit of adventure but had to talk to him sternly about breaking school rules.

The year dragged on and work became more and more dreary. The only human contact I had was with the kitchen staff and the waitresses, my immediate boss being an unpleasant little man, who made up for his lack of height by his domineering manner. I was quite pleased therefore when one of the waitresses came to me in tears, saying that he persisted in touching her inappropriately when she was serving his meal, and could I do something about it as she did not want to lose her job. I arranged to meet with his superior who heard me out and instead of agreeing to speak harshly to the offender, he laughed in my face. I was deeply affronted and asked him to take it more seriously. He said something non-committal and I swear his hand wandered inappropriately below my waist as he ushered me out of his office.

I hated the job from then on and it became a grinding effort to get to work on time every day, as I felt I had let the waitress down and gossip soon spread below stairs that I was ineffectual as a manager. I was also probably a figure of fun with the executives upstairs, "One of those women's libbers."

Around this time, I had to renew my passport and apply to the Home Office for permanent residence as commonwealth citizens no longer had freedom to come and go without stay permits. It was a matter of some pride to me when I received my European Community passport in the mail – I was no longer a British subject but a citizen of Europe. It suddenly seemed important to me that I was no longer a second-class resident of Britain, a member of the commonwealth without the status of being born in the United Kingdom. From then on, I took a closer interest in politics and the debate about the European Community that still raged on in certain quarters in the press and Parliament. The UK had joined the Common Market in 1973, ratified by a referendum in 1975. I was appalled when Brexit happened forty years later, and the UK withdrew from Europe.

But in the meantime, my personal winter of discontent had turned into a whole year. When I should have moved ahead on my own at last, with both the children settled and happy, a reasonably well-paid job and a flat I could afford, I became paralyzed instead. I had taken the first step toward going back to school but was unable to take the next. What was happening to me was that I thought I was drinking too much because I was unhappy. Instead, I was unhappy because I was drinking too much. And I began a slow spiral downwards into addiction and spiritual despair.

20. London 1980-1983

Not Waving but Drowning

Nobody heard him, the dead man,
But still he lay moaning:
I was much further out than you thought
And not waving but drowning.

Poor chap, he always loved larking
And now he's dead
It must have been too cold for him his heart gave way,
They said.

Oh, no no no, it was too cold always
(Still the dead one lay moaning)
I was much too far out all my life
And not waving but drowning.
Stevie Smith (from Brain Pickings)

Towards the end of the year, Chris broke his leg playing rugby at school and as he would be unable to manage taking suitcases and Sophie on the plane trip to Washington for Christmas, it was arranged that I should go too. John had rented a townhouse in Falls Church, outside the capital, and we arrived to a snowy landscape and colder weather than I had anticipated. I needed warmer clothes and John took me shopping at his expense, and I found some smart suits and dresses for work at a fraction of London prices. Our sightseeing was limited by Chris being on crutches, and most museums were closed for the holidays, but we did visit several former friends from Khartoum and Jordan days.

I found those visits difficult, with conversation awkward and stilted. People were too polite to ask about Alan or why John and I were living in separate countries. While maintaining a reserved but friendly relationship with John, for the sake of the children, I had no desire to sit around drinking with his friends and reminiscing about the past. I preferred to drink on my own, only too aware of the foolishness of people, especially John, when they had had too much to drink. I was happy when it was time to return to London, helping Chris onto the train to Dover and Sophie back to Frensham Heights.

Sophie in her costume for a school play

I went back to work the day after New Year's Day and was surprised to get a phone call from my sister, inviting me to come over and cook dinner for an American friend whose wife had recently died. I agreed without thinking, forgetting I had already arranged to have a drink with the waitresses at a nearby pub in Shepherd's Market. So I turned up late in a taxi, to find that dinner was over of course, and Jane was not pleased with me. However, the guest was delighted as I had brought a bottle of Scotch, and we settled down together with a glass each, on the hearth rug in front of the fire, both of us finding Jane's house too cold for comfort. I was pleased I was wearing one of my smart American suits as I found him charming, witty, and attentive and for the first time for a very long time, I felt appreciated both as a person and a woman. His name was Jerry, and when he dropped me off at my flat and asked me to have dinner with him the next day, I agreed immediately.

Jerry had been born in Pittsburgh but was a New Yorker at heart, having lived there since he was 14. Nearly twenty years older than me, he had a fund of amusing jokes which he produced at apt moments – timing is everything, he would say. It was wonderful to be laughing again, to have someone who would open car doors for me and who was able to talk on a dozen subjects without ever mentioning agriculture. His attention was urgent and flattering – he had been very lonely for six months since his wife had died of cancer and the fact that I had a Cordon Bleu diploma was a major attraction. He admitted he was tired of tuna salad sandwiches, his sole culinary endeavor, and disliked eating alone in restaurants. We quickly discovered we had a lot of interests in common, politics, music, books, and the theatre, and I was soon staying overnight with him in his lovely apartment in one of London's more fashionable Georgian squares.

One night, a few months later over dinner at our favorite Thai restaurant near Harrods, he looked at me seriously and said, "What is the thing you would most like to do with your life?" Without having to think twice, I replied, "Go back to University and get an English degree." "We can do that', he said decisively, "and I think it's time you left Maida Vale and moved in with me." I promised to think about it while he was away on one of his frequent business trips to New York, as I was reluctant to commit to another man, having only just become independent. But I was certainly not enjoying my freedom on my own, so I felt very confused about who I was and where I was going. He was away for three weeks and during that time, I found it easier to have a bottle of wine each evening and sleep soundly instead of worrying about a decision.

I hated myself for my lack of courage and lack of direction, and found myself sinking deeper into a depression, probably because Jerry was offering me a future that I wanted to have achieved on my own. But I knew I was not doing well by myself and while I was muddling along in a job I hated, neither married nor divorced, I was becoming sick and tired of myself and my indecision. Looking back, I wonder why it took me so long to understand that my drinking was the cause of my inadequacies, not the other way around. It took one dreadful morning, when I simply could not face the day and had to call in to work saying I had a migraine, and I sat on the floor feeling an abject failure and in complete despair. I had nothing to fall back on, no spiritual support, no one to call for help, and it was that rock bottom that eventually got me to AA.

It took nearly a year of attempts to give up drinking and I realized the insidious power of alcohol addiction and how it drains the soul. You are ready for AA "when you are sick and tired of being sick and tired", one of the catch phrases I learned at my first and subsequent meetings. I would walk down to St Andrew's Church at the end of Cadogan Place every Monday night and gradually, all the unhappiness of the past was behind me as I learned humility, hope, acceptance, and courage from a whole new world of supportive friends. Life suddenly became infinitely more meaningful and precious and though it was not always easy, I began to live with more integrity and more purpose. And instead of feeling threatened or trapped by another relationship, I was finally able to love Jerry with a whole heart.

21. London 1983-1988

God grant me the serenity
to accept the things I cannot change;
courage to change the things I can;
and wisdom to know the difference.   The AA serenity
prayer

I was never happy with the word God in the prayer
that ended every AA meeting. I thought of myself as an
atheist or at least an agnostic as I appreciated there were
many gods in world religions. I had distrusted Christian
dogma ever since I was told to leave a Presbyterian
confirmation class in Fiji when I was thirteen. The elderly
minister became annoyed when I questioned him about faith
and belief.

I asked, "If I don't believe in God but you tell me to
have faith, isn't that being dishonest?", remembering some of
my father's discussions about scientific truth and reason. I
was told I did not belong there, which upset me at first as I
wanted to stay with my friends from school. I told them later
that I was a Communist and that Karl Marx had said that
religion was the opiate of the masses. I may have had my
father's silent approval but not that of the girls in the
confirmation class.

Many years later, it was another Presbyterian church that created a pivotal moment in my life, this time the Scottish Church of St Andrews, where the AA meetings were held in the basement. I met some wonderful people there and made lasting friendships as I began to understand the nature of addiction and the power of supportive friends and the AA program. When I complained about the word God, I was told, "Just add an extra "o" to the word," and sure enough, the collective power of Good in the rooms was enough to turn my life around. We all had shame to overcome, guilty secrets, damaged relationships, and personal disasters of many kinds; the details may have been different, but a similar sense of loss and despair was shared by us all. With the help of new friends, and many tears and much laughter over mediocre coffee in many more church basements, I slowly regained my integrity and my sense of self, with a new humility and respect for the process.

Jerry and the children were supportive, though I think that Jerry never quite understood that I had to stop drinking completely instead of just cutting back. He was happy that I continued to pour his evening whiskeys and would join him with a Perrier instead, and our life together became even happier as I was able to live and love without the black dog nipping at my heels, as Churchill described it. I also managed to stop smoking, a different addiction and in some ways harder to achieve as it did not have the same social stigma. I persevered however, and after many months I was finally able to be in a room with smokers and feel revulsion rather than a craving. I was finally free.

I was accepted as a "mature student" in the BA program at Westfield College, a campus of the University of London in Hampstead. Originally a women's college, it still had a faintly Victorian air of respectability. In Britain in 1982, not only was higher education free but students also received a book allowance of several hundred pounds. That allowance was ended by Margaret Thatcher the following year, and the year after that we were charged an annual fee, so I managed to get in before it became a major expense. The campus was a mix of old grey stone buildings and new red-brick lecture halls and library, with mature trees and lawns and, unusual for London, adequate parking. Jerry bought me a car, a second-hand Peugeot to make the commute simpler, and resigning from my job with enormous relief, I began my new life as a full-time student.

I was utterly happy to be learning again, to be told to read books, instead of considering reading a guilty pleasure. I met three other women in my year about the same age, and it was good to have new friends beyond AA. One of them, Diana, lived nearby and we would meet and walk together in Hyde Park, helping each other learn enough Anglo-Saxon to pass the required exam on Beowulf. Chaucer's Middle English was much easier to cope with. I wrote my papers on Shakespeare and Victorian novelists with increasing confidence and enjoyed meeting with my tutors, who were around the same age as me, so we had a mutual respect and understanding.

In 1981, four members of the Labour Party had defected and formed a new party called the Social Democrats. This intrigued me because I certainly would never vote for a Conservative and I felt no affinity for the Labour Party which I felt at the time only represented coal miners and Union members. The Social Democrats, on the other hand were pro-European and represented the new face of British politics, absorbing the best of the old Liberal party ideals and reflecting social democracy as it was manifested in Sweden and Germany. After years of being on the outside of politics, a New Zealander living in third world countries and never having voted, I found these ideas exhilarating. Some years later I read the book by British political philosopher Tony Judt, *Ill Fares the Land (2010),* which encapsulates all that I believed at the time and since. Social democracy underpinned the merging of the new party with the old Liberal party, first becoming the Alliance, then renamed the Liberal Democrats in 1989. I became an enthusiastic and active member of the Social Democrats with Jerry's encouragement and discovered a whole new world of political activism.

Protesting with Charter 88 in Trafalgar Square

At the same time, I was rebuilding a relationship of trust with my children and when I spoke to them about my drinking in the past, they were not very impressed by my achievement, as they said that they had not really witnessed anything to forgive me for. That was a great relief. Obviously, it created a little distance between us as they understood something about the social stigma of alcoholism, and I was sad about their loss of innocence regarding their mother. I felt the best I could do for them was to become a stronger, more loving mother and I hoped they would be proud if I worked hard for a degree, became active in the political world and even started writing again.

I felt very safe and protected with Jerry in my life. I told him once that he was everything to me, father figure, lover, husband, and friend, and while I think he was momentarily pleased, I was also aware that I had given him perhaps too much responsibility for my happiness. He needed me just as much, if not more, in different ways. A younger wife was good for his male image and a loving companion and housekeeper would end his fear of becoming a lonely old man. He enjoyed the role of mentor and making it possible for me to return to school, but he also needed me home on time each day to cook our dinner.

I loved hearing stories of Jerry's early years in New York when he had rejected his Jewish faith, influenced by his socialist uncle who was a labor organizer in the garment district on the Lower East Side. He upset his mother by refusing to be bar mitzvahed and left Pittsburgh when he was fourteen to live with his Aunt Fanny, a teacher, in Brooklyn. He excelled at school and won a place at City College of New York, "where all the clever, poor kids went" and after early graduation in 1942, he joined the Army and went on to officer training school. He became a lieutenant in Military Intelligence and was posted to Frankfurt towards the end of the war. His anecdotes were sometimes amusing, sometimes grim and he used to say that all he learned from his army experience was a hatred of standing in line. His job in Frankfurt involved the de-Nazification process, and he was appalled by the readiness with which Germans could accuse a neighbor of being a Nazi, just so they could take over their shop or land. The war had destroyed more than just the landscape, and when he returned to civilian life, he was aware of the persistence of anti-Semitism in his own country. He wondered what it was all for, when he was still unable to join a country club because of his religion, and would quote Groucho Marx, who said, "Any club that would accept me as a member is not worth joining."

He started to work for Time magazine in the sales and promotion department in 1948 and spent his entire career there until he retired forty years later, continuing as a consultant for several more years. He loved New York, and when Time management announced they were shifting their corporate headquarters from the Rockefeller Centre to Alexandria, Virginia, Jerry was appalled. He did not want to live and work in what he considered the suburbs, and when he was offered a position in London, in the Time Life Books department, he accepted right away. He and his wife Evelyn settled in London and their only child, Ellen, stayed in the US to follow her college career. Ellen had hidden the fact that she was gay from her father, and he found out only when a colleague at the office had seen Ellen interviewed on some local TV station. He was deeply hurt, not that she was gay, but that she had kept it from him, confiding only in her mother. Their relationship had been tense for some years, so when he announced she was coming to visit us with her partner Joan, I was somewhat apprehensive.

It was difficult from the start. Ellen was only five years younger than me, so when she said, rather rudely, "I hope you don't expect me to call you Mother," I was shocked. "Of course not," I said, "I am not your mother. I am Jerry's wife." She and Joan spent much of their time sightseeing in London, and I was glad I had classes to keep me busy. I had cooked a meal for their first night, but they decided to go out together instead. I tried to be friendly and it was easier with her partner Joan as she had been married and had a son. I suspect my warmth towards Joan was another reason for Ellen to dislike me, and thankfully everyone stayed polite until the visitation ended. It was only after they had gone, that Jerry confessed that he had told Ellen I was a recovering alcoholic. I was upset and hurt that he had betrayed my anonymity and I never trusted him completely again. It was a bitter lesson and a sober reminder that a person you thought you loved totally can still disappoint you. I forgave him of course, but it took a little time. I had learned through AA that forgiveness meant that you no longer had to hit back. As one of my favorite writers, Anne Lamott, said, "It's better to be kind than to be right."

Jerry and I were married in March 1983 at the Chelsea Registrar's Office, a place popular with celebrities and divorced couples re-marrying. My sister Jane and her husband Jack were present as witnesses and Sophie had the day off school for the occasion. We all went to Claridge's after the ceremony for a champagne lunch, with Perrier for me, and it was all horribly expensive but rather wonderful. Jerry drank a little too much and I was pleased that I was driving, when we took off that afternoon for a honeymoon weekend at Chewton Glen, a fashionable five-star country hotel with a famous chef. It was an easy drive to the New Forest in Hampshire and the hotel staff gave us a warm welcome with champagne in the honeymoon suite and again with dinner. By this time, Jerry was tired from the excitement of the day, and had indigestion from too much champagne and rich food, so we went early to our four-poster bed and watched television until we both fell asleep.

Marriage did not change things much, but it did mean that because Jerry put a notice in the Times of London Births, Marriages and Deaths section, the titled lady who lived next door finally acknowledged me, instead of politely ignoring me when we met on the street. I had said to Jerry earlier that I was happy to live in sin with him for as long as he wished, but he insisted that I get a divorce and become a respectable woman. When I finally went to a solicitor and sent John papers to sign for a divorce, I was taken aback when he expressed his surprise. We had lived apart for ten years, with occasional visits for the sake of the children and I could not imagine why he thought this should continue indefinitely. I suppose it was a blow to his self-esteem to be finally formally rejected, though if he had been a thinking person he should have felt that many years ago. I found it yet another example of his mental laziness about me as a person and his continuing obsessive concentration on his career at the expense of all else.

He visited London later that year and had an awkward meeting with Jerry at our apartment. I deliberately refrained from asking Jerry what he thought of him, as it was obvious from his unusually polite conversation. I took Sophie to John's hotel the next day as they were flying to New Delhi for the school holidays. We walked into the hotel foyer, and sure enough, there was John at the bar, drinking with some casual acquaintance he was probably regaling with stories about Vietnam. "There she is, my beautiful ex-wife," he shouted across the expanse of hotel carpet. "Why did I let her get away?" I was furious and should have turned round and left with Sophie there and then. But she was excited about going to India, and I made sure that that was the last time I ever had to see him again.

Jerry's apartment was in a building in a Georgian square where the lease was running out. Most property in Central London could not be purchased freehold, and the leases were usually for 100 years. With seven years left, the title to Jerry's apartment in the Cadogan Estate was becoming attractive to investors and we began to talk about selling and moving. I was secretly delighted as the furniture and pictures had all been chosen by Jerry's late wife Evelyn and it was still very much her home. We soon found a spacious apartment in a 1970s mansion block in South Kensington, still within walking distance from Harrods, and with three bedrooms and a bigger modern all-white kitchen, I loved it right away. I chose curtains and new sofa covers in muted colors of grey, blue and cream, tactfully replacing some of Evelyn's exuberant Mexican décor. Without realizing it, I had chosen the colors of my Siamese cat, Nijinsky and a friend teased me about my coordinated cat.

The kitchen was a joy to work in, as I had not given up my interest in food and cooking and I loved the fact that Jerry's colleague and good friend at Time Life Books was editing the new Good Cook series. I was willing to test recipes and we enjoyed meals with the editor Kit and her husband Tony over the years. Jerry's London and New York friends were all good to me and welcoming, and one of them confided to me that they were so pleased to see Jerry with a quieter, more loving wife. Evidently, Jerry and Evelyn were known by their friends for their loud arguments at parties. One friend said it was like being on the set of "Who's Afraid of Virginia Wolf." It made me feel a little more relaxed knowing that, and I was happy to plan dinner parties for his friends from then on, where at least I would be the sober one.

Believing the adage, "all politics is local," I joined the neighborhood branch of the Liberal Democrats in Kensington and Chelsea. I had a lot to learn about the different personalities of the members, and as I began to take more of a leadership position, I had an inevitable clash with Roy, a chain smoker and fast talker who wanted to keep control of the rather ineffectual local group. I managed to sidestep his attempts to dominate and found it much more satisfying to attend the Liberal Democrats' National Conferences held four times a year in different cities. There we would debate the finer points of our new manifesto and hear from our charismatic leaders, the two Davids, David Owen, the charismatic leader of the SDP and David Steel, the quieter but no less passionate leader of the Liberal Party. David Steel had taken over the leadership from Jeremy Thorpe, whose career had ended in scandal when he was accused of trying to have his homosexual lover murdered. His son Rupert was Sophie's age and attended her school, the two becoming good friends over the years.

The two Davids unfortunately did not work well together and the Liberal Democrats only became a real force in British politics when Paddy Ashdown later became leader. Handsome, articulate and a former paratrooper, he brought the party together and for a while, we believed that third-party politics was going to change Britain for ever, replacing the old binary split between Conservative and Labour. All the women candidates were a little in love with Paddy, and when he walked into a room, you could feel the electricity. I was pleased to be asked to be secretary to the Candidates Association which meant helping to train new women candidates for positions at city, county, and national level. We held regular workshops in public speaking, which was one of the main issues holding women back from seeking public office, and the trainer Liz, an attractive and confident actress, became a good friend over the years. She went on to become a Member of the European Parliament and retired only recently.

It was always exciting for me to attend press conferences at the Houses of Parliament, to walk the corridors and recognize Members of Parliament from seeing them on television at Prime Minister's Question Time. I always felt like a privileged tourist, rather than someone who might belong there and had no ambition beyond trying to achieve something on a local level and maybe run for City Council. With the help of colleagues in the local party, I helped to start a newsletter for neighborhood residents, struggling with the layout on my newly acquired computer and enjoying the process of writing articles about missing streetlight bulbs, uneven sidewalks, dog poop and dangerous pedestrian crossings.

I talked to local business owners and shop keepers and started the South Kensington Association of Traders, or SKAT for short. Happy to be known as the lady from SKAT, my biggest achievement was getting an unsightly and unhygienic public toilet replaced. I persuaded the City to provide us instead with an elegant French loo, wrought iron decoration on top, with an automatic sliding door and a self-cleaning mechanism. Inevitably, there was a letter in the paper from a patriotic retired General asking why we had to have a French toilet when British ones had served us well in the past.

From my kitchen window, I could see the roof of the Royal Albert Hall and the spires of distant churches. I was beginning to love London at last, seeing it through Jerry's eyes as well, and we enjoyed going often to the theatre and to concerts. With the South Kensington station just across the road, it was so easy to travel in central London on the Underground, enjoying theatre at the Festival complex across the river or in the West End. A favorite Sunday outing was a walk and a pub lunch in Chelsea, followed by a concert in the Wigmore Hall.

We also discovered the countryside together in the weekends. We found picturesque villages with good restaurants, went several times with friends to Oxford, and visited my friend Fiona in Cambridge as both Jerry and I loved the two university cities with their colleges and "dreaming spires." Fiona was also a mature student and had won a place at Cambridge, far more prestigious than London University, and it was a privilege to visit places with her that were not open to the public. Once we went down to the basement of the library at Kings College and were able to hold – with gloves - a Gutenberg Bible. She also invited us to Advent services at the King's College Chapel, dating back to Henry the Eighth, and we both found the glorious music and the whole experience incredibly moving and memorable.

Sometimes we would pick up Sophie from school and take her with us, though she did not enjoy long drives in a car as she suffered from car sickness. I remember one outing when we found a Fair being held on a village green and we bought her a ride on a merry-go-round. Each time she came round to where we could see her and wave, she was greener and greener, until she finally threw up. It was more fun for her when some of her school friends could meet her in London, a popular place being the swimming pool at the nearby Holiday Inn. She started taking flute lessons and I loved hearing her practice, but she was not sure what she wanted to concentrate on - music, art, dance, or drama. We sent her to a summer school for classical ballet, and that did not satisfy and then a drama course in Oxford the following summer, but that was still not the direction she wanted to pursue. I worried about her dissatisfaction with herself and her abilities and thought it was just a part of adolescence, and at least she always had her drawing and painting to fall back on where she showed talent and commitment.

While Sophie was settled at Frensham Heights, Chris turned 18 and was reaching the end of his time at Dover College. He was Head of the School, quite an honor, and I drove down to Dover for his final speech at the prize-giving ceremony at the end of the year. I had bought a pink suit and a rather silly pink feathered hat to match – arriving only just in time to take my seat and embarrassing Chris when I waved to him up on the stage.

Sophie, 14, with the Royal Albert Hall and monument in the background.

He had failed to get into a British medical school, which he had insisted that he wanted to do. The required math and science subjects however were not his forte, and I wish he had been persuaded by his teachers to do languages and history instead. His excellent command of English and his desire to travel, I felt would have been a great basis for a career in journalism.

He decided to try again in New Zealand and went to live with my brother Robert and his family so he could attend the local high school and get his New Zealand University Entrance qualification. He got into Massey College but again failed to get into medical school because rugby, girls and beer proved more distracting. He then took off on a life of adventure for the next few years, working in a copper mine in New Guinea, drilling for water in Central Australia and working in housing construction while living with his father in Washington DC. That did not last long as there was some dissension about wet towels left on the bathroom floor, though I suspect the underlying antagonism was deeper than that. Chris then came back to the UK and worked on an oil rig in the North Sea for a time. I remember Jerry saying to him, "Chris, you can make all the mistakes you need to until you reach the age of 30. But by then you should have worked out what your life is about."

My work in the neighborhood was being noticed by Liberal Democrat officials and I was asked to be a candidate for the Kensington and Chelsea Council. I was quite nervous at the thought but understood I had no chance of winning as the Borough was overwhelmingly Conservative. I continued to work with Brian, my friend and agent from the local organization and together we put in many late hours, writing and delivering the newsletter in which I featured as editor, rather than candidate. In Britain, campaigns are limited to six weeks before an election, and a limit was placed on the amount of money that could be raised and spent. As I was only a" paper candidate", we were not running a serious financed campaign, but the Liberal Democrats star was in the ascendant and when the results came in, I had done better than anyone expected. I was still surprised when I was asked if I would then be a candidate for Parliament in the national elections. "Who, me?" I thought, worried about my lack of experience, my New Zealand background, and my still quite recent sobriety. But Jerry made light of all my hesitancy and was proud and supportive. So I agreed, and the next exciting chapter of my life began, as candidate for the Liberal Democrats in the constituency of Kensington and Chelsea.

My official candidate photo

22. London 1988-1992

. What we call anger is often simply the unwillingness to live the full measure of our fears or of our not knowing, ...in our wanting the best, in the face of simply being alive and loving those with whom we live. Maria Popova, Brain Pickings.

I was sitting in the House of Lords tearoom one summer afternoon, drinking Earl Grey tea and having hot, buttered crumpets with Lord Ezra, thinking to myself, "How did Susan Lamont, a New Zealander from Fiji, get to be here, in the political heart of the United Kingdom?" It was probably the most meaningful experience I would have as a parliamentary candidate, and Lord Ezra, my sponsor in the House of Lords, was charming and interested in all I had to say. He agreed that it was difficult being a candidate in a constituency that I had no chance of winning. A statistical study of voting results over the last fifty years showed that Chelsea and Kensington was the safest Conservative seat in the country, and even with a massive percentage shift, it would remain Conservative. There would be no funding from the national party, and I was on my own to do what I could. He told me that the party appreciated what I had achieved in just a short time, with SKAT and the newsletter, and he also knew of my work on the Candidates Association. I left feeling more exhilarated and self-confident than I had for a long, long time.

With Lord Shaughnessy, a Liberal Democratic supporter

I sometimes thought of the metaphor of the calm and elegant swan, smoothly gliding over a lake. No one can see those little feet, paddling like crazy to stay afloat and on course. As the months and years went by however, I gained courage from Jerry, my children, and my friends as I was able to loosen the knot of shame and remorse and let it all go. I began to feel safe in my new universe knowing I did not get there on my own, but grateful that one day at a time, I was approaching my goal of calm and wise spiritual health. And because I did not want to spend a whole year of my life on the lost cause of the election, I went back to school, this time to do a master's degree in Anglo American Literature. The campus was the University College in Central London, with its evocative atmosphere of old buildings with historical and literary associations.   I got great pleasure each time I walked past the glass case enclosing the mummified body of Jeremy Bentham, on display according to his Will. He was a leading theorist in Anglo-American philosophy of law, and a political radical whose ideas influenced the development of the welfare state. He advocated individual and economic freedoms, the separation of church and state, freedom of expression, equal rights for women, the right to divorce, all very enlightened ideas for his times.

This was the London of the Bloomsbury group, which included the novelist and critic Virginia Woolf and her husband, the Fabian writer Leonard Woolf, the novelist E.M. Forster, the biographer Lytton Strachey, the art critic Clive Bell, the artists Vanessa Bell and Duncan Grant, and the economist John Maynard Keynes.

Just around the corner from the college, T.S. Eliot had worked for forty years for the publishers Faber & Faber in Russell Square, and it was his poetry, essays and plays that became the center of my studies based on his sensibility as an Anglophile American living in London. Henry James was another focus and gave us a reason one fine weekend for a drive to his former home, Lamb House in Rye in East Sussex, a lovely old Georgian house near the sea and now a National Trust museum. I read, wrote, and absorbed all I could about American writers who came to England and English writers who went to the United States to live and write there. There was so much material that I found it difficult to identify a theme for my dissertation, but eventually settled on the aspect of their search in another country for a Utopian vision of a richer life with a deeper meaning.

I enjoyed writing it once I had discovered the new world of computers. Instead of sitting on the floor, with scissors and glue and spending many hours typing and retyping, I bought an Amstrad word processor and learned to love it. I called my dissertation "Impossible Dreams: Some Aspects of Utopian Imagination in American Literature," and one of the books I quoted was *The Oasis* by Mary McCarthy. In it she portrays an idealistic commune and their attempt at progress toward perfection, but she ended the book with a pessimistic impasse, not with cynicism or despair but with a realistic appraisal of the misguided but well-intentioned ideals within a small community. I was intrigued with the subject and with her as a person because of her friendship with my intellectual political guide, Hannah Arendt. I wrote my first and only fan letter to McCarthy to which she replied promptly, to my great surprise and pleasure, and I quoted from it at some length in my dissertation. She said that "good intentions are no safe refuge when their pursuit requires people to ignore the truth," and that "ultimately Utopia would fail; that was to be expected."

"Morality," she went on, "did not keep well, it required stable conditions, it was costly, it was subject to variations and the market for it was uncertain." This was echoed by Hannah Arendt, in her statement about the need for tangibles in life.

She wrote," The point, as Marx saw it, is that dreams never come true." McCarthy concluded that idealistic communities need something more tangible than morality and suggested that the Oneida Community survived because it had a product, the Oneida Plate, instead of just Utopian dreams.

This tension between individual and community fascinated me; politics always seems to involve the cult of personality in conflict with community. A party responds to a charismatic leader because democracy often brings with it too much conformity. Reinhold Niebuhr, another writer I was excited to discover, said," The brotherhood of the community is indeed the ground in which the individual is ethically realized. But the community is the frustration as well as the realization of individual life." I was to think of this concept often in the future when I became part of a group formed to establish a co-housing community in Colorado. After years of workshops, discussions, planning, and arguments, it still has not been built – but that is another story.

I was also alerted to the nature of nationality and citizenship as the books I studied were often on the theme of rootlessness, identity, and the concept of home when living in a foreign country, which had all been part of my personal experience. A Booker Prize-winning novel by New Zealand writer Keri Hulme called *The Bone People*, caught my attention as an expatriate Kiwi and also because its theme was on alcoholic child abuse. I read it twice, appalled that it should have a happy ending. I discussed it with my tutor, and he asked me to write a letter about it which was published in The London Review of Books in December 1985.

"Keri Hulme's Booker Prize-winning novel, The Bone People, discussed by D.A.N. Jones (LRB, 21 November) and on the Letters page by C.K. Stead (Letters, 5 December), leaves me, as a New Zealander, with a sense of painful recognition and of deep disappointment. Is this the best that New Zealand can offer the world?"

My final paragraph was rather censorious.

"The ending is a reunion of Joe, Kerewin and the child in a drunken, incoherent, sentimental coming-home: 'all good cheers, and covered tears and matey friendship'. Kerewin has made peace with her estranged family and everyone is 'aching with love to give, smothered by love in return'. There is no examination of the uncomfortable truths which haunt this book, and which haunt New Zealand. Beneath all this togetherness, and the notion of a racial or cultural solidarity which accompanies it, there seems to be a dangerous exclusiveness. The sterility of the island mentality is not confined to places like New Zealand, of course – it exists in inner cities throughout the civilized world. But I would have thought that if this novel depicts the present state of its nation, then New Zealand still has some spiritual growing-up to do."

Reading this many years later, I feel I was a little unkind, but as a recovering alcoholic, I was very aware of the bad faith behind drunken sentimentality. There may be many reasons for bad behavior but no excuses. I remember with some bitterness, my mother saying, "Well, I did the best I could at the time." I snapped back, "But your best was not good enough." Good intentions are not enough if they are based on a morally wrong action, as Hannah Arendt pointed out in her book on Eichmann. This may be rather an extreme parallel, but it was one I was making for myself as I sorted out the difference between reasons and excuses for my past actions. Forgiveness of oneself and others is one of the hardest lessons in sobriety.

As my interest in literature and politics deepened, I was at the same time attempting to restore a relationship with my family. Mother was a constant reminder that I had failed her as a daughter, just as she had failed me as a mother. After my father died, she developed some personal resilience but then it all vanished with a medical mishap. She had gone into hospital to have her gall bladder removed. The policy of the free national health service in New Zealand includes the need for hospitals to train surgeons from the Pacific Islands. My mother had the ill fortune to be operated on by a trainee Samoan surgeon who failed to remove a suture, which then for the next eighteen months caused her much pain and suffering. She went to so many doctors that she gained a reputation of being a malingerer, until she finally persuaded the hospital to operate again. They removed the sharp suture which had been irritating the inside of her rib cage, followed by a further operation to remove some damaged bone. By now, Mother had become a victim in her mind of an uncaring health service and any contact with her by phone or mail resulted in a repeated litany of her grievances.

We had a welcome visit in 1986 when my brother Robert came to see us in London with his new partner Jen. Robert and his first wife had divorced, acrimoniously, and I had always wondered how their marriage could be sustained after such an unhappy beginning. Jen was quite different, quiet-spoken, practical, an accomplished horsewoman and trainer and she had managed to cut down on the excessive drinking that had also been such a destructive part of Rob's life. I sometimes gave credence to a theory that alcoholism is hereditary, the "curse of the Lamont clan", but believe now that it is the result of a family dynamic rather than a gene.

Robert and Jen, London 1986

Rob and Jen were pleasant guests and we also got to meet Jen's son who was working in a London bank, another example of the generational urge to leave New Zealand for the wider world of challenge and opportunity. Sometime after their return, we received the shocking news that Rob had colon cancer. He had assumed his stomach pains were due to stress from the divorce and worries at work, and by the time it was diagnosed, his days were numbered. We spoke at length over the phone and I apologized for not being a better big sister. I had always been the buffer between him and Jane's spiteful mischief when we were little. "Nonsense", he said, "You didn't abandon me, it was the other way round." He reminded me how furious I had been with him and our parents when they decided he should have his first baby adopted, yet he had ignored my advice and gone ahead with their decision.

As the weeks went by, Jen kept me informed about his condition and Jerry finally insisted I fly out to New Zealand to see him before he became too ill to know me. Jane had already left and was staying with her son and family in Auckland, and after an unsatisfactory reunion with Mother, who refused to accompany us, we flew down to Wellington together where we were joined by our little sister Juliet. It was a strange and bittersweet time – Rob had insisted on getting up and dressed to meet his three sisters, and I was distressed to see how painfully thin he was. We Lamont girls had much to talk about when Rob was sleeping, while Jane went into a flurry of buying organic fruit and vegetables which she turned into healthy smoothies for Rob. He made a valiant effort, I think to please her, but could only manage a few mouthfuls.

Juliet and I took a long walk although the weather was unpleasant, the city living up to its name of "Windy Wellington." She told me the saga of her first pregnancy and her baby that had been adopted. She had gone home to our parents in the last months of her pregnancy, telling me, without bitterness, that Mother had asked her to take her daily walk at night so that the neighbors could not see her. I cried when she told me about her post-partum depression, her attempt to reclaim the baby, and her subsequent committal to a mental health institution. "I looked out the back window of the van as we drove away, and saw Mother turn her back and walk into the house." I wondered how Juliet could ever forgive her and her life had certainly not been completely happy since. Her marriage to a handsome German, Manfred, ended when he went off with another woman, and Mother had not been helpful with the children when Juliet had to go back to work. "No wonder Mother didn't want to come to Wellington, "I said. "She would have had to face a lot of emotional baggage from the three of us, not only because Rob is dying."

The second day we were there, Rob again made a valiant effort to dress and come downstairs as he wanted to talk to us. "I have met my first child," he said, with a lovely tranquil smile. "Her name is Mary, and by the strangest coincidence she actually was working in the same building where I had my law practice. She had found out who I was some time ago and when she heard I had cancer she decided it was time she introduced herself. "

We were astonished and delighted for him when he went on to say that she refused to consider that forgiveness was necessary. She had had a good life, she told him, with loving parents and she was only sorry that she had not made herself known to him a little sooner. She had been a constant visitor to their house over the weeks, bringing flowers and books for Rob, she and Jen becoming particularly close, and they had enjoyed a gentle and unemotional time together as he became more and more ill. We were so thankful for Rob having achieved closure on such a painful time in his life and sat with him while he struggled to share it with us.

No one could quite remember the last time the four of us were under one roof, but we were certainly aware that there would not be another opportunity.

Two days later I returned to England, and was met at the door by Jerry, a serious expression on his face. He had just got off the phone with Jen. Rob had died while I was on the plane, halfway between our two separate worlds. I was sad for many days, not just for his death, but for all the lost opportunities when I could have been more supportive to my younger brother and sister while I was living in other countries and they had stayed in New Zealand. We had exchanged fairly regular letters, but I am sure things would have been easier if we had had the internet in those years.

Several years later, Jerry had a business trip to Australia and New Zealand, and I went with him. We took Mother the small sewing machine she wanted and took her on an excursion up to the Bay of Islands in our rental car as she wanted to visit Keri Keri again, where she had been happy with my father. It was not a great success – she talked constantly about her grievances with the New Zealand Health Service, and conversation was difficult as her hearing had deteriorated. Jerry had a silly anecdote about a deaf aunt of his, who used to exclaim at inappropriate moments, "Raining, raining, who said it's raining?" We tried to explain this to Mother, but she was not amused.

We also spent time with Juliet, who was looking so well I thought, having lost some weight, and had allowed her lovely naturally curly hair to grow to a flattering length. She had my father's deep blue eyes and was most like him of all of us. She talked warmly of her work in promoting organic farming, and of her two boys and then told me quietly that she was being treated for cancer. I was devastated. It seemed that the generations were the wrong way round, and the preoccupation with Mother's health had overlooked the possibility of illness in her children. Robert's death had been tragic enough, and now this.

Juliet had been teaching at a Rudolph Steiner school and had married a fellow teacher, also German, who had been a loving parent to her two boys, Thomas and Simon. Mother had scoffed at the spiritual aspect of her beliefs and was disturbed that Juliet may have been relying on prayer and diet instead of medical intervention. I kept a letter that Juliet wrote to Mother, who she addressed as "Dear Cecile", and in it she wrote, " My attitude to it all is to accept my illness with dignity and call on my courage which has helped me through life so far, so why not now?

It broke my heart reading of her struggle to keep the boys close while she was in the Hospice and could not go home as the process of buying their new house had been delayed. "My poor children - camping in a strange house without their familiar things and most of all without their Mum, of course they aren't feeling the best. They're just devastated by all of this and the pain in their eyes is just heart-breaking." Whenever I read my little sister's letter, I become unreasonably angry with my mother all over again. This was surely a time when she could have put aside her own problems and got herself on a plane or train to be with her daughter to offer some unconditional love to her and the two grandsons. Juliet died the way she wanted to, without surgery or chemotherapy, and I was distraught that I could not fly from London in time as she had been too proud to tell me that it was imminent.

I had asked her if she had been able to forgive Mother for the misery she had caused over Juliet's first baby. "Not really," she said, "but we had called a truce." Through New Zealand's open adoption system, she had found out where her son was living and arranged to meet him when he was eighteen. He told her he had had a happy childhood and was working as a car mechanic in Auckland. I gather that there was not any real resolution in their meeting – he was a little embarrassed by the situation and did not ask many questions so there was much left unsaid.

I held Juliet tightly when she told me about it, and said tearfully, "How I wish I had kept you in Fiji and brought you up like a daughter. I feel that I've let you down terribly." "Please don't say that", she said, "I made my choices and I knew you were always there if I had really needed you."

Somewhere in Wellington there is a memorial rose garden with two yellow rosebushes we had planted for Rob and Juliet, and over the years, Jen and I kept in touch with letters at Christmas time. I reflected on the irony that I had lost the members of the family that I had cared for most, my father, Juliet, and my brother Rob. I was left with Jane and Mother, two difficult women who alternated between spite and sentimentality where I was concerned. In AA I had learned that these relationships are described as toxic and are best avoided, and I was therefore content to be in London, with my mother in New Zealand, and Jane in France where she and Jack had retired to a mountain village.

I had more to do with my life than grieve about the past, and with Jerry's encouragement I went back to school again. This time, I would do a master's degree in International Relations at the University of Kent campus in London, which happily was a short walk away from our apartment. I was about to stretch my mind from local politics to the international arena, which would enable me to examine more closely the world I had lived in when I was young and sad and angry. This time, I wanted to paraphrase T.S Eliot and say, "I had the experience, but did not miss the meaning."

23. London to Santa Barbara 1992

Fulfillment was to be reached not by avoiding pain, but by recognizing its role as a natural, inevitable step on the way to reaching anything good.   Alain De Botton (from Brain Pickings)

The Conservatives won the 1987 election again with John Major as their leader instead of Margaret Thatcher. The Iron Lady had been relegated to history, along with our weekly enjoyment of the wonderfully satirical TV show, Spitting Image, where she was portrayed in men's clothes and smoking a cigar. John Major was the epitome of a somewhat boring banker and bureaucrat, and probably what the country needed after the national upheaval and angst of the Falklands War. In dramatic contrast, our leader Paddy Ashdown brought fresh excitement to the newly combined parties of Liberals and Social Democrats. Jerry and I became enthusiastic supporters, and Jerry always enjoyed the parties we gave in our large South Kensington apartment, especially when we entertained Liberal Democrat Members of Parliament who drank the same brand of Scotch as Jerry.

I was putting in the footwork as well, by volunteering in by-elections around the country. One memorable weekend was spent with a friend Jennifer, a member of our local party, when we drove together to a constituency in North Yorkshire to help deliver election material. I was happy we were not going to Harrogate, with its bad memories, and instead we walked miles in suburban York, through sleety snow showers, putting leaflets through mail slots with frozen fingers, hoping not to be bitten by the inevitable growling dog on the other side of the door. Each evening, when we returned to the local pub which served as temporary campaign headquarters, we were met by a band playing and a noisy crowd of young people talking politics accompanied by beer and cigarette smoke. It was always fun to see the bizarrely dressed eccentric Screaming Lord Sutch, the third Earl of Harrow, who was a perennial parliamentary candidate for the Official Monster Raving Loony Party. Sadly, he died by suicide in 1999, but when I knew him, he was an amusing and colorful reminder that politics had a less serious side, bringing people together to celebrate our mutual urge to change the world for the better and have some fun at the same time.

Jerry would accompany me to our Party Conferences, held four times a year in different cities. He would explore the town while I was in a Convention Hall voting on a point of policy, and together we would visit cathedrals and galleries before returning to London. One city we found to be a major disappointment was Blackpool, with its tacky seafront and garish tourist attractions, but we loved cities like Lincoln with its stately cathedral and Georgian elegance. Jerry joined me once for an evening rally in Liverpool when the keynote speaker was better known as Basil from the British TV series Fawlty Towers. The actor, John Cleese, also famous for the Monty Python Show, was a keen supporter of the Liberal Democrats and had the audience roaring with appreciation, with Jerry joining in the standing ovation. I was to see John Cleese occasionally in later years, when we both lived in Santa Barbara, California, but never had the courage to introduce myself and speak to him. I was content to admire him from a distance, as I knew he had been battling with his own personal demons of depression and was a very private person at heart.

Our London apartment was popular with American friends as we had a large guest bedroom and bathroom, and we kept it very warm in winter. A regular visitor was Jerry's friend, Joe Heller, author of Catch 22 and his second wife Valerie. He had signed a copy of one of his books "To my good friend Jerry Broidy, who gave me hundreds of ideas for my books, none of which I ever used." Valerie and I used to escape to go shopping at Harrods or Harvey Nichols, leaving the two men to argue, laugh and reminisce over their whiskey. We took some memorable road trips together, to Bath one year, and to Winchester where I was surprised that Joe was reluctant to enter the cathedral, because he was Jewish. "Come on Joe," Jerry said. "The ceiling hasn't fallen in on me yet." He reluctantly came in to note Jane Austen's tomb and then we all retired to a nearby pub for a good lunch.

Joe and Valerie Heller outside Winchester Cathedral

I was grateful to Joe on one visit when he agreed to meet with my writing group. He charmed them with his New York wit and my friends were suitably impressed to have met a famous writer. Our group had met on a retreat in Devon a few months previously, when I had packed my word processor and drove through the summer countryside to the idyllic farmhouse that had been the home of the poet Ted Hughes and his wife Sylvia Plath. My friend Rosie from AA was there too, and we had fun taking turns cooking the evening meal and talking about books and writing in the evenings. It was a splendid hot summer, and I wrote each day in the cool thatched barn with the wide doors open and swallows swooping in and out. I had brought a book of Ted Hughes's poems with me and it was an odd feeling to imagine him perhaps at the same desk where I was sitting. His poem about writing, *The Thought Fox,* haunted me. It begins,

I imagine this midnight moment's forest

Something else is alive

Beside the clock's loneliness

And this blank page where my fingers move...

The poem ends;

Till with a sudden sharp hot stink of fox

It enters the dark hole of the head.

The window is starless still, the clock ticks,

The page is printed.

I was inspired while in Devon to start writing a novel about Vietnam, achieving three or four chapters in Ted Hughes's barn. The yellowing pages have followed me to America, and get unpacked and put aside again, a work in slow progress. I had already finished a novel I called *The Peacock Angel*, an adventure story set in Iraq. I wrote it as an escape from getting our second bathroom remodeled. Jerry wanted a walk-in shower, so we removed the bathtub and hired a cheerful contractor who turned out to be quite incompetent. Jerry enjoyed his company however, so I gritted my teeth, went into my study, and shut the door and wrote. The bathroom and the book took three months.

It needed much more critical editing, but Jerry liked it and sent it off to his friend Paul in New York. Paul was a lawyer who specialized in representing authors. Harold Robbins was a major client and Paul had many anecdotes about his efforts to keep Harold sober while working in exotic parts of the world. Paul thought well enough of my manuscript to show it to his friend at St Martin's Press, who returned it with compliments but regret.

I had also shown it to an editor in London who really wanted me to write about becoming sober in AA, which I was hesitantly considering. Maggie was also enthusiastic about *The Peacock Angel,* and kept me on tenterhooks for months, as the London publishing world was going through mergers and attrition until ultimately, Maggie and with her my book became redundant. I have vowed to look at it again someday, but as the old Amstrad discs cannot be transferred to my present computer, I am reluctant to start typing it all over again. I know it will need a complete rewrite, as I was trying to write to a formula, and I knew it had no real integrity.

The lectures and reading for my course on International Relations kept me busy and I was delighted when one semester was held at the famed London School of Economics, a hotbed of left-wing philosophy. The class on Environmental Justice was attended by several young African men whose fathers were running countries as presidents or generals – I think they viewed me as a relic of the old British Empire and I stopped trying to argue with them. I became interested in a book that was being widely discussed at the time, *The End of History and The Last Man,* by Francis Fukuyama. He proposed that history progresses in a straight line, with Western liberal democracy becoming an inevitable end point. I took exception to his theory in my dissertation, because I still had echoes in my mind of Hannah Arendt's *Rise and Fall of Totalitarianism.* Also, my experience of living in the Middle East had made me somewhat cynical about liberal democracy becoming inevitable there. I was justified when my analysis of Fukuyama's book proved to be correct, as sadly, democracy has not become perfected over the years but instead, has become distinctly tarnished.

Life was not all politics and college work in my life with Jerry, however, as we travelled often. During a sales meeting in Southern Spain, when I eagerly accompanied him, he agreed that this could be a wonderful place to retire to. To my intense delight, he bought us a holiday apartment in Calahonda, a beach between the two tourist towns of Torremolinos and Marbella. We had rented it for a week and loved it. On a wide curving bay with the mountains behind, it was beautiful, and Jerry particularly loved the rocky headland which curved again into another smaller bay where the beach clubhouse had been built. We had discovered some good restaurants in the area, including a Belgian one which was sometimes a welcome change from the inevitable gazpacho, fish, and salad. When Jerry told me he was going to buy it, I was overwhelmed. It was not the white-washed Spanish farmhouse I had once dreamed of, but it would be our own retreat from London's weather, our very own sea, sun, and sand. We would fly to Malaga, pick up a rental car and drive to our apartment in about five hours from door to door. We went there at least twice a year for the next five years – once we made four trips and I almost managed a year-round suntan.

View from our balcony, Calahonda, Spain

We took Sophie with us once as a change from her flying out to stay with her father during school holidays. We promised her some authentic flamenco and I was pleased that she was so impressed. I loved the music, with its undertones of heartbreak and despair, like Portuguese fado in which you could hear the Arab cadences. We had a late dinner and drove to a night club near Marbella where we had to wait till past midnight before the show began. It was genuine gypsy flamenco, the women fiery and passionate, the men serious, lithe, and elegant. After a while they started encouraging people to come and join them and learn the zapateado, or fast footwork. Sophie did well and I was happy to see her so absorbed in the music.

Jerry and Sophie in Spain

Sophie had become a little quieter and more withdrawn as she got older which I put down to adolescence. I had spoken several times to her headmaster at school about her and was delighted to hear that he had held a study group for her class, based on the book *"The Road Less Travelled"* by

Scott Peck. It was almost required reading for my group of friends in AA and I was pleased that Sophie was hearing about it in a different context. I felt it saved me from having to keep explaining myself, which in retrospect was rather a cowardly way of avoiding awkward conversations about addiction. One good thing came out of it all – neither Sophie nor Chris had shown any interest in smoking and they thank me for that.

I loved our visits to the Costa del Sol. We visited the mountain towns of Ronda and Mijas that I knew from my earlier stay in Spain, and drove to Cordoba, Granada, Seville, and Cadiz absorbing the sunshine and the culture hungrily after too much grey London weather. Granada was a favorite, the beauty of the gardens, pools and fountains contrasting with the somber cathedral interior with its dark wood and massive black wrought iron doors and candelabra. One day we were in the Alhambra gardens and came by chance on a concert being performed by a guitarist playing Bach. We sat by the long reflecting pool and watched the swallows diving round the cypress trees as the music filled the tiled cloisters with its elegant precision. "I will remember this forever," I whispered, and Jerry took my hand in agreement.

On another trip to Cordoba, we hired a horse carriage as an easier way of exploring the narrow streets. Jerry was delighted when we turned into a little square and there was a statue of the Jewish philosopher and physician Maimonides, who was born in Cordoba in 1138.

With Jerry in Granada, Spain

We were less happy when we came unexpectedly on an Easter procession in Granada one year, the hooded penitents having an uncomfortable resemblance to the Ku Klux Klan. It was compelling to watch though, with the huge wooden platforms for the saints' highly ornate statues being carried by a succession of young men taking turns to duck under the ponderous catafalque as it made its way down the street, emerging after a while, hot and sweaty, for another to take his place.

One trip Jerry and I did together, which I almost wish we had not, was to Fiji for my school reunion. The two grammar schools combined the boys and the girls, and anyone who was able, no matter which year they had left, was eligible to come. I was ready for a sentimental journey back to Fiji after thirty years but was unprepared for the heat and humidity which Jerry hated even more than me, and he was tormented by mosquitoes which somehow left me alone. I was embarrassed to find I had forgotten so many names and faces and realized that all my former schoolfriends had kept in touch over the years as most of them lived in Australia or New Zealand. Nobody seemed particularly pleased to see me. I remembered Jane's spiteful storytelling about me to her school friends and I wondered if perhaps that was still on their minds. Also, I was the odd one out – I had never kept in touch with anyone and had gone off to see the rest of the world instead. I was grateful however, for one of my brother's former school friends who came up and offered his condolences. He had heard of Robert's death somehow and I was pleased to know that he had not gone unremembered.

We went on a boat trip to a nearby island, with Jerry muttering about mosquito bites, and on the way to Suva, stopped for lunch at the Hotel Fijian, where John and I had spent many weekends when the resort was being built. I found it depressing – the buildings looked their age, and the sea was a muddy brown instead of the crystal blue I remembered. Years of pollution and tourists walking over the coral had killed it and ruined the beautiful beach. There seemed to be the same level of poverty amongst the cane farmers in the countryside as we drove by on the now tar-sealed road. Independence had not changed much for the better, it seemed, except for the road.

When we got to Suva, everything I remembered seemed smaller and shabbier than it was thirty years ago. The house where I lived the year before I married, was barely recognizable as trees had grown up to change its aspect dramatically. Our walk past Government Buildings and Radio Fiji was ruined by an aggressive Fijian wanting to sell us poorly carved wooden masks, which Jerry bought just to get rid of him, and which we later abandoned in our hotel room. At our farewell dinner, I found myself sitting next to a woman named Barbara whom I had barely known as she had left school some years before me. She started talking about John and said she had gone out with him long before he had met me. I introduced Jerry and explained I was divorced. "You know, we wondered about you, " she said." John Greenfield had a terrible reputation for drinking too much and driving too fast. He picked me and my mother up once from the airport and drove so fast we were terrified. He refused to slow down when we begged him. I never went out with him again."

I was quite taken aback and wished I had had friends at the time who might have shared this sort of information with me, though I may not have believed it or cared. "I thought I could change him," I said, feeling uncomfortable as Jerry was getting irritated. Barbara gave me a thoughtful smile, knowing that there was a lot of unspoken sadness there, and gave me a little hug. "I'm so glad you're happy now", she said. I became almost tearful and couldn't speak, overcome to realize that I had not been invisible after all when I was younger and that there could have been friends like Barbara if only I had let them into my life.

We left Fiji the next day and I was pleased to leave it all behind. Jerry told me, "You can't go home again," referring to the Thomas Wolfe novel with that title. We agreed that nostalgia is a sentiment that is best done away with if one is to grow and change. Real maturity comes with acknowledging things as they are, and we should no longer look back "through a glass darkly." After the discomfort of the reunion, I was content to be on our way home to England, sure of who I was and safe with Jerry.

Back in London on one of our Sunday afternoon visits to an art gallery, we both stopped in front of a painting which was dramatically different from the other works on display. In muted greys and blues, it was a mountain scape that suggested a mystical, dream-like world and although it had a SOLD ticket on it, we asked the curator for the artist's name and contact information.. That was the beginning of our friendship with Ivor Davies, a Welsh painter who lived in Penarth, in Wales. We drove down one sunny weekend to visit his studio and bought a large painting which has dominated our living rooms ever since. The mountains in the background are taken from an old sketch by the traveler and geographer, Alexander von Humboldt, who visited New Zealand in the 1880s. The mountains no longer exist in the same contours, a fact that fascinated the artist, as they were partially destroyed by a volcanic eruption of Mount Tarawera in 1886.

Ivor told us," As a Welshman, I have always had a love and reverence for mountains, so I was intrigued by these mountains that exist only in my mind and now on canvas. I think that map makers have a certain temerity if they think mountains can be explained by contour lines in an atlas. The Welsh know that mountains are more meaningful than that."

He framed the painting and brought it up to London a week or so later and stayed the night with us, the beginning of a happy relationship. Jerry and Ivor became close friends, an unlikely combination of witty New Yorker and gentle, mystical Welsh artist, each enjoying the novelty of each other's company. Ivor's visits to London when he stayed with us were a pleasure, and several times we accompanied him to galleries and gained a new perspective of modern art through his eyes. I think we were all a little mystified by Jasper Johns however, and his many reiterations of the American flag.

Jerry was approaching retirement and as a way of detaching gradually he was offered several consultant assignments with Time Life which had now become Time Warner. He did some work with HBO but did not really understand cable TV and could not see a future for it. We did enjoy a sales meeting in Cannes however, where I was delighted to see David Niven at the airport, close enough for him to hear my surprised recognition and to give me a lovely smile. After our years of visiting Spain, we had decided we wanted to retire somewhere where we were not foreigners, and neither of us was ready to leave London. Sophie still had a year left at Frensham Heights so we were both delighted when Jerry found a part-time position with the Macmillan Fund. This was the leading charity in Britain for cancer relief and research, and because his first wife had died of cancer, Jerry felt it was an appropriate foundation to work for. It did not take them long before they recognized his expertise in donor management and fund-raising and he soon became a fixture in the London office.

The patron of the Macmillan Fund was Prince Charles. There were several lords and ladies on the Board and once they got used to Jerry's somewhat irreverent humor, he became a favorite, as long as he remembered not to call a certain Countess "darling". A New York lawyer friend, Mark, then based in London, had lunch with Jerry one day, and the two men planned the creation of American Friends of the Macmillan Fund. Mark had many wealthy American clients in London and knew how to approach them for donations, and in return, Prince Charles agreed to host a reception at his home in the country.

I tried not to get too excited about accompanying Jerry to Highgrove in Gloucestershire, as I was a European citizen now and not a humble British subject. But I was pleased and planned a new outfit suitable for cocktails with a Prince. It was a cool and drizzly day, when about a dozen of us went in a small bus through the lush countryside, the Americans eager to meet royalty and some of the women overdressed in hat and gloves.

His Royal Highness The Prince of Wales
requests the pleasure of the company of

Mr & Mrs G Broidy

at a Reception at
Highgrove
on Tuesday, 30th June, 1992

R.S.V.P.
Mrs. Mark Angelson,
32 Matida Avenue,
London W2 1ST

6.30 p.m.

Dress: Lounge Suit

One I remember wore the most beautiful pale lilac
suede shoes, and I felt sorry for her when Prince Charles took
us on a tour of his organic vegetable garden on rather muddy
footpaths. I had already told Jerry I was not going to curtsey,
but when it was my turn to meet the Prince, I tripped slightly
on the edge of the rug. "You curtseyed!" Jerry whispered in
my ear later and I replied, "I did not!"

Highgrove was a quintessential country house, with
muddy wellies by the front door, and shabby chic chintz
covered furniture. Two dogs had to be shooed out of the
room when we gathered for cocktails. Prince Charles was a
charming host and I enjoyed our conversation about my
Liberal Democrat ambitions and my work in the Borough of
Kensington and Chelsea. As his London home was the
Kensington Palace, he was a constituent and spoke of his
interest in recycling the Palace trash. When my friends back in

London asked, "What did you talk about?" I was amused to reply, "We talked rubbish."

As Sophie approached her seventeenth birthday, she was becoming more and more remote. I became very distressed when she would not communicate and there more frequent lapses in her behavior that caused me a lot of grief. She went to a party once and did not come home till the morning. I had had a sleepless night waiting up for her, trying to tell myself that this was normal, angry with her for not trying to find a phone, and worried because of a recent tragedy on the Thames when a party boat had capsized and over one hundred teenagers had drowned. She had been out with a friend of her friend Rupert Thorpe, David, who was a good-looking young man from Dartford, the "wrong" side of London. Our snobbish old porter, Alf, disapproved of him and came up once to our door to complain about David parking his motorbike in the wrong place. "He's not our sort, ma'am", he said.

I tried to reassure Sophie that it was her safety I worried about, not the accent of the latest boyfriend, and she wrote me a thoughtful letter from Delhi later, admitting that she had been "embarrassed and afraid " that I would not approve of him. "There is nothing sordid or secretive about me," she wrote, "I am just a little confused about priorities and responsibilities." She also said," I'm so sorry that I made you feel so unhappy before I left, anyway that's all over."

Her last term at school was rather disappointing as she did not do well in her A-level exams, having misread the Art paper instructions, and answered six questions briefly instead of three in depth. Fortunately, the headmaster wrote an obviously glowing testimonial with her application which enabled her to get a place at the University of Wales in Aberystwyth. When it was time for the long drive to Wales, she clung to me and wept, and I thought at the time it was just the emotion of leaving London and home. I had no idea there was anything deeper, or that she was living with secrets that would take years to uncover. As I said goodbye to my beautiful, talented, insecure young daughter, I took comfort from re-reading the ending of her last letter to me, "I love you so much!"

Sophie's 17th birthday

It was approaching time for Jerry to retire completely. On our travels to the States and beyond, we had talked about where he wanted to live when he retired. We had decided against Spain, though I was sad when the time came to sell our apartment in Calahonda; and we had also decided against London, New York or Paris, the three places Jerry often said were the only places worth living in. We had driven up and down the California coast several times, visiting friends in Carmel in the north and Rancho Santa Fe in the south near San Diego. I began to think that California was a place where we could belong.

We had had a memorable trip with Sophie and Chris one year, starting in Laguna Beach where we had exchanged houses with a couple who we hoped were enjoying the use of our car and apartment in London. As we drove through Santa Barbara, heading for Carmel and San Francisco, we were all impressed by its beauty and setting, the beach and mountains very reminiscent of our part of the Costa del Sol. The coastline was stunning, and we were lucky there was no sea fog to detract from the view as we drove up the Big Sur, stopping for lunch at the Nepenthe outdoor café. Hang gliders were drifting over our heads, one so close I felt I could reach up and touch his feet. As we were returning to the car, the barman came running after us with Sophie's purse. We thanked him profusely and as we drove off, he gave us a cheerful blessing, "May all your babies be born naked."

"What was that about?" Sophie said. We were amused and mystified too and decided it was just the California vibe that we would have to get used to. As we drove back through Santa Barbara on the return trip, I said to Jerry that maybe this was where we should come to live.

"No way", he said cheerfully, "This looks like the sort of town for tourists only."

"But it's a college town", I said, "and I could go back to school again and get a PhD".

"Well, I'll give it some thought", he said. "As long as it doesn't close down at six o'clock each night, and there's something else besides milk to drink with my dinner."

The four of us in Carmel, California

As it turned out, Jerry belonged to an active Time Life alumni association and when he went through the directory, he was pleased to see that several old friends had retired to

Santa Barbara. We would be among friends, and so it was decided.

Before we returned to London, Jerry had arranged to meet his old friend Paul, the literary lawyer from New York, who was in Palm Springs visiting his client Harold Robbins. I was glad Chris was driving when we set off from Laguna Beach to meet at a specified restaurant, as it meant I could enjoy the scenery and keep out of the discussion about which highway to take. Chris and Jerry argued at every intersection until finally I prevailed, and we stopped and asked at a gas station. We were miles off course and finally arrived at the restaurant to discover Paul had a famous guest with him, Betty Friedan, who was hungry and very unhappy about having to wait so long for lunch. I was mortified, as I would have loved to talk with her about her life and work, but she had had several Bloody Marys and was in no mood to deal with strangers.

Once she had eaten and left, we followed Paul to Harold Robbins's house, where we sat by his pool and were entertained by his outspoken good humor. "Keep talking," he said to Chris, "I just love that crazy Aussie accent." He was in fairly good shape considering his life of excessive drinking and drug taking, and he seemed genuinely pleased to meet us, which made up for Betty Friedan's grumpiness.

Jerry and I had things to do before we left England. Over the years we had had some great road trips to the Lake District, the Cotswolds and Devon and Cornwall. Apart from a brief trip north of Aberdeen for the wedding of a friend's daughter, I had not been in Scotland since Coronation year, when I had waved a flag for the new young Queen in Edinburgh. I wanted to see Scotland once more, and I did a little research into the Lamont clan. I had always liked the thought of being half-Scottish and my father had some books about the clan, though had little to say about his own father's history, whose family had been coal miners. I had probably formed my more romantic ideas from reading Walter Scott and Robert Louis Stevenson, and as Jerry and I drove North, I was intrigued with the idea of seeing where my ancestors came from. I was not disappointed.

The weather was cool and grey, and we stopped in Glasgow to see the Burrell Collection of great paintings before driving to Dunoon the next day. I was pleased to be in Lamont territory and wished my father were still alive so he could hear about my pilgrimage. The clan is said to descend from an Irish prince who settled in Argyll but by the end of the 14th century, almost all of Clan Lamont's original territory had been lost to their ancient enemy the Campbells.

I must have been around seven years old when I first became aware of the enmity between Campbells and Lamonts. It was school sports day, and as we were lining up for the junior 100 yards, my father said, "Don't let yourself be beaten by a Campbell,' nodding towards the freckled, red headed boy next to me. I was never sure if he was serious, but I ran like the wind and Lamont honor remained intact.

It was a lovely drive skirting the shore of the Firth of Clyde, passing old Toward Castle and the expansive grounds of Knockdow Estate, two historic homes of the Lamonts. Knockdow House was built in 1760 and was extended in 1920 by the laird at the time, Sir Norman Lamont, formerly Permanent Private Secretary to Sir Winston Churchill. Another more recent Norman Lamont was Margaret Thatcher's Chancellor of the Exchequer. We stopped at the memorial at Dunoon, a Celtic cross that commemorates the massacre in 1646 of around two hundred Lamonts at the hands of Sir Colin Campbell and his men. We drove on to the little Inverchaolain Church, as the mist thickened and became close to rain. Jerry chose to stay in the car while I wandered through the graveyard, noting that many tombstones bore the name Norman Lamont, my father's name. I also saw many names of Thomas and Jean, my grandparents' names, which made me feel closer to them even though they are buried in New Zealand. Ancient family ghosts were all around me as I absorbed the atmosphere and sense of history in this hallowed place, imagining the pain and grief of my ancestors, now at rest.

Our last few months in London were a little dislocating. We had sold our apartment to Lady Baring, whose husband had owned Barings Bank in the City.

The graveyard at Inverchaolain Church, near Dunoon, Scotland

We were delighted to find out that she had been one of the Bletchley Girls during the war and had worked with the codebreakers of the German Enigma cipher, along with the more famous Alan Turing. As I was still finishing my dissertation, we moved to a friend's house for the last month, with our furniture already on its way to California. The only one really upset by this was Nijinsky, my beloved Siamese cat.

I was ambivalent about leaving the UK, the place where I had known so much anguish and yet so much happiness once I had met Jerry. I had my Green Card and would eventually have yet another passport, shedding my Britishness and becoming American. Jerry was looking forward to returning to his own country, meeting up with other retired friends from his Time Life days in New York and establishing a new home in sunny Santa Barbara. And so we left London behind and flew off to yet another new world for us both in California.

24. Santa Barbara 1992-1996

"Age has given me what I was looking for my entire life - it has given me "me". It has provided time and experience and failures and triumphs and time-tested friends who have helped me step into the shape that was waiting for me. I fit into me now. I have an organic life, finally, not necessarily the one people imagined for me, or tried to get me to have. I have the life I longed for. I have become the woman I hardly dared imagine I would be."   *Anne Lamott (from Brain Pickings)*

Santa Barbara was warm and welcoming in late September when we settled into a furnished rental house near the beach while we looked for a house to buy. Nijinsky the cat followed the sunshine around as it streamed through windows and patio doors and was in cat heaven. We bought a car and after driving so often in Spain, it was an easy adjustment for me to drive on "the wrong side of the road" once more. Jerry had long ago decided he was never going to drive again, and I was happy to take on the role of chauffeur as well as American housewife, another easy adjustment.

I had an introduction to a professor of Political Science at the University of California, Santa Barbara and decided to go talk to him as soon as I could before we settled into a routine. I wanted to see what would be involved in a PhD course specializing in International Political Ethics. Someone jokingly said, "That's an oxymoron", but I felt I wanted to study the role of the United Nations more deeply. Western democracy was flawed, and I thought the work of the UN could produce a viable substitute through international treaties, Bills of Rights, and obligations.

I was invited to audit the graduate course on International Relations and soon realized that this was not what I wanted. I had been spoilt by the British system, where I met with my tutor once a week to discuss progress on my dissertation. He was the stereotype of an English professor, long hair, velvet jacket and flowing cravat, and he would stretch out on a chaise longue and say, "Read to me Susan, read to me." The American system however, required intensive tutorials three times a week with daunting reading lists and would take far too much time away from Jerry. I was pleased to have tried the course and to have decided against it instead of thinking wistfully about a lost opportunity.

We bought a small white house on a hill overlooking the Montecito Country Club golf course, with a glimpse of the sea beyond. It was perfect for the two of us after some renovations and a new bathroom. We decided this would be our home "forever" as we were both aware that eventually I would be on my own because of our age difference. I had been 40 and Jerry 60 when we met, and it was not such an issue then. Now twelve years later, Jerry was beginning to have prostate and digestion problems that we were able to deal with but were an uncomfortable reminder of what could lie ahead. So I worked at making the house and our routine as peaceful and ordered as possible, with a healthy diet and long walks on the beach.

All too soon however, we were caught up in a social life beginning with a party at the home of the friendly UCSB professor and his wife. No sooner had we walked into their lovely home in Montecito, than a woman came running up to Jerry, threw her arms around him and kissed him. "Jerry Broidy!" she said," I haven't seen you since you visited our home in New York!"

Eva and her third husband Yoel became good friends over the next five years and we spent many happy evenings in their lovely home overlooking the ocean. Eva was Hungarian and Jewish and had managed to escape the Nazis as a teenager with her little brother during the war. She told me a little of her ordeal and her hard life until she worked her way to success in London, Paris and eventually New York. She was active in Santa Barbara society at many levels and on the boards of arts and social justice foundations both locally and nationally. She promptly got us involved in one of her many interests, WEV or Women's Economic Ventures, which offered courses and start-up help to women entrepreneurs. Jerry particularly enjoyed assessing the business plans while I became busy with the Arts Foundation.

At the same time, I joined the League of Women Voters and the American Association of University Women to satisfy my political interests. The local Democrats welcomed my willingness and energy, though I was taken aback when they said I could not register voters because I was not yet a citizen and Jerry would have to sit with me at a table at the Farmers Market to make it official. He loved it, fortunately. "Hi, my name is Jerry and I'm here to make your day!", he would get people smiling and interested right away.

With Hillary Clinton, Santa Barbara 1995

Wherever we went, Jerry was the center of a group of people, laughing and enjoying his company. We soon had a wide circle of friends beyond the Time Life colleagues who had also retired to Santa Barbara. We became active volunteers on the committee to elect Bob Ream, a young PhD student in Education who had decided to run for the State Assembly. Bob was hard-working and idealistic and asked me to host a gathering of people to introduce a new curriculum on peace studies for elementary schools. We rented some folding chairs and were amazed at the crowd who turned up, including the Chancellor of the University and his wife. A woman I did not know came in a little late and got the last chair. After the presentation, she came up to Jerry and there was almost a repeat of the welcome given him by Eva.

"Jerry Broidy! I haven't seen you for years!" They had met some years previously in New York and now Sara was living in Montecito and running Sage Publications after her husband's death. One of the biggest publishers of technical and academic books, Sage had offices in London and New Delhi and was a highly successful business. Sara and Jerry had their New York Jewish background in common and they renewed a warm friendship from then on. I will always remember the night Sara came for dinner and I cooked mussels in white wine and cream, without thinking of kosher restrictions. Jerry put on a record of klezmer music and Sara danced around the kitchen.

"If Mother could only see me now" she said, "Eating treyf and dancing to klezmer!"

It was a joy to have Sophie visit from London where she had quickly found her place in the thriving world of computer graphics. She had done a master's degree in computer design since finishing her BA in Aberystwyth. Her second year had been spent in California as an exchange student at UC Riverside, and she had gained a lot of confidence in the art department there and had had her own exhibition in a downtown venue.

"This could never have happened in London', she said, and I was thankful that she was beginning to feel comfortable as an artist who used a computer, instead of the other way around, a computer geek who happened to be artistic. One of her first jobs in the real world was working on a book called *Sophie's World,* written by a Danish professor to help his own young daughter understand philosophy. Sophie designed the graphics for the CD-ROM and went to Denmark with a photographer to gather material. I was immensely proud of her and was not surprised when she was offered positions with new companies starting up during the so-called dot-com bubble and was soon the head of a department of 20 graphic artists.

She visited us in Santa Barbara one year with her current boyfriend, Giles, a graduate student at the prestigious Royal College of Art in London. Giles was very academic, using ten words when one would do, and I think found California too casual for his British ways. We were at a seaside restaurant for lunch one day when he ordered a ham and cheese sandwich. "Black Forest or honey cured?" asked the waitress. Giles looked blank. "Cheddar, provolone or Swiss?" she persevered. Giles was silent. "Sourdough, whole wheat or rye?" the waitress offered hopefully. Giles went red in the face and said, "I give up. You decide."

I think he tried to dazzle Sophie with his academic approach to art and belittled the commercial aspect of her work. I was pleased when she eventually met Rob, an Australian working and studying in London. He was a more rounded person and I felt they had a healthy respect for each other. That was the beginning of a long relationship which included marriage, divorce and now a lasting friendship. She and Rob left for Australia together when Sophie's company asked her to go set up an office in Sydney. Unfortunately, the dot-com bubble burst just as they arrived, and the plan did not materialize. They became part of the expatriate community in Sydney of freelancers in their field before they eventually found steady careers.

Chris and Sophie on the beach in Santa Barbara

With Sophie so far away, it was not so easy to see her for Christmas or birthdays. Jerry had always been marvelous to me for Christmas Day, my birthday, and we had some great trips to celebrate, going to Morocco once and a cruise on the Danube another year. A memorable Christmas Day was spent in New York at Madison Square Garden where I saw my first American basketball game, ate hot dogs, and learned which team to cheer for. Jerry certainly made up for John's disappointing gift to me one year – a pair of earrings separately wrapped, one labelled Happy Birthday and the other Happy Christmas.

On vacation in France, 1995

The summers in Santa Barbara were delightful because of the Music Academy nearby, set in tree-filled gardens on a promontory by the ocean. Students came from all over the world for the Master Classes which were open to the public and they also gave evening performances which we enjoyed with friends after a picnic in the grounds. We had season tickets for the Santa Barbara Symphony which was more of a social event of meeting and greeting friends and an excuse for dinner at a restaurant beforehand; the music was not of such high quality and Jerry always muttered, "The French horn is flat again."

Life was not all sun-drenched, dreamy days however, as we were rudely awoken early one morning by the Northridge earthquake. Our house was undamaged, but a large tree had fallen across power lines and for two or three days we were grateful that our neighbors had an RV parked in their yard. We barbecued what we could from our defrosting freezer on their gas barbecue and made coffee together on their camp stove. We also had a dramatic storm one year with torrential rain and high winds, fortunately leaving us unscathed but some lives were lost with mudslides and local flooding. And then of course, there were the wildfires, alarming when we could smell and see the smoke, but again, we were fortunate that they always seemed to be on the other side of the city.

Just when I was beginning to wonder if Chris was ever going to settle down, he called us before we left London to say he was getting married. He had met Laura in the Cayman Islands where he was running a scuba diving boat for tourists; I am not sure if they really did meet underwater, but it made a good story. Laura had studied photography in her hometown of Rochester, New York, and in her photos looked like an all-American girl, blue-eyed with long blonde hair. The wedding date was set for February and Jerry, Sophie and I flew to Rochester together, with strict instructions from Chris not to wear my fur coat as the family were animal lovers and vegetarians.

Laura's grandmother had arranged for us to stay at the Country Club where the ceremony would be held. I was surprised by the informality of the guests at the dinner we hosted the night before and the general lack of occasion. Only the grandmother made friendly conversation as she and Jerry soon discovered a mutual taste for Scotch on the rocks. I hoped Chris would be happy but suspected that this was another family dominated by alcohol and its destructive influence. Laura had little to say and I thought it was because she was shy. I hoped that would change as we got to know each other better. Jerry did not usually comment unkindly about people but said privately that she was almost un-American in her reticence. It was bitterly cold in Rochester, with snow on the ground and I was pleased to get back to London and my fur coat.

Sophie, me, Chris, Laura and Jerry, Rochester, NY. 1996

Chris and Laura then set off on an adventurous life of scuba-diving and attempting to make a living from underwater photography. It was a crowded field, and not well-paid, and Chris said once, "All I own in the world is a swimsuit, a pair of flip flops, an old bicycle and an expensive underwater camera." After living in Aruba, the Cayman Islands and Hawaii, they would eventually come to Santa Barbara to settle down and start a family. In the meantime, we were learning to love California and were enjoying the beaches, the inland valleys and the occasional trips to Los Angeles and San Francisco.

When Jerry had been a rebellious boy in Pittsburgh and left home to live with his Aunt Fanny in New York, he was idolized by his young cousin, Joan. I was delighted to get to know Joan and her family as they had moved to Santa Barbara when her husband Jerome had retired from teaching near Pasadena. Cousin Joan became an important part of my years in California, a dear friend with whom I shared a love of books and poetry and whose gentle sweetness was a welcome addition to my life. Her children and grandchildren were often part of family gatherings which Jerry enjoyed, and we regularly met for breakfast at our favorite seafood restaurant on the Santa Barbara pier.

Joan taught Literature and Creative Writing in the Adult Education department at the City College, and when I thought of getting a teaching qualification she suggested I speak to the head of her department first. Instead of enrolling as a student, I ended up teaching right away in the new TANF program for young mothers on welfare who were required to go back to school to get the equivalent of a High School diploma. It was a perfect part-time job as I was always home in time to get lunch.

I supervised a curriculum for two hours but was given carte blanche for the last hour of the day, so I brought my sewing machine to school and taught some of the young women how to make stuffed toys for their babies or cushions for their sofas. I got permission to use the demonstration kitchen for some cooking and nutrition classes, and I also brought my laptop with me and gave basic computer lessons. It was rewarding when some of the students responded and made the most of the opportunity, but disappointing when some of the young women became pregnant again and dropped out, or simply failed to turn up to class for various reasons. One student confessed that she could not bear to leave her little girl at nursery school because she was afraid she would be molested, as she herself had been when young. Another young mother told me that her boyfriend was out of jail at last and would not let her come to class anymore.

I became more involved in the broader aspects of the welfare -to-work philosophy and legislation, meeting with social workers and attending conferences to devise a better way of educating the young mothers so they could have the confidence to improve their lives. I had two successes– Jamie, who went on to graduate from UCSB and Shelly, who left her abusive truck driver boyfriend and started writing wonderful imaginative short stories and went on to college in Washington state.

I was busy and happy. Jerry and I loved our house on the hill and he would take his coffee onto the patio in the mornings with his crossword puzzle. We would end the day there also watching the sun set over the broad sweep of green lawns, beyond the bird sanctuary to the palm-fringed ocean. I was glad that he was so content and had found enough to do in Santa Barbara without missing life in big cities. We made several trips back to New York and each time I think he found it changed so much that he was pleased to get home again.

"Time magazine is being run by accountants now instead of the visionaries when I was there", he said. He had admired the company policy in the past of being generous to public school libraries and buying up small struggling publishing houses to try to keep them afloat. "All that is gone now," he said. "The bottom-line rules."

I lived hearing his anecdotes about the good old days when he worked at Time Life in Rockefeller Plaza. There were several stories that always produced laughter, one about a certain frustrated writer who was renowned for throwing his typewriter out of the tenth floor window, and then there was the famous party for Jerry when two students were hired to streak naked across the stage. I enjoyed staying with friends from Time Life Books – Carol in New York and Betsy in Vail, and Joan Manly who had been the first woman president of a Time division. Jerry had been renowned for his fairness toward women employees, promoting them when he felt they deserved it. He was one of the first to hire a black secretary, and then surprised people who had admired his liberal outlook when he fired her "for incompetence." He encouraged another of his secretaries to go to law school, by instituting a Time scholarship for her and she is now a judge.

To celebrate my 55th birthday, our friends Eva and Yoel offered their lovely home for a party. I would do the cooking and Eva would handle the guest list; I was grateful that Sophie was visiting again that year and able to help me as about 50 people were invited. It was a black tie occasion and I was a little taken aback when Eva introduced me to one of her friends, the famous chef and food writer Julia Childs, who said, "Quite good food, my dear." and I had to be satisfied with that. It was a splendid party and it was the first time I had had so many well-dressed people singing Happy Birthday to me.

After we had recovered from the party, we decided to go to Mexico for Christmas, not to a tourist resort, but to Mexico City see the art galleries and museums Jerry had loved on earlier visits. Friends had recommended a small hotel that had been a monastery in the 17th century, within walking distance of the Zocalo or main square. Once we got used to the hard mattresses – "I don't think they've changed these since the first monks were here," Jerry grumbled, - we loved the atmosphere of the charming building with its flower-filled courtyard and cloisters where we had breakfast before exploring the city.

On Christmas morning we walked to the Zocalo and were amazed to see hundreds, maybe thousands of people in an orderly queue, filing forward to receive a free meal from a local charity. They were the city poor and downtrodden, with many barefoot peasants in colorful ethnic clothes and many, many children. They were quiet and patient and I marveled at their stoicism and their obvious need. It made Jerry uncomfortable because he always hated being in situations where he was so obviously a "rich" American, the reason why he had no interest in going to India or Africa. We walked past the huge crowd to the main cathedral and stood just inside the door for a while, listening to the music. A children's choir was singing Christmas hymns -their untrained voices loud and in tune, but harsh somehow, as if they were more used to singing in the open air. It was very moving and an exotic contrast with an English boys' choir.

We visited the Palacio de Bellas Artes and The National Museum of Anthropology in Chapultepec Park and took a day trip to the pyramids of Teotihuacan and the shrine of Guadalupe. I noticed for the first time on our travels how Jerry was more frequently looking for somewhere to sit and rest awhile and was also complaining about indigestion, which we conceded was probably because of Mexican food.

25. Santa Barbara 1997

The triumph of love is in the courage and integrity with which we inhabit the transcendent transience that binds two people for the time it binds them, before letting go with equal courage and integrity. Maria Popova (Brain Pickings).

Jerry seemed quite uncomfortable by the time we were on our way home and promised he would see a doctor as soon as we could get an appointment. I was not fond of his doctor at the Santa Barbara Clinic. He was a Republican and I had made the mistake of talking to him about Britain's National Health Service, which was free, excellent, and accessible to all. He teased me about being a communist and was totally against the concept of Medicare for everyone. Perhaps if he had paid more attention to Jerry instead of arguing with me, he would have diagnosed Jerry's colon cancer earlier. We were both devastated when we heard the result of the many tests and scans that Jerry had over the next few months.

He had surgery, chemotherapy and radiation and our life revolved around trips to the Clinic, waiting for tests, waiting for test results, waiting for doctors, therapists, technicians. We began to hate waiting rooms. His good days were suddenly so precious, and I remember sitting with him on our patio, with his whiskey at hand while he was doing a crossword and I said,

" Is there anything in the world you want to do, that you regret not doing?" He looked at me and then at our ocean view and said with a sweet smile, "I'm doing it right now."

After a disappointing visit to his oncologist, when she showed him the scan of the tumors in his liver, he asked how long he should plan on living. "About nine months," was her sober response. Jerry determined to prove her wrong and in fact we had eighteen months together, living with the knowledge that time was running out and that every day had to be sufficient unto itself.

We took a road trip to Vancouver at Jerry's insistence to get away from doctors and clinics for several weeks. I found it a deeply moving experience, driving along the splendid Californian coastline and then through forests and cities that were new to us both. We stopped at cafes that looked promising for wonderful seafood, sometimes choosing a funky little motel and sometimes a more comfortable hotel where we could get our laundry done and enjoy room service. Jerry said he felt close to his homeland as the miles unfolded with such great natural beauty and so much space and light. As we drove north, it was a pilgrimage of celebration and farewell and I felt it was meaningful and fitting, with tears and laughter and happy arguments about which route to take, as always.

On our last road trip

Jerry loved visiting aquariums and of course we stopped in Monterey to see the otters. The aquarium in Vancouver was also spectacular and its white orcas gave him much pleasure. I would have preferred to visit the famous gardens, but this was Jerry's time and I sat with him and watched while the orcas dived and circled, majestic wild creatures which should have been in open waters. While in Vancouver, we had dinner with an old school friend from Fiji days, whom we had enjoyed seeing again at the school reunion. Raewyn and her husband were very considerate and hospitable, and Jerry enjoyed a gentle evening with them before we faced the long drive south again.

We went back on Interstate 5 instead of the coastal route and enjoyed the day with Mount Shasta a constant companion in the distance. We stayed a night in Ashland, home of the Oregon Shakespeare Festival and had one of the best Thai meals we have had outside of Thailand, but by then Jerry was too tired to see a play. He said, "Once you've been to Stratford upon Avon, Shakespeare goes downhill." He was getting restless and uncomfortable by the time we got close to home and both of us were pleased to be out of the car at last, in our own bed and with our own washing machine. It had been a strange and bittersweet homage to Jerry's America, a farewell to his country that had welcomed his parents from poverty and pogroms in Europe, a country he had fought for during World War Two and now after travelling the world, was to be his final home.

One of his major concerns in his last months was my immigration status. I had been eligible for citizenship for two years and still my file had not reached someone's desk for the next step. We asked Congresswoman Lois Capps to help – a good friend and an active campaigner for Healthcare for All long before she stepped into her husband's position in Congress after his untimely death. Her office was able to get me an appointment in Los Angeles and slowly the bureaucratic process got underway, and I was finally able to become a citizen in September with Chris as witness, as by then Jerry was too ill to travel by car. I had a flash of remorse as I recited the words "and forswear all foreign potentates," thinking, "Oh well, Queen Elizabeth, here's where we part company." But I was happy to become a citizen along with over 2000 others in the huge Convention Hall, and held my little plastic flag, Made in China, all the way home.

Jerry was pleased as he said he did not want me to feel stateless and adrift once I was on my own. He was comfortable knowing that I would have no barriers to staying and working here and no reason not to consider America my home.

I become a US citizen on the 6th September 1997.

Our days together were a careful mix of gentle activities and rest for Jerry, and I did my best to provide meals that he wanted, as it seemed a little late to be worrying about vitamins and calories. He loved cottage cheese and radishes and Trader Joe's pork dumplings so that is what he often had for lunch. We had more frequent visits from his daughter and her partner Joan, when Ellen would quiz me about medical details until I felt irritated enough to suggest she speak to Jerry's oncologists herself. She had the unfortunate knack of making me feel he had not had adequate medical attention and that it was my fault. I was careful not to show this to Jerry, but often took the opportunity to go shopping or to see Cousin Joan when Ellen and Joan were in town, giving them time with Jerry without me being there.

Then came the day we had been dreading – Jerry woke one morning feeling weak, disoriented and in pain so we went straight to the ER and he was admitted immediately to the cancer ward. Cancer had invaded his colon again, and we both knew that little could be done except to keep him comfortable and pain free. We had both discussed this moment, but now it had come we did not want to face it after all. I kept up a silent litany of "No, no, it's too soon, I wanted more years with you," and he and his doctors discussed elaborate medical procedures that might bring him more time. I was very distressed when Jerry agreed to undergo a very painful experimental procedure, being told that it would help future patients. It was noble of him, but it may be only gave him an extra week.

Jerry was incredibly brave however, for a man who used to make a fuss about a paper cut. It was Halloween while he was in the cancer ward and the nurses were dressed in a variety of costumes, which I privately thought was too frivolous at such a time. But when a nurse came in wearing a witches' mask with warty nose and long grey hair, Jerry took one look and said, "Mother! What took you so long!" I could hear the nurses laughing all the way down the corridor as Jerry's comment was recounted again and again.

I was thankful that Chris and Laura had decided to return to Santa Barbara to live. Chris was a great emotional support for me and helped me with the discussion about hospice care. We decided that it would be best for Jerry and everyone else if he went to the Hospice recommended by the clinic. Set in lovely gardens, with his room looking out on a tree-shaded patio, the hospice became my home too for the next three weeks. Sophie arrived to be with me, unbidden, and I was very appreciative that she decided to take time off from her work in London. We took brief walks together in the grounds of the hospice, green and lush with a view of mountains and ocean, and she was a great comfort to me, although there were no words really to express fully what we both felt. I spent most of the day there and tried hard to maintain some emotional balance while living with the sick dread of losing him. I would find myself becoming breathless during sleepless nights as if I had forgotten how to breathe, and I stayed several nights with Jerry towards the end, listening to him trying to breathe in his morphine induced sleep. The hospice nurse was wonderfully compassionate and told me when the end was near. I held Jerry's hand until it grew cold and sat there with him, stunned by the realization that he had gone. Chris arrived as soon as he could and took charge from then on.

Although I had been losing him day by day, for eighteen months, I had not foreseen the reality of his death. I moved through the days that followed in my own world of locked down grief, numbed by the finality and finding little comfort in the counselling sessions recommended by the Hospice.

"Time is really the only healer '" she said. "It sounds like a cliché, but it is so true."

Friends brought food and flowers and I hope I was appreciative. Our friend Eva took over the planning of a memorial service for Jerry which was quite overwhelming. She had invited everyone of note in Santa Barbara and the outdoor service was led by our mutual friend the Rev Sarah from the Santa Barbara Unitarian Universalist Church. The most moving moment was when a young Polish cellist from the Music Academy played a melody based on a Jewish prayer, and I told myself that this is the way I would remember Jerry – music, sunshine, and the ocean as backdrop.

I had some dreary moments; once when trying some retail therapy at Nordstrom's some weeks later, I gave up and started to drive home. I backed into a pillar in the parking garage and burst into tears, as a woman ran up to see if I was alright.

"I saw it happening and couldn't get you to stop", she said. "My husband died, " I said, weeping as I had not wept before and she patted my shoulder and handed me tissues until I had calmed down and was able to drive safely again. I also had a bad moment when Ellen and Joan arrived to take what they wanted from the house. I had put aside several books that had New York Public Library stamped inside them with Ellen's name below and some photographs of Jerry that I thought they would like to have. They wanted however the one thing I was quite attached to, the carved figure of the Japanese happy monk Hotei, also known as the happy Buddha. It seemed to have so much of Jerry's spirit in it and was a beautiful piece of carved wood. I was sad to see it go and pleased to see Ellen and Joan go as they had been difficult to deal with over the last few months. Ellen had complained that they were not given enough notice about the memorial service, and I tried to explain it was because Sophie had to get back to England. She was also upset when I told her that I would honor Jerry's wish for cremation with his ashes to be scattered at sea. She wanted a Jewish burial where she could visit and lay a stone each year and was not mollified when I suggested she could think of him more often every time she went to a beach. I was sorry we did not part on better terms, but the relationship was fraught from the beginning.

I listened to the advice of friends who told me – "Don't make any major decisions for at least two years. It will take that long for you to come to terms with your new life." So I resolved to stay in Santa Barbara and begin the process of facing life alone, again.

Jerry, wearing his Urban League equality pin, as always.

26. Ojai, California 1999-2008

It is not enough to weep for our lost landscapes; we have to put our hands in the earth to make ourselves whole again."
Robin Wall Kimmerer (from Brain Pickings)

Almost two years to the day after Jerry's death, I sold the house in Santa Barbara and moved some twenty miles inland from the coast at Ventura to the Ojai Valley, where I bought a house with nearly two acres of land. It was mainly weeds and dust, but at the back were some magnificent California oaks and to one side were three fenced corrals where the previous owner had boarded horses. The house was set back from the road and I felt an almost primitive excitement about owning a piece of land that was all mine and I could do whatever I wanted with it.

Jerry had been a real New Yorker when it came to gardening; when I fretted one day about the state of the front garden in Santa Barbara, his response was, "Pave it, pave it!" But now I had room to grow, personally and horticulturally. I bought the Ojai property on La Luna Avenue on September 9th - 9.9.1999 - and felt that was propitious somehow. I made some needed changes to the house and cleared the land of rickety fences and an old hot tub and hen house and then set about creating a garden and making this my home.

The small town of Ojai is set in a lovely valley which was the background for Shangri-La in the movie based on the 1933 novel *Lost Horizon*. The town is noted for its avant-garde music festival held each year in the open air and is home to many artists and musicians, and actors who have left Hollywood for a better way of life. Surrounded by the TopaTopa mountains which are snow-capped briefly most years and with the Ventura River flowing through it, it was a perfect place to live.

I had worked for the Nuclear Age Peace Foundation for a year in Santa Barbara before making the move. Without Jerry, it had been important to have a reason to get up every morning and go somewhere and I was thankful for that. But the work at the Foundation was boring – simply recording the names and emails of thousands of students all over the world who had signed our online petition to ban nuclear weapons. When I asked David, the Foundation President, what we were going to achieve from this, he looked taken aback. I did not feel that simply gathering signatures was sufficient to achieve world peace and soon realized that the Foundation was more of a single-minded passion of David's, supported by raising money from wealthy people in Santa Barbara. I did enjoy the rather irreverent humor of Christof, a German PhD scholar of International Studies, who felt the same as I did as we worked together collating signatures. He and his wife and son moved to Ojai and it was good to have them as near neighbors. The annual Foundation dinners were rather fun however, with visiting celebrity speakers such as the Dalai Lama and Queen Noor of Jordan, and I was given the opportunity to travel to Boston for a Ploughshares Peace Conference and to a Sikh community in Arizona, to present them with a Foundation cheque for their work towards world peace.

Ojai was also famous for its past when the philosopher Krishnamurti lived there for some months each year along with his devotees and patron, Annie Besant. Every May for twenty years, he gave lectures at Oak Grove in Meiners Oaks, now the Oak Grove School. He also founded the Happy Valley School in Upper Ojai, since renamed to honor Annie Besant. Krishnamurti's worldwide reputation attracted many celebrities and intellectuals to the valley such as Aldous Huxley, Jackson Pollack, Charlie Chaplin, and Greta Garbo. I enjoyed the tenuous link with my father's interest in philosophy. He had told me of travelling to Wellington when he was a young man to hear Krishnamurti speak during his New Zealand tour in 1934 and was deeply impressed by his discussion about patriotism and the need to become a conscientious objector rather than blindly go to war.

Krishnamurti was originally associated with the theosophy movement which is still active in Ojai at the Krotona Institute. He eventually went his own way when the Theosophists became too closely associated with Madam Blavatsky, hailed as a holy guru by some and a charlatan by others. She did help however to bring a knowledge of Eastern religions and philosophy to the West. Another reminder of those early Theosophists in Ojai is Taormina, an idealistic community founded for members of the Theosophist Society. One of the qualifications was that residents must be celibate; needless to say, the community did not last long, and it was now a charming area not far from my property, its small houses much sought after by realtors. I liked living close to a place significant for the philosophy that my father had admired..

Ojai was recognized in the 1880s as having a perfect climate for people with tuberculosis and it became renowned as a health spa. The sons of a Yale professor bought a ranch on a hillside overlooking the Ojai Valley as a place for a fresh air cure, and soon other young men were sent out by their parents for tutoring and for the outdoor life. This became the prestigious Thacher School, where students today go hiking and rafting and each student has a horse of his or her own to care for.

Jerry and I had visited the Thacher School a few years previously. His friend Mark in London, with whom Jerry had set up the American Friends of Macmillan Cancer Relief, had an anonymous client who wanted a cheque delivered to the school. Jerry and I were pleased to be the couriers and contacted the headmaster who set a time for us to meet. That was our first trip to the Ojai Valley, and I fell in love with it immediately, as it had such a palpable sense of place. The mountains created a stunning backdrop for the orange groves and oak trees that filled the valley with lush greenery and the elusive scent of orange blossom. We were welcomed by the appreciative headmaster and as we handed over the cheque for $100,000, felt a glow of benevolence ourselves even though it was not our money.

So Ojai was a natural place for me to move to after Jerry's death, and I was eager to be gardening again after so many years of window boxes in London and temporary houses in foreign countries. I had met Margie Grace, a landscape architect who became a good friend and with her plans and the work of Dave, an AA friend who installed the irrigation system, we began to create something stunning. Ojai's climate was perfect for roses and lavender which we planted in lavish quantity and we built two substantial pergolas for wisteria and climbing roses, creating shaded areas for outdoor living and dining. As the plants became established, I grew more settled and contented, getting a deep satisfaction from my new trees, shrubs, and flowers.

I had not been long in Ojai before I was offered a job in nearby Ventura, which I was delighted to accept. My interest in Democratic politics had expanded considerably and I was often at meetings where congressional and state elected representatives were present, so I got to know many of them well. I became the Field Representative for State Assemblymember Hannah-Beth Jackson in her Ventura office, about 20 minutes' drive away. It was interesting work, mainly problem solving for constituents and attending community and Council meetings and presenting awards on behalf of the

Assemblymember. One day, a woman came into the office to seek help over some issue concerning the annual Livestock Fair at the Ventura Showgrounds. She had in her arms a baby goat, which, if it was designed to get my undivided attention, it certainly worked. We became friends and in no time, I was putting the old corrals at my house into use for keeping goats.

My first two adopted goats were former 4H projects whose young owners could not bear to sell them for goat meat. After Harry and Tex, I acquired Rosie, an ancient pygmy goat, who needed a retirement home where she would be safe. The word spread in town, and next I was given two surplus mohair goats who were not so friendly and loved to butt me when I turned my back for a moment. I ended up with nine – the last being little Twinkle who was happy to follow me around in the garden like a dog. I loved them all and their different personalities, and only resented them briefly when I had to feed them early in the morning in the rain before driving off to work.

By the third year, the garden was luxuriant and beautiful. Margie and Dave came out occasionally to advise and keep the irrigation system functioning and I had to employ a gardener once a week for the lawns and basic maintenance. I also hired a local High School student to rake out the goat pens every Saturday morning and put the manure on the rose beds, then trim the roses and feed the cuttings back to the goats. It was a lot of work and expense, as the water bills went up and up each year. But it was deeply satisfying, and I loved it when there would be a knock on the door with friendly strangers asking if they could walk around the garden. It was featured on the Ojai Garden Tour each year and in the Lavender Festival as I had planted 17 varieties. It was also photographed and written up in an issue of Better Homes and Gardens magazine, which gave me great satisfaction.

It was also a pleasure to be able to offer the garden for political fundraisers or gatherings for organizations such as the League of Women Voters when I would provide an English afternoon tea. Chris and Laura had stayed with me for a few months while they were finding their way in Santa Barbara, and by the time they had their two children, Alex and Ashley, my house and garden became a great place for them to visit. The goats were not such a success however, as the children preferred to feed them through the fence rather than join me inside the pens. Over the next few years, I had visits from Jen and her new partner, and from my nephew David and most pleasant of all, a visit from my dear friend Fiona from London. She is a good cook and helped me prepare for a gathering I was hosting. She and I still correspond regularly and I am hoping she will be able to come for another visit, this time to Colorado. Sophie and her Rob also came to stay, and I was beginning to feel very established as a homeowner and gardener as I got to know more and more people in the area.

Some evenings I would become almost dizzy with the heady perfume of the rose garden, my favorites being David Austen varieties with their peony-like petal structure which all too soon fell apart in the Californian summer heat. The many bushes of hardy white roses were more rewarding as they had a long blooming season and looked eerily beautiful in moonlight or on misty mornings. I planted about one hundred South African proteas and hoped to make some money selling the blooms to florists, but they did not thrive, and the water bills continued to mount so I did not persevere. It was all getting too much for me with often long hours at work and the weekends being all too brief.

I had a welcome break from weeding with two trips to Australia.. The first was for the birth of Sophie's first child, Adam, who was born on my birthday, Christmas Day. I had planned to arrive a few days before he was due, but when Rob met me at the airport, it was with the news that the baby had arrived already, and both mother and child were fine. We went straight to the hospital, and Sophie and I met in the corridor, both in tears of joy and relief. Sophie was in that state of shock and euphoria that I remembered so well when my first child was born, and I was so thankful that I was there in time to be of some comfort. I had found a motel quite close to their tiny apartment and walked up through the shopping center of Crows Nest each morning with ingredients for breakfast or lunch, giving Rob a chance to have a break from domesticity. I tried to time my visits so that I was not being an overbearing mother-in law, as I had forgotten how generous Australia is with parental leave and Rob was often around.

The same issue arose the following year when I flew out for Adam's first birthday and Christmas and rented a house by the beach for a week, so Sophie could have a break from non-stop baby-care. Rob came too, and while he was polite enough with me, I could feel the tension and regretted that we could not have an easier relationship. Sophie was in tears on several occasions and would not share with me the reason, but I guessed Rob was wanting me out of the way. I insisted on buying Sophie some new clothes as she was looking a little overwhelmed by being a young mother with no income of her own at that stage. That was probably seen as a veiled criticism by Rob and I think we were both pleased when the visit ended. There was no danger of me returning the following Christmas because the stock market crash intervened, and I could no longer afford to travel.

Sophie with Adam and Blake

After nearly five years, I was pleased to leave my job in Ventura to have more time for the garden, and one of my first moves was to acquire Bitsy, a little black poodle mix from the Animal Shelter. She joined the two cats and became an integral part of my life as I began to work part-time with the newly established Ojai Performing Arts Foundation, the brainchild of a long time Ojai resident, Joan Kemper. Joan was a delightful person, with a deep interest in Ojai, the theatre and Democratic politics and I enjoyed working with her as administrative assistant and grant writer. The plan was to build a theatre complex with classrooms on the grounds of the local Nordhoff High School. She had two major patrons in mind, Larry Hagman, of Dynasty fame and Otis Chandler, former owner of the LA Times, both Ojai residents and supportive of the project. For several years we worked on plans, wrote grant applications, and lobbied our Congressional representatives for state funding. Joan put on local concerts and plays to publicize the idea and generally we were totally absorbed in what looked like a viable and popular concept. But with uncertain economic times and a change in the school board and administration, the momentum slowed. We even considered asking the Republican Governor of California, Arnold Schwarzenegger, to speak at a fundraiser but we could not find a good time to make it happen and the project came to an end.

My grandson Alex and Bitsy

I began to realize that there would not be a permanent or even a part-time job for me with the Foundation and I became increasingly concerned about my finances. Without an income, I was relying on the stock market to generate enough profit to cover my mortgage and my garden expenses.

Then came a torrential rainstorm that proved I needed a new roof, followed by the discovery that mold had become established between the inner and outer walls of several rooms. All this became alarmingly expensive and I sadly decided that seven years of gardening had satisfied that basic need in me to get my hands dirty and to grow something beautiful. It was time to be more practical and think of my future.

I was sad to see my goats go to their new homes when I sold the house to appreciative new owners who loved the garden and the space for their grandchildren to play. I bought a condo not far away in a small community known as Hitching Post. It had patios front and back for plants and I soon volunteered to be on the landscaping committee with the Homeowners Association. I also acquired another little dog, this time a white poodle named Honey. Honey had been briefly owned by a Hitching Post resident who I suspected of wanting a little poodle as a fashion accessory. She complained to me that the dog followed her around all the time with a slipper in her mouth. I tried to explain that that was the nature of rescued dogs, but she found it so irritating that she was pleased to hand her over to me permanently. I promptly reverted to her original name of Honey and she was happily welcomed by Bitsy.

Ashley, Chris and Alex in my Hitching Post condo

I now had time to increase my involvement with the local Democrats and was delighted to renew my acquaintance with Helen Conly from Santa Barbara days, as I admired her intelligence and sense of fun and her ability to make politics enjoyable. We worked together on many occasions, trying to build up membership in local clubs in Ojai and Ventura and travelling together to party meetings and Conventions from San Francisco to San Diego.

We both came from the school where we tended to ask for forgiveness rather than permission as we decided to set up our own committee of two to increase voter registration in our county. Vote Blue was a lot of work, but we were so effective that we turned the county "blue" for the first time historically, achieving a majority of Democratic registered voters. We received recognition with the award of Volunteers of the Year at the Convention in Sacramento, irritating a lot of older men in the party who had said it could not be done. I think that gave us more pleasure than the actual award.

I was appointed to the Ventura County Area Housing Authority because of my long-standing interest in affordable housing, attending monthly meetings and trying to advocate for housing in the Ojai Valley. I was already on the board of People's Self Help Housing, which was an organization similar to Housing for Humanity, where potential homeowners could put in sweat equity by helping to build their homes. Jeanette Duncan, the founder and President of Peoples Self Help Housing was an effective and dynamic fundraiser and had the ability to attract layers of funding through a mixture of loans, grants, and investments which she called "lasagna funding", achieving much more through her vision and drive than a government agency could. I had a fondness for Jeanette as wherever she built affordable communities along California's central coast, she planted rose gardens as well.

I maintained my friendship with Sara Miller McCune from Sage Publications and was happy to drive her on several occasions to her holiday home in Yosemite in her Jaguar. It was a pleasure to be in her comfortable six bedroomed "cabin" and to enjoy the beauty of Yosemite without hordes of tourists. Sara appointed me to the board of her Sage Foundation which gave out grants each year for organizations working for social justice. The work was challenging and enjoyable as I reviewed the grant applications and made field visits. It led to me being a founder member of a giving circle for Ventura County called the Social Justice Fund, which made grants to smaller start-ups and groups working for social change.

One year, Sara bid for and won an auction prize of a week in Tuscany in a villa owned by a woman who also lived in Santa Barbara. Sara was having difficulty walking, due to arthritis and several recent falls and asked if I would accompany her to help with luggage and driving. I accepted with alacrity and we set off for Florence and then the drive to Montepulciano. Sara found the stone stairs leading up to our rooms a problem and when we explored the nearby towns of Siena and Pienza, neither of us had realized that parking for the car was outside the town walls and we had to walk from then on. In retrospect we should have rented Sara a wheelchair as she was unable to do all she wanted.

I had read a book by Iris Origo, Marchesa of Val D'Orcia about the war years when she and her husband gave food and shelter to partisans, deserters, and refugees, including thirty-two small children. The late 15th-century villa of La Foce had been restored by Iris and her husband in the 1920s with the impressive gardens designed by the English architect Cecil Pinsent. When I discovered in talking to our villa owner that La Foce was a short drive away, I went exploring on my own as Sara wanted to rest.

It was a magical experience and although the building was not open, I wandered round the garden and tried to imagine how it was under the German occupation. Today it hosts an annual music festival which I imagined would be a great experience in such a stunning setting and put it on my "bucket list" of things to do some day.

We also learned that we were not far away from a wonderful gourmet experience. In the small village of Cetona was a restored 13th century monastery run by an organization called Mondo X. Originally built by St Francis of Assisi in 1212, the monastery is now used as a rehabilitation center for troubled youth with addiction problems. In the surrounding gardens and orchards, vegetables and fruit are grown for the gourmet kitchen where young residents are taught to become cordon bleu chefs. We had a wonderful lunch overlooking the Tuscan countryside, a tasting menu of twelve small and delicious courses with wines to match which Sara enjoyed. I have never paid so much for a meal, but felt I owed it to Sara as she had paid for much of the holiday's expenses. The experience was meaningful in a way that I could not share with her, not wanting to confess that I had been a "troubled youth" myself.

We went on to Venice, which again was a problem for Sara with her limited mobility. Venice is definitely a walking city and I would help her to a café table and go off on my own for brief explorations, remembering a little from a past visit with Jerry but still getting happily lost and finding my way again. I looked for but never found the church again where Jerry had decided he had had enough of pictures of saints dying gruesome deaths. "No more Saint Sebastians," he had said, so we gave up on churches that day and visited a gallery of modern art instead. Sara wanted to buy some Venetian glass, so she hired a vaporetto and we sped over the lagoon to the island of Murano where we had a fascinating time watching the master craftsmen create glass artifacts using the millefiori technique. Sara bought half a dozen large pieces and arranged for them to be shipped to her home in Santa Barbara. I was not envious as the multi-colored glass was not to my taste, but I was glad to have had the experience.

2008 became a turning point for me with the stock market crash where I spent anguished months watching my bank account dwindle from nearly one million dollars down to $300,000 when I finally cried stop. My broker told me to hang in, but I was frantic, with credit card debt mounting and visons of it all disappearing forever. I withdrew what was left and transferred it to Ameriprise with the help of their local representative, Olga Jones, who has been a good friend and adviser ever since.

At the same time, and possibly what helped to keep me sane, we had a Presidential election to win. The Obama campaign was heating up and we decided to rent a downtown storefront which became a nucleus of Democratic activity in the valley. It was an exciting time. I really appreciated the transformative power of dedicated people working together for a single vision. It was heart-warming to have total strangers coming into our headquarters to volunteer, donate or simply sit around and talk about the news on our big TV screen that I had bought second hand. I got to know Pam, who volunteered to organize our "boutique" where we sold T-shirts, caps, and pins with the Obama logo, getting a local designer involved so we had our own fashion line. Pam and I had an unfortunate bond – she had lost all her savings because of Bernie Madoff.

We organized evenings at a local high school theater with visiting speakers, well-known politicians, or writers, usually with a reception before or after, so that our predominantly educated liberal community had plenty of opportunities to be part of the campaign. I had great support and encouragement from people like the actor, Peter Strauss and local business owners who offered space for fund raisers and phone-banking.

It was an exhilarating time and we knew that California would vote for Obama but were unsure about the conservative heartland. On Election Day I supervised a polling station so was kept there till long after the polling closed, counting and recounting the ballots before delivering them to the County pick up point. It was late when I ran into our headquarters saying, "Did we win? Did we win?" and the crowded room erupted in cheers as I cried a little and was overwhelmed with hugs and laughter. Victory was sweet and for days afterwards people I barely knew would stop me in the street for a hug and congratulations. Our Obama campaign had certainly brought our town together as a community and I knew I would miss it if I ever had to leave.

Chris and Laura had by this time sold their house in Santa Barbara and moved to Colorado, a state with better education for the children and housing that was certainly cheaper than Santa Barbara. They settled first in Monument near Colorado Springs but were not entirely happy there. Chris had spent three months in Greenland as the medic for a scientific expedition, which was measuring ice melt amongst other things. Laura appreciated the extra income but was not happy on her own and they moved after a year to Longmont, buying a house in a neighborhood, Chris told me, "where we saw the most Obama signs on the lawns."

When the phone rang one day a year or so later, I was sad but not surprised when it was Chris who said, "Mom, would you consider coming to Colorado? We're getting divorced and I need your help with the kids."

I was pleased to be needed, and thankful that I had a clear direction at last. I stopped struggling to pay my mortgage, let the bank take over my condo, entered a debt resolution program and started packing. I would be able to live modestly on what I had left in my IRA and would no longer feel like a second-class citizen with my Santa Barbara friends.

Chris flew out to California, I said farewell to friends and with a U-Haul towing my Prius, we drove to Longmont, with Bitsy and Honey on my lap and my heart in my mouth as I wondered what was next. I had left so much behind. One thing that cheered me up however, was my decision to save on hairdressers and let my hair go naturally gray. I also thought of the poem, Warning, by Jenny Joseph, which starts:

When I am an old woman I shall wear purple

With a red hat which doesn't go, and doesn't suit me.

Now was my time, I thought, to be a grandmother and to try to grow old gracefully, but I would always have a secret hankering for a pair of purple boots.

27. Colorado 2009-2020

Even if things should last, human life does not. We lose it daily.
As we live the years pass through us and they wear us out into
nothingness. It seems that only the present is real, for "things
past and things to come are not."   Hannah Arendt *(from*
Brain Pickings).

Colorado was an exciting state to live in. It was on the
verge of becoming Democratic after years of being dominated
by conservative ranching and oil interests. Now with the
emphasis on technology, young families were moving from
California and other states for better jobs, housing, and
education. The state had retained some of the old frontier
spirit, mixed with the cosmopolitan influx each year in the ski
resorts along with the renaissance of downtown Denver and
the boom in technology jobs. The small city of Longmont
however, lacked the energy of Denver or Boulder with its
college atmosphere, and was largely a bedroom suburb for
the nearby cities. It suited me however, to be in a small town
instead of an anonymous big city.

The apartment I moved to was on the edge of town by
Lake MacIntosh, with views of meadows and mountains which
made up for the absence of the Pacific Ocean. The dogs and I
loved our morning walks past the ground squirrel colony down

to the water's edge and while the landscape was bleak in winter, there was always the breathtaking backdrop of the snow-covered Rockies to lift the spirit.

I needed something to hold onto as it had been a profound shift for me to have been a homeowner, a Housing Commissioner, a Regional Director for the California Democrats, and now to be just a widow and a grandmother in a rented apartment in a small town in Colorado. I did my best to be a loving and understanding influence in the children's lives, but Ashley and Alex were difficult because of the stresses and tension at home and I wished I could enjoy their visits and sleepovers more. I felt so inadequate when they fought with each other so viciously, and I tried to set reasonable boundaries which they completely ignored. Laura was her usual remote self and Chris was overworked and overtired, so the move to Colorado was not quite what I was hoping for. I was lonely and needed to find part-time work to help with expenses and I hoped that would give me a better sense of being grounded in my new identity.

I was hired right away to work for Measured Progress for about three months each year, grading test papers for Education Departments all over the country and was also hired by Professional Home Health Care as their evening and weekend on-call person. This was stressful as it involved fielding calls from patients complaining that their nurse or caregiver was late or from nurses or caregivers calling to say they were ill and could not work that shift. This gave me a new insight into the business of home and companion care, and I thought this could be an avenue to pursue, especially as it could be an experience to share with Chris, with his career in nursing and health care. I did extensive research into setting up my own small business and then attempted to form instead a cooperative of like-minded caregivers, but there was no viably financial way I could be administrator and caregiver at the same time. It was best to go it alone.

The months turned into years and I felt some satisfaction with what I was doing but missed the immediacy of California politics. The local Democratic party had some dynamic women members whose company I enjoyed when we had work to do during elections, and I became a committee member and precinct worker. Some excitement was generated when a benefactor decided to rent a disused storefront on the Main Street and turn it into the headquarters for progressive action for social justice. I had learned from the Obama campaign how important it is to have an actual office space where people could meet regularly and relished the thought of helping to turn it into a viable center for social change.

The Longmont Democrats encouraged other organizations in town to use the space and I had visions of regular coffee meetings, political book discussions and somehow helping to raise money to defray expenses. It was not a great success despite our best efforts – the space was distinctly shabby despite a coat of paint and meetings tended to be dominated by a few fervent and sometimes eccentric members. At the same time, there was great energy being generated in town by the MoveOn movement whose younger liberal members preferred evening meetings with potlucks in each other's homes rather than the down market atmosphere of the Progressive Center. I no longer had the income to help support the running of a rented space as I had in Ojai and was sorry that it never really became a viable center and movement. After a year or so, the benefactor withdrew his support and announced he would no longer pay the rent of the building. His wife, who evidently controlled the family finances, had decided it would be better spent on missionary work in Africa and so our headquarters had to close.

I had attended several conferences and meetings about affordable housing and Health Care for All, but never really found people with the same progressive drive and passion I once had shared with my Ojai friend Helen.. It was not just that my income was reduced, it was my energy level also, as yet another birthday reminded me each year. My interests really lay with my own age group now and I was happy to be appointed to the Boulder County Area Agency on Aging, where I could concentrate on promoting programs that would help seniors. One of our mantras was "Aging in place, with dignity and grace," a concept I heartily endorsed.

My mother died in New Zealand in her 95th year, after being in ill health for more than forty years. I was tempted to write "after enjoying ill health" as her preoccupation with her medical mishap had been her obsession for many years. But that would be unkind. She was not really a hypochondriac but someone who turned her loneliness as a widow into a permanent condition of being a victim living in constant pain with no one to understand her. She had been placed eventually in a nursing home by my sister Jane and in her last years her dementia meant she no longer knew us. I was sad to hear the news, but not as sorry as I had been over the years when she had abandoned me emotionally.

Jane sent me an email to let me know of Mother's death and said that perhaps now she was gone we could become friends again. I wrote back and said, "Now she has gone, there's even less reason for us to be friends again." I refused to forgive and forget all of Jane's petty spitefulness, including an email she had sent to a friend and by mistake also to me where she had complained about having to put up with a visit from Jerry and me. The last straw had been her comment to my Santa Barbara friend Eva, to whom in a weak moment I had given Jane's phone number in France, because Eva and her husband were travelling to nearby Geneva. Eva called me when she got home.

"You know Sue," she said, "I didn't like your sister Jane at all. She had obviously had too much wine when we spoke on the phone and she insisted that you had married Jerry for his money." I was appalled. I had to apologize for my sister's crass behavior and tried to turn it into a joke by saying, "If I had wanted to marry for money, I would have found someone richer than Jerry." I was distressed for weeks afterwards, wondering what other indiscretions Jane had shared to undermine me and was similarly shocked and saddened sometime later when I was speaking to my niece. She said that Jane had told her children years previously that I had had an affair with her first husband Bernie.

"No wonder you kids were standoffish with me over the years," I said in dismay. "What a wicked lie. I wonder what drives her to say such things." I resolved to never have anything to do with her again and the relief was remarkable. With both my mother and sister out of my life, I no longer needed to look for love and understanding from either of them and I would never again be rebuffed or betrayed.

The years went by in Longmont, marked by dramatic seasons after California's benign weather. The novelty of snow in winter soon became unwelcome when I had to scrape ice off my windscreen and snow off my pathway. Chris and Laura were engaged in a bitter divorce with the new man in Laura's life being particularly difficult about Chris's presence in the children's lives and he would take Chris to court for every perceived infringement of their mediated settlement. It meant I had to help Chris with loans to pay ineffective attorneys and his stress was becoming more and more evident. I was thankful when he got a job in nearby Fort Collins and after some lonely years, he eventually met an ER nurse and began a relationship with her. Unfortunately, the children were incompatible and there was no possibility of combining the two sets of teenagers in an adult and respectful way. Everyone was angry and disappointed with each other and I was unable to help.

Alex was sixteen by now and emancipated himself and went to live at the Inn Between, a refuge for teens from troubled families; Ashley stayed on with Laura and her new husband John when they moved to Missouri. I decided to move to Fort Collins as a way of seeing Chris more often. By then, I had been working as a companion caregiver for some time, having met a woman from Jewish Family Services who found me private clients in Boulder. One was Rabbi Deborah, a retired liberal rabbi who needed help several times a week with cooking and transportation to doctor appointments. She was a delightful person and it was a privilege to know her. As the months went by, I became more of a friend than an employee. We went shopping together, I took her dog for walks when Deborah was too tired, and I helped in the garden. Her wisdom and strength were of more help to me in the long run, I believe, than my presence was for her. She was greatly loved by her congregation and had many friends who kept closely in touch with her. I loved the occasions when I would drive her to services at the Har Hashem synagogue and she would ask me to stay. I felt close to Jerry as I listened to the Hebrew prayers and wondered how he could have turned away from the loving fellowship of the Jewish faith. Perhaps he would have maintained his Jewishness if he had discovered a liberal congregation.

I had found a spiritual home by then in the Unitarian Universalist church, first in Santa Barbara out of gratitude to the minster who had led Jerry's memorial service. I went on Sundays and stayed because I discovered there the liberal, intellectual, and spiritual support I had lacked all my life. When I moved to Ojai, I attended the UU church in Ventura and followed its relocation from an old wooden house on a hill to its new bigger home in downtown Ventura with wonderful space for social justice activities, meetings, workshops – all the things that I had hoped to bring to the Progressive Center in Longmont. For a liberal community to thrive, I learned, it needs not just the right space but also charismatic leadership, and this I discovered was more likely to come from younger women ministers in the UU community. I found myself responding with more empathy to a more feminist message from the pulpit than that provided by "old white men." Rabbi Deborah's influence helped to balance my awareness of the breadth and depth of universal religion, based on love, family, action, and compassion. It is not easy to be a truly good person, but at least now I had a framework and a support system for my search.

When I moved to Fort Collins, the first Sunday I was there I found the UU church and immediately knew I was among friends. I loved my new apartment which had a garage attached and at last I would not have to scrape ice and snow off my car during winter. Chris worked in Loveland, about twenty minutes away, and I was pleased to have left the stress of Longmont behind. Another reason for my dissatisfaction with Longmont was because my little dog Bitsy had finally succumbed to her heart condition and I had to have her put to sleep. Then a year later, Honey, my little poodle was savagely mauled by an off leash adopted greyhound, and she also had to be put to sleep. I had since acquired Muffin, a shitzu terrier mix, to replace Bitsy and then I succumbed to my grandchildren's pleas for a playmate for Muffin and adopted Chloe, a poodle bichon mix from a puppy mill rescue charity. It felt good to take my new pups to new surroundings with no sad associations and while we missed our walks round Lake MacIntosh, we had a park right at our doorstep and a pathway past a tree-lined pond for our daily walks.

I would have liked some private clients again, but I needed to earn right away and signed on with a home care agency. Some of the clients I was sent to were a test of my compassion, as they were Medicaid patients often at the end of their time for independent living and in need of the move to residential care. Their health and their homes had been neglected and I often had to do some serious cleaning and counselling and go beyond what I was supposed to do. Some patients had mental health and addiction issues, some were hoarders whose living conditions were appalling and there were a few patients who I loved and cared for at the end of their lives. That experience made me want to do specialized training in hospice care, so I joined another agency who promised me this opportunity. Unfortunately, they were still waiting months later for some state accreditation and in the meantime, I had the same problem with patients who needed their floors scrubbed rather than have me cook a Cordon Bleu meal. I eventually left that agency and became a Visiting Angel with a well-respected agency dealing with private pay patients only. At last I had clients who appreciated my homemaking and cooking skills.

I had been in Fort Collins for almost a year when I was shocked to find out that a man had been murdered in the apartment complex where I was living. It made me very uneasy and shared this with a new friend at church, who said, "But you must move to Affinity, where I live!"

Affinity was a new apartment complex for active seniors – 55 and over- with wonderful facilities and a small number of subsidized apartments, one of which I was lucky to get. Chris and Alex helped me with yet another pack and move operation, and I loved the safe, new atmosphere with opportunities for book groups, lectures, movies, and potlucks all within the building. My friend Linda from Longmont decided to move there also, and I felt that finally I was in a safe place and among friends.

I had to keep working as even the subsidized rent was a bit of a stretch, but I knew I could manage as long as I stayed healthy. The preceding Christmas had been an important occasion for me as my daughter and her two boys came to Colorado. Sophie and I had looked at Affinity together during her visit and while she felt that it was too "institutional" I think she was relieved to know I was moving to something safe and secure.

Her visit was long awaited as I had not seen her for ten years and had never really met the boys as Adam had been just one year old on my last visit to Australia. It was a very emotional reunion and it was good to see my son and daughter together again under my roof and to watch the grandchildren getting acquainted. Adam and Blake had never experienced snow and I had bought sleds for them to try out on the slopes nearby. It was more successful when we went up to the cabin I had rented in the YMCA of the Rockies, where the dogs joined in the fun. I had hoped Alex would have been more of a team leader with the younger boys and organized outdoor activities with them, but unfortunately he caught a bug of some sort and had to go home.

The whole mountain experience was a bit of an anti-climax, as the two young Australians preferred to stay indoors with their phones and laptops, so we returned to Longmont for the last week of their visit. I was a little disappointed and Sophie seemed somewhat restrained and unenthusiastic after staying a few nights with Chris and his girlfriend. I realized I had been naïve to imagine that everyone would automatically get along beautifully just because we were family. It takes more than proximity to create relationships and we had all spent too many years apart, living our own lives in different countries. I was sad to see Sophie and the boys leave and I felt it had been a lost opportunity to achieve a sense of intimacy that I had been yearning for. I felt I had failed Sophie somehow and felt quite distressed as I realized I simply had to get on with my life alone and be grateful for my work and my women friends in the UU congregation. Once I had settled in Fort Collins, I enrolled in a poetry class at the college and gained much insight and solace from reading poetry again. Mary Oliver was a special comfort and I loved the message in this poem of hers;

I go down to the shore in the morning

and depending on the hour the waves

are rolling in or moving out,

and I say, oh, I am miserable

what shall, what should I do?

And the sea says

in its lovely voice:

Excuse me, I have work to do.

28. Fort Collins 2018

The challenge of recovery is to reestablish ownership of your body and your mind — of your self. This means feeling free to know what you know and to feel what you feel without becoming overwhelmed, enraged, ashamed, or collapsed. For most people this involves (1) finding a way to become calm and focused, (2) learning to maintain that calm in response to images, thoughts, sounds, or physical sensations that remind you of the past, (3) finding a way to be fully alive in the present and engaged with the people around you, (4) not having to keep secrets from yourself, including secrets about the ways that you have managed to survive.

Bessel Van der Kolk (from Brain Pickings)

It began as any ordinary day. I had taken my two little dogs to a nearby park where they had watched some rabbits and chased a squirrel - for them, a highly successful walk. The phone rang and I learned from my daughter Sophie of the death of her father. We agreed that it was good his suffering was over as he had been unwell for over a year with some rather mysterious neurological condition. I restrained myself from suggesting it was brain damage due to his excessive drinking over the years.

"You know Sophie, I can't pretend I am sorry. That man caused me a lot of grief over the years". She was silent for a while, then talked of her disappointment that there was no money in her father's estate for her or Chris apart from sharing a $10,000 life insurance policy.

"That's outrageous," I said. "Have you seen a copy of his will?"

"His partner Sandra assured me there was nothing left." Sandra had been living with my ex-husband for about twenty years and had benefited from his income over the years to become a successful real estate agent and investor.

Although they had never married, John and Sandra had been together long enough to be considered man and wife under New Zealand law, but I still felt that my children deserved something. It felt like the ultimate betrayal of his children and evidence of his total lack of regard for conventional decency.

I was appalled by his bad faith towards his children and reflected on the role alcohol had played in our marriage and the insidious nature of alcoholism through the generations. My parents were idealists when they were young – my father a Quaker by inclination if not practice and Mother presumably had the moral underpinning of Christian Science. They both drank at the end of the day to relax and being together so much during those early years – the babies, the war - their lives were shaped by each other rather than a wider circle of friends. So I believe their moral imaginations became stunted, and their lives unfolded with my father bearing unresolved grudges, first against his father, then against the NZ Dept of Agriculture with my mother being the co-dependent consoler.

They created a self-perpetuating aura of bad faith which failed their children and estranged us all in different ways – the unnecessary hysteria over Jane getting married so young and pregnant, the abandonment of me, the participation in Robert's first child being adopted and similarly though more tragically with Juliet, who was literally driven mad by their decisions.

I had carried on family tradition – a life of bad faith, too much alcohol, unrealistic hopes of being able to live a good life and wanting to be true to myself but not knowing how. I cooked, I cleaned, I baked, I sewed but that was not enough to be a good wife. A responsible wife would have admitted that John was not a good husband and certainly not good material as a parent. Once I realized I should never have married him, I should have left.

He rarely read a book, he did not care for classical music, he drank beer and not wine. I thought I could change all that, but I was only 19 and he was 29. He had always resented the fact that his older brother Peter was sent to boarding school and there was not enough money for him to go too, so he had to make do with the local Napier Boys High School. He was sensitive about having only a Diploma in Agricultural Science and not a degree, and always scorned those who had PhDs in particular, regarding them as theorists instead of practical agriculturalists like himself. This was the narrative he lived by and used as an excuse to pursue his single-minded selfish ambitions without any concept of the need for integrity, morality, or spirituality.

John had been a United Nations expert, and I love Frank Lloyd Wright's aphorism; "an expert is a man who has stopped thinking because 'he knows.'" John was that man who had stopped thinking.

Erich Fromm said it best:

Narcissism is an orientation in which all one's interest and passion are directed to one's own person: one's body, mind, feelings, interests... For the narcissistic person, only he and what concerns him are fully real; what is outside, what concerns others, is real only in a superficial sense of perception; that is to say, it is real for one's senses and for one's intellect. But it is not real in a deeper sense, for our feeling or understanding. He is, in fact, aware only of what is outside, inasmuch as it affects him. Hence, he has no love, no compassion, no rational, objective judgment. The narcissistic person has built an invisible wall around himself. He is everything, the world is nothing. Or rather: He is the world.

.....Nevertheless, he wants everything for himself; has no pleasure in giving, in sharing, in solidarity, in cooperation, in love. He is a closed fortress, suspicious of others, eager to take and most reluctant to give.

I will never understand why I was so willing to pack and follow over the years, hoping that each new country would mean something different in our marriage, when the ingredients remained just the same. Sophie's father's death was a benchmark for me and it brought me closer to my daughter after years of misunderstandings.

Over the next few months I developed severe back pain which meant I could no longer carry on working as a Visiting Angel. I also had had a car accident one snowy evening when I was driving reluctantly to a client in a blizzard. My car was a write-off and new car payments plus the exorbitant new insurance rate meant I could no longer afford to stay at Affinity, the retirement community where I had spent a safe and pleasant year. I sold my replacement car and moved to a more affordable senior housing complex which had just been built in Fort Collins.

I loved the new apartment and made new friends among the residents there and was grateful for Chris visiting fairly regularly. I relied on my closer friends in the UU fellowship for their friendship as I faced an uncertain future. The services on Sunday were often relevant and I found them inspiring and helping to underpin my week. I carried on working as much as I could, using a friend's car to get to clients and to the chiropractor for my aching back. heart and

When Chris asked me if I would move back to Longmont to a rented house where we could be together, the three generations of us, I did not hesitate. Here I go again, I thought, leaving a place with unhappy associations and being childishly optimistic that the future would be better and happier. But this time, I thought it would be alright. The worst is behind me. My search for peace and understanding may be a little tentative now, but at least it would be all uphill.. I decided that memories of John and my mother and sister have lost their power to distress me. Illness, old age and even death can be met with a new resilience now. And as I approach my 80th birthday, I have the next ten years to look forward to, running forward, like Mary Oliver's dog Percy.

Percy (Nine)

Your friend is coming I say

to Percy, and name a name

and he runs to the door, his

wide mouth its laugh shape,

and waves, since he has one, his tail.

Emerson, I am trying to live

As you said we must, the examined life.

But there are days I wish

there was less in my head to examine,

not to speak of the busy heart. How

Would it be to be Percy, I wonder, not

Thinking, not weighing anything,

just running forward.

29. Colorado to New Mexico 2019-20

Because self-knowledge is the most difficult of the arts of living, because understanding ourselves is a prerequisite for understanding anybody else, and because we can hardly fathom the reality of another without first plumbing our own depths, art is what makes us not only human but humane.
Maria Popova (from Brain Pickings)

Living in the United States in the year of the coronavirus has been interesting. It is ironic that the apocryphal curse, "May you live in interesting times" originated, like the pandemic, in China. The virus has sharpened perceptions of life and death, loneliness and community and reshaped family relationships. The all-pervasive dread of catching Covid19 has made many people more aware, more sensitive, and more appreciative of what they have and need to hold onto. It has made us turn isolation into an art instead of an imposition.

Mary Oliver has prescient questions for us as we consider how our lives were spent and how to proceed with what is left of them: *"Tell me, what else should I have done? Doesn't everything die at last and too soon? Tell me, what is it you plan to do with your one wild and precious life?"*

The beauty of nature, the warmth of friendships, albeit distanced, and the kindness of strangers are no longer taken for granted. We are in a world with a whole new reality and a whole new paradigm. Life itself and our manner of living are immediate, yet transient with a new urgency. If we had fears of old age, cancer, Alzheimer's – these fears are now relegated to second place. Something more alarming stalks our conscious moments as we watch the mounting daily toll of infection and death.

My return to Longmont was happy enough for the first six months. I had a real house again to furnish and clean, a yard to keep tidy and with Chris coming back for a week to ten days each month from California, I had his presence to look forward to and his help with assembling furniture. His visits to Colorado became more infrequent however and I was not surprised when he announced that he had met Ella, an attractive ER nurse, twenty years younger and with two small children and that he would therefore be spending more time in California. This coincided with the onset of the pandemic and his need to work extra shifts transporting critically ill Covid19 patients to hospitals in Southern California.

I was pleased for him but dismayed to realize I was now alone in the house with my grandson Alex and his partner Hale. From the start I had been made aware that they were totally uninterested in having a family relationship. Most of the time they just ignored me, and went in and out through the garage, the three of us leading our separate lives.

I realized that Chris was defensive of his son and I should have become aware sooner that my health and happiness were way down his list of priorities. Nonetheless it was a shock when I appealed to Chris to talk to Alex about his lack of concern for me during the pandemic, when four of their friends suddenly appeared in the kitchen for a barbecue on the deck, without giving me any warning and with no obvious use of hand sanitizer and certainly no wearing of masks.

Rather than make an effort to be an honest broker, Chris had opted for the narrative that the kids were entitled to live as they pleased and that I should "learn to get along" or find alternative accommodation.

I was devastated. I had thought our new relationship was based on something stronger and that Chris had a new awareness and responsibility for my well-being. I was used to his inability to express his feelings and his usual reaction of angry withdrawal if he felt criticized, but I was not prepared for his hostility. His one brief visit in six months had not been friendly or communicative which I had initially attributed to his exhaustion working with Covid19 patients in California.

I agonized for some time about what to do. When hurt feelings had subsided a little, I would try to remind Chris of his parental responsibilities and his promise to visit his children once a month. With Alex nearly 21 and Ashley 18, I no longer felt able to be a substitute parent, compensating for Chris's remoteness. Clearly I no longer understood my son or my grandson and I reflected somewhat bitterly that their regard for me had coincidentally evaporated along with my depleted income. I could no longer lend or give them money and I was the one feeling abandoned.

It was clearly time I took back responsibility for my own health and happiness and moved on. In time, the disappointment I felt became balanced by the optimism of another fresh start. I did not exactly shut my eyes and put a pin in a map, but I settled on Albuquerque as it has the dry summer heat I love, and the winters would be milder than Colorado's. I would never have to rake leaves or shovel snow again.

I would be moving to a brand-new development in an over-55 affordable "resort-style" complex, much like Affinity where I had enjoyed a year in Fort Collins. Without a car, I would have everything I needed under one roof or within walking distance and the dogs would have a dog park to play in again. Above all, I would be with people my own age and stage in life and I would feel at home immediately in the UU congregation in Albuquerque.

I will never be sure how much of my sense of isolation has been due to the coronavirus pandemic and the need to stay at home alone for months on end. It was certainly not helped by my son's absence both physically and emotionally and I became dependent on my once a week Skype calls with my daughter in Sydney as a way of feeling more centered. Even my granddaughter's arrival in Longmont did little to ease my growing sense of dislocation and unease. Ashley is a sweet and communicative young woman, independent with her own car and happy to be out most of the time with her friends from her former school days in Longmont. Her final year of high school was achieved online and it was clear that she did not have a pressing need for me in her life; and as her other grandmother lives in Longmont and they are in touch regularly, she had someone to call on if needed.

The pandemic has certainly sharpened my sense of my own mortality. Ten-year plans and bucket lists seem irrelevant now with imminent death from Covid 19 a nagging possibility. The random nature of infections meant that even if I wear a mask, wash my hands frequently and try to keep six feet away from other people walking their dogs each day, there is still the possibility of the grandchildren and their friends being asymptomatic carriers. They are understandably somewhat nonchalant about it as they have no idea of what it is like to live knowing your time on earth is running out fast. I have had my Biblical three score and ten years and as I approach my 80th birthday, there is not only an urgency to complete this memoir but also to write the book that has been in the back of my mind for some years.

In writing my story and examining my choices, motives, and decisions, and those of other people, I have been very conscious of the concept of bad faith. This is defined as "a philosophical concept used by existentialist philosophers Simone de Beauvoir and Jean-Paul Sartre to describe the phenomenon in which human beings, under pressure from social forces, adopt false values and disown their innate freedom, hence acting inauthentically."

I have read and thought about it a lot, especially the issues of false values and inauthenticity, and how in childhood we are so quick to notice when something is not fair, when a parental decision is being made based on expediency rather than what is morally right. That innate sense of right and wrong is soon altered or conditioned by authoritarian, family, or societal relationships, exhibited in its most grotesque form by Eichmann, as Hannah Arendt explored so vividly in her book *The Banality of Evil.* Eichmann was an unimaginative bureaucrat, concerned only to please his Nazi bosses and to achieve his job targets in a timely fashion. He was incapable of empathy and unable to expand his consciousness to include the universality of humanity and their right to life, liberty, and dignity.

At the other end of the spectrum of inauthenticity was another book that affected me deeply – Scott Peck's *People of the Lie.* He wrote that ordinary people can unconsciously make the cruelest decisions based on false values, with the belief that they are doing the right thing. The example that sticks in my mind is of the Midwestern parents, in a gun-friendly community, who decided to give their young son a rifle for his birthday because he seemed depressed and they thought it would cheer him up. I am sure they were horrified when he committed suicide with the rifle, but they were also unable to accept moral responsibility for their decision or his act. Scott Peck describes this banal ignorance and lack of imagination as a form of evil. Certainly, it is an extreme example of bad faith.

This concept was a reminder when I was researching my grandfather's life and writing. I reflected on his experience in the Cook Islands as a missionary teacher and speculated about his commitment to Christianity and how he viewed the work of the Church in the islands. So much has been written about the harm done by missionaries in the Pacific over hundreds of years with arguments on both sides continuing at a scholarly level. Missionaries may have stopped cannibalism, but they destroyed cultures. They stopped barbaric native wars but introduced measles and chicken pox instead which took many more lives. The early missionaries were particularly puritanical and unimaginative as they tended to be relatively uneducated men and more likely to interpret the Bible literally. They were convinced of the righteousness of their calling and on many occasions were over-zealous and even cruel as they preached the Word. Over the years, as more educated missionaries and qualified teachers went out to the Pacific, their teaching became somewhat more liberal and enlightened but there were still some egregious examples of what I can only call bad faith.

So as I start the process again of sifting out my possessions, selling my pottery and classics collections and getting quotes from moving companies, I am buoyed by the thought that I shall continue researching and planning my new book about missionaries in the South Pacific. The working title is *Bad Faith* and it will be a novel, though heavily based on an interpretation of my grandparents' lives. In between exploring my new surroundings and learning to love the red rocks of the high desert of New Mexico, I shall be back in my imagination in the humid tropics of my childhood in the South Pacific. I will pack my copies of Mary Oliver's poetry and will try to follow her advice, to live within each moment and be attentive and intentional in all that I do from now on.

Maybe I can safely plan for the next ten years of this "one wild and precious life" when there is an effective and readily available vaccine against Covid19. This year of 2020 will be a bad memory to be forgotten; certainly, it will be a rock bottom to build from, as the world struggles to readjust economically and I personally to the new reality of a post-coronavirus world. While we make plans, God laughs , but I need to believe that I will see my daughter Sophie again, that I will outlive my two beloved little dogs and that I will live out my days in New Mexico, without any more instances of bad faith, half-truths or broken promises while I "age in place with dignity and grace".

The experience of living in a similar environment in Affinity confirms that I will find friends in my new home who will share my interests and politics. And I know that I will get to meet dog-owners immediately as my Muffin is always ready to announce her presence.

And this time, I have finally learned that I do not need to go it alone. There have been so many good women who have touched my life over the years, and I may not have even known or acknowledged it at the time. Too proud to admit I needed help; I have wasted a hundred opportunities. I have the courage now to ask for help and to appreciate the opportunity to further a friendship in doing so, and I intend to continue to live my life accepting the things I cannot change, changing the things I can and developing the wisdom to know the difference. This time, I will have the experience of living an examined life and this time I do not intend to miss its meaning.

Acknowledgements

I am grateful to Maria Popova for her permission to use the quotes that head my chapters. They are from her weekly compilation of wisdom and inspiration, *Brain Pickings*, which has provided me with so much food for thought. I have been inspired to read again many of the writers who have influenced me in the past – Simone de Beauvoir, Hannah Arendt, Mary McCarthy, Ann Lamott, and the poet Mary Oliver. *Brain Pickings* also has introduced me to many new writers, such as Rebecca Solnit and Bessel Van Der Kolk, whose work has the integrity and authenticity I admire so much.

I must thank also all those anonymous people, whose presence at AA meetings over the years has helped to give me the courage and wisdom I needed to transform my life. I also want to pay tribute to the lecturers at the University of London whose encouragement enabled me to open my mind to the wider world of literature and politics and to the late British philosopher Tony Judt for helping me to realize I was a Social Democrat. I am also grateful to those who helped during my quixotic run as a parliamentary candidate for the Liberal Democrats.

I am deeply grateful to my writing friend and mentor Linda Bendorf, of Blue Sage Writing, whose sensitive commentaries each chapter enabled me to reach the end.

And of course, none of this would have happened without my late husband Jerry, whose love and wit and wisdom I still miss every day. Life has only become bearable now because of his memory and because of my closer relationship with my daughter Sophie.. This book is intended as a tribute to her and hopefully will create some closure for us both as we move forward.